GLOBAL SIGNIFICANCE OF INDO-RUSSIAN STRATEGIC PARTNERSHIP

GLOBAL SIGNIFICANCE OF INDO-RUSSIAN STRATEGIC PARTNERSHIP

Editor
V.D. Chopra

Publications

KALPAZ PUBLICATIONS
DELHI - 110 052

On Behalf of
International Institute for Asia–Pacific Studies, New Delhi

Global Significance of Indo-Russian Strategic Partnership

Rs. 750

ISBN : 81-7835-400-4

Published in 2005 in India by
Kalpaz Publications,
C-30, Satyawati Nagar,
Delhi-110 052
Email : kalpaz@hotmail.com

Lasertype Setting by: Tact Computer Graphics, Delhi
Printed at: Mehra Offset Press, Delhi

Contents

Preface

In this book entitled "Global Significance of Indo-Russian Strategic Partnership", this subject has been examined on the basis of concrete data when the international situation is witnessing certain basic changes. In this sense, the Indo-Russian strategic partnership is not merely a bilateral relationship between India and Russia, but it has its own global dimension. That is the main thrust of this book and it has been conceptualised and compiled in this framework.

Before we underline the main content of this book, one basic development in the beginning at the 21st century needs to be emphasised. This relates to unipolar character of the world order in which the only superpower that is the United States of America is the most powerful military power.

The main dimension of the present world order, particularly after the collapse of the Soviet Union, rise of the internalised market economy, which in economic idioms is called globalisation of the world economy and growth of political globalisation and above all exposition of the theory that now an era of limited sovereignty of each country under the supervision of the sole superpower - USA - are some of the main features of the new world order. This characterisation of the present international order may look to be too sweeping. However, if one goes by recent developments, political, economic and military, one tends to come to the conclusion that this assessment is nearer to the reality than what appears on the surface. It is relevant to mention here that the three 'wars' launched by the transnational elite so far (Iraq, Yugoslavia, Afghanistan) have been aimed at securing the stability of the new world order in economic and political dimensions by crushing any perceived threats against it

As against this, parallel developments are taking place in the various parts of the world in Asia and Eurasia. The chief among them are Indo-Russian, Sino-Russian and Sino-Indian relationship. In this triangular relationship, each one of them stands on a different footing with their own specific characteristics. Sino-Russian and Indo-Russian relations stand at higher level than Sino-Indian relations. Nevertheless, in the totality of the situation, these relations between these three countries are developing and deepening. If there are no conflicts and irritants between India and Russia, all the disputes between Russia and China have been resolved and their relations are developing and deepening. On the other hand, Sino-Indian relations are revealing new trends including solution of long standing border disputes between them. Similar trends are unfolding themselves in other parts of the worid.

It is in this background that Indo-Russian relations should be objectively assessed and their global significance analysed. It is precisely this objective of this book.

This book has three main components.

Firstly, global significance of Indo-Russian relations has been examined.

Secondly, the impact of Indo-Russian relations in the various parts of Asia and Africa has been assessed.

Thirdly, a study has been made of the economic potentialities and the problems of Indo-Russian relations.

Finally, it may be mentioned here that academics, researchers, and scholars from Delhi University, Jamia Millia Islamia University and Jawaharlal Nehru University and strategic experts have made rich contribution, in this book. I profusely express my gratitude to all of them in making it possible to bring out this book. I am also grateful to Mr. Manohar Singh Batra for revising the manuscript of the book. I hope this book will serve as a source of information to the academics, researchers, scholars and policy makers.

V.D. Chopra

List of Contributors

1.	Prof. V.P. Dutt	— Former Pro-Vice Chancellor of Delhi University and Former Member of Parliament. Leading Expert on International Affairs.
2.	Prof. R.R. Sharma	— Former Vice Chancellor of Jammu University. Dean, School of International Studies, Jawaharlal Nehru University, New Delhi and an Expert on Russia.
3.	Mr. V.D. Chopra	— Former Head of Economic Department in D.A.V. College, Rawalpindi, Former Chief Editor, *Patriot Daily* and *Link* Weekly, Vice-President of International Institute for Asia-Pacific Studies, New Delhi and a well known author.
4.	Prof. K.R. Singh	— Former Professor, School of International Studies, Jawaharlal Nehru University, New Delhi.
5.	Mr. Manohar Singh Batra	— Former Deputy Director General, All India Radio.
6.	Maj. Gen. (Retd.) Afsir Karim	— Security Expert and Editor, *Aakrosh*, Journal on Terrorism.

7.	Brig. Chandra B. Khanduri	— AVSM, Senior Fellow ICHR, ABI and USI.
8.	Prof. Ravi M. Bakaya	— Former Professor, Jawaharlal Nehru University, New Delhi.
9.	Prof. Kalim Bahadur	— Former Professor, Jawaharlal Nehru University and an Expert on Pakistan.
10.	Prof. B.K. Srivastava	— Former Professor, Centre for American Studies, Jawaharlal Nehru University, New Delhi and an Outstanding Expert on the United States.
11.	Dr. A.K. Pasha	— Chairman, Centre for West Asian and African Studies (CWAAS), School of International Studies, Jawaharlal Nehru University, New Delhi. A Leading Expert on the Gulf Countries.
12.	Dr. Jagdish Prasad Sharma	— Associate Professor, Specialist on Afro-Arab and Asian Affairs, Deptt. of African Studies, University of Delhi.
13.	Dr. R.K. Wadhwa	— Asst. Professor, Indian Institute of Foreign Trade.
14.	Prof. Shri. Prakash	— Professor, Academy of Third World Studies, Jamia Millia Islamia University, New Delhi.
15.	Prof. G.M. Shah	— Lecturer, Academy of Third World Studies, Jamia Millia Islamia University, New Delhi.

1

India-Russia Strategic Relationship in a Changing World: Overview

V.P. Dutt

India-Russia strategic relationship has to be related to the overall strategic environment in the world and the international situation. The unilateral attack on Iraq reflected the rise of the neoconservatives in the United States and their belief that US overwhelming military power could overcome all problems and its use did not require anyone else's sanction. We now take note of some of the changes in the world situation so as to put Indo-Russian relations in their context. Many significant changes have taken place in the meantime.

The power of neoconservatives in the United States has *weakened somewhat*. They continue to occupy many important positions both at the top and the middle level in the Bush administration and it is too early to say whether this weakening is only temporary or not. But whatever small erosion has taken place is directly the result of the fallout from the Iraq war. The game plan of the neoconservatives has gone awry. There comes a point when you cannot spin reality.

As Steven R. Weiseman wrote in the *New York Times* (5 September 2003) "the harsh realities were the American military strength was able to win a war but could not fashion peace had virtually overwhelmed other calculations"[1] or as Ivo Daaldar and James Lindsay have pointed out in their recent book "the President's unilateralist policies produced quick victories in Afghanistan and Iraq, but have also fractured the nation's alliances and as a result, the world system is more chaotic and unfriendly and the United States is less secure". The deeper problem is that "the fundamental premise of the Bush revolution - that American security rested on an America unbound—was profoundly mistaken". They pinpointed: "another abiding characteristic of the administration is foreign policy has been its belief that forceful US leadership would cow the US enemies and bring wavering friends into line".[2]

The failure to win the peace in Iraq was evident from the grim picture that Donald Rumsfeld himself painted in a speech at the Pentagon.[3] That George Bush had to rethink was evident from the constitution of an Iraq Stabilisation Council, headed not by Rumsfeld but by Bush's Security Adviser, Condeleeza Rice. To use the colourful words of Maureen Dowd in the *New York Times,* "Condi has gaslighted Rummy. The so-called Iraq Stabilisation Council is infact evidence that the war over the postwar.. is now as heated as the war over the war itself."[4]

The second evidence of this weakening of the neoconservatives was Colin Powell's ascendancy and Bush's volte face over the involvement of the United Nations in the Iraq imbroglio. Powell was reported to have seized on a delicate and painful moment for Bush in the Iraq war to convince him that American allies were essential to paying the military and economic cost of securing and rebuilding Iraq, not to mention bringing troops home in 2004. It is worth noting that the Pentagon estimates that the cost of military occupation of Iraq is around $4 billion a month, while the loss of oil revenues and the cost of operating a civilian government in Iraq amounts to some $20 billion for the year 2004.

The American plan, rather the Paul Bremer plan to hand over power to a handpicked Iraqi council has had to be thrown out of the window. Mr. Bush had no other option but to request the UN Secretary General to take over the process of instituting a new government in Iraq, even though the United States retains its overall power and authority there. The problem was compounded by the increasing resistance of the Iraqi people to the US plan to foist a non-elected government over their heads. There was a general demand that only a genuinely representative government can assume the attributes of sovereignty in Iraq.

George Bush had broken some of the unwritten rules of US intervention abroad and, therefore, had to backtrack. Michael Ignatieff has enumerated five basic rules that America had followed in deciding upon intervention abroad. Rule No.1 was never to pick on someone of your own size, which meant someone with nuclear weapons. Rule No.2 was never to fight someone who was more willing to die than you were. This rule was proven in Vietnam, but Bush broke it when he attacked Iraq. Rule No.3 was never to intervene except with overwhelming force in defence of a vital national interest. It has aroused intense debate and division whether the Iraq war was in defence of a vital national interest. Rule No.4 was never to use force except as a last resort. Bush decided to use force as the first resort. Rule No.5 was that when force was used as a last resort, avoid American casualties. This too became Bush's nightmare.

As the powerful neoconservative, Deputy Defence Secretary, Paul Wolfowitz admitted that the "bureaucratic" reason, that is the presence of weapons of mass destruction in Iraq, was not the main or the deciding factor. The real reason was to rebuild the pillar of American influence in the Middle East. It is debatable how far the Bush administration has been able to achieve this objective.

The Bush retreat has also been hastened by his declining popularity. His poll rating nosedived from over 70 per cent to just about 50 per cent. A democratic hopeful Kerry leads Bush by 4-5 points. This point, however, need not be exaggerated. Bush describes himself as a war President and through resurrecting a more moderate conservative programme could romp home in the coming elections. To a large extent, US elections have been determined on the strength or weakness of the economy.

Examining all these developments, Putin's versatile diplomacy also merits attention. He has not allowed his relations with the United States to deteriorate without abandoning his basic stances and has simultaneously consolidated his relations with Europe; all this while cultivating a new relationship with China and cementing the old strategic relationship with India.

Putin has pursued a complex policy in regard to the United States. He voiced his dissent with the United States quite strongly, on the issue of the war against Iraq. He did not yield to American pressures on many international issues ranging from the Iraq war to assistance to Iran in the nuclear energy field. Yet, he has succeeded in maintaining a non-antagonistic and non-combative relationship with the United States. He continued to affirm that he was with the

United States and a member of the international coalition against terrorism. His success can be measured by Condeleeza Rice's comment that the American policy was to punish France, ignore Germany and forgive Russia. George Bush continued to call him a good friend - no mean achievement considering the US administration's anger against all those who opposed the Bush war in Iraq. Putin has achieved this not only without ignoring Russian interests but also without a let-up on Russia's defence preparedness, evident from the recent successful experiment with the supersonic ballistic missile.

Yet, Putin has, at the same time, established a closer relationship with Europe, recalling without his saying so Gorbachev's reference to a European home with Russia included in it. He retained close relations with France and Germany throughout a difficult period when America was engaged in a war with Iraq and a war of words with Europe over the latter's failure to line up the United States. With Germany, particularly, Russia established a partnership which was described by some as "a beautiful friendship". Vladimir Putin and Gerhard Schroeder meeting in Russia signed a raft of political and business deals symbolizing the two countries' increasingly close ties. As Ben Aris put it in *the Guardian,* "once again at the heart of an enlarged Europe, no western European country has moved faster or further than Germany to cement ties with Russia since the fall of the iron curtain. Russia has quickly reestablished its importance in Europe and flexed its political muscles for the first time earlier last year during the stand-off between Europe and America over the need for war against Iraq."[5] Germany is already by far Russia's biggest trading partner in the European Union.

Putin also consolidated his relations with China. As both sides acknowledged, their relations have never been so good as today. China and India are amongst the largest military purchasers from Russia. 70-80 per cent of Russia's arms exports are to these two countries. Indeed, China's trade with Russia is much higher than India's with Russia. Yet, Putin took into consideration India's security concerns while supplying arms to China. Konstantin Maklenko of the Moscow-based Centre for Analysis of Strategies and Technologies noted the differentiation Russia made in supply of arms to China and India. Certain state-of-the-art weapons were supplied only to India.[6]

Nevertheless, we should not overlook the fact that Putin is still playing from a weaker hand and that there are too many divisive, if not destructive, forces working in the Russian federation. There are serious differences too between Russia and America and Russia and Europe over issues that impinge on Russia's internal developments. But the United States and the European Union are highly critical of Moscow's handling of the Chechen conflict which Moscow regards as a war against terrorism while USA and Europe criticize the human rights abuses by the Russian armed forces. USA and Europe also remain critical of the increasing consolidation of power in Putin's hands. His moves against mafia capitalism in Russia have elicited repeated concerns from America and the west European capitals about the diminishing space for democracy in Russia. Moreover, Russia's economy is just turning around and it would take many years of sustained efforts for Russia to catch up with the West. Putin has to keep in view all these contrary facts of his national and international situation.

There is a clear sentiment of irritation with one another on domestic developments in Russia among USA and Europe on the one hand and Russia on the other. Putin's consolidation of power in his own hands, and his open confrontation with Russia's mafia capitalists and his moves to get rid of the Yeltsin's legacy and its supporters within the government has aroused widespread unease among Western governments and the media as compromising democracy and the steady return of authoritarianism in Russia. On the external front too, there are areas of tension between the two sides. NATO's enlargement towards almost the borders of Russia has visibly irked the Russian opinion. Some even deplore Russia's incapacity to respond adequately.

Not a few knowledgeable circles are apprehensive of the possibility of a new cold war between Russia and United States. To take one instance, the noted US expert on Russia, Prof. Steven Cohen of the New York University, talking to students of the Russian State University for Trade and Economics in Moscow feared that "a new cold war is beginning between the United States and Russia". Cohen listed several reasons for the returned hostility. Apart from the legacy of the cold war, the replacement of Boris Yeltsin who followed a policy of concessions to USA, with Vladimir Putin, who was pursuing a policy dictated by Russian national interests raised new questions for Washington. Cohen also worried that George Bush was "creating a new, autocratic policy. We are now being saddled with the ideology of a new American imperialism". Yet another fact, that he listed for the revival of antagonism was the tendency of the United States to demand concessions from Russia but offering nothing in return. To this was added, in Cohen's view, NATO's Eastward expansion, a policy bound to disturb Russia.[7] However, the United States continued its dual approach towards Russia. While the US continued with the policy of NATO's Eastward expansion, it sought to allay Russian apprehensions in this regard. The Bush administration also found some virtue in Putin's reelection as President and the installation of a new government in Moscow. The State Department took the view that there were some encouraging signs that Putin's new government will pursue reforms despite his "tainted reelection and moves to consolidate power". The Assistant Secretary of State, Beth Jones told the House International Relations Committee that the focus of the new cabinet seemed to be on economic reforms. "This is a good track for him to be on". She hoped that pressure from Russia's middle class "will move him towards reinstituting and enhancing democratic institutions".[8]

Within Russia, however, Putin continued to be highly popular. He dismissed the last hangover of the Yeltsin's era, Prime Minister Mikhail Kasyanov and chose his own team headed by Mikhail Fradkov, who was earlier Chief of the Federal Tax Police Service. Many in the new cabinet were considered to be technicians. Alexsander Zhukov, the sole Deputy Prime Minister in the new cabinet, is reportedly a specialist in the field of currency, tax and customs law. The new Foreign Minister, Sergey Lavrov, had been Russia's permanent representative to the United Nations and was seen to be particularly involved in matters pertaining to Iraq.[9]

There was no real challenge to Putin and he won the presidential election easily on 14 March 2004. His mandate, in his own view, was to strengthen, stabilise and modernise Russian economy, protect Russian interests in the international fora and restore Russia's position in the comity of nations. Putin had a two-thirds majority of voters voting in the elections and interestingly, the 6,000 Russian voters in Israel also handed him a two-thirds majority.

In the context of these international developments, what is the strategic substance of India-Russia relationship? This writer would not like to overestimate its importance for the world, but for India, the relationship is substantial and is of strategic significance in the preservation of its fundamental interests and there is reason to believe that the relationship has some significance in Asia and the world.

India's biggest foreign policy challenge has been that of terrorism, particularly sponsored from outside. Indian and Russian perceptions have coincided whereas the United States adopted an ambivalent and dual policy. Washington recognizes the role of foreign-sponsored terrorism but has continued to pat Islamabad on the back over its contribution to the fight against terrorism. The United States has its own compulsions as the Al Qaeda operates from the borders between Pakistan and Afghanistan. The US administration believes that it needs Pakistan's continued cooperation in fighting the Al Qaeda. Russia, on the other hand, makes no distinction in the patterns of terrorism and its policies in this regard are in full alignment with those of India. The joint working group established by India and Russia on terrorism meeting in April last year took the common view that the anti-terrorist drive could not be selective. Terrorism was terrorism and had to be countered no matter where it came from.[10]

The American approach, on the other hand, has been highly differentiated. President Bush publicly acknowledged that terrorist activities against India could not be described as struggle for freedom. But the Bush administration has also been highly protective of Gen. Musharraf's regime. While exerting pressure on Pakistan downsized the terrorist camps in Kashmir and elsewhere, a major US objective has been to dissuade India from taking any retaliatory action. One might also add but that is the route the Indian government also took-depending on the United States to exercise pressure on Pakistan.

What happened after the terrorists attack on Indian Parliament was the most inglorious instance of this dependence. Reacting to the attack, the government mobilised the armed forces on the border but then–nothing happened. It allowed Pakistan time to marshal its forces on the border as well. Obviously, the government hoped that the US would come to its assistance by pressurizing Gen. Musharraf to bring about some visible reduction in terrorist violence sponsored from across the border. Gen. Roy Choudhary (Retd.) described the entire operation as a fiasco.

In fact, even the recent thaw in Indo-Pak relations, besides the link with the general elections in India, has an American input in it. The process started with Washington brought both sides into a dialogue and intervening on crucial moments to bring about the desired results. US Secretary of State, Colin Powell, acknowledged this much in his comments on the Indo-Pak decision on comprehensive talks. He told the *US News and World Report* that "we pitched in and broke the ice".[11] As mentioned earlier, a primary objective of the United States was to support and protect Gen. Musharraf because his help appeared to be crucial to the Bush administration for the fight against bin Laden and the Al Qaeda.

USA's dual (some say double?) approach was evident from the manner in which it had handled relations with India and Pakistan in more recent months. India was a friend but Pakistan was an ally, and the ally had a better claim than a friend. The "strategic partnership" between India and USA lay in tatters with Secretary of State, Colin Powell, coming to India and breathing not a word about the impending elevation of Pakistan as a non-NATO ally and then going on to Islamabad and announcing a new formal alliance with Pakistan that would enable it to tap the US for more advanced military supplies.

History appears to be repeating itself. In 1974, Dr. Henry Kissinger, the then Secretary of State, came to India soon after the successful emergence of Bangladesh. At a banquet hosted by the then Foreign Minister, Y.B. Chavan, in which many intellectuals were invited to interact with the US Secretary of State, this writer quizzed Dr. Kissinger about the US intentions. The core problem between USA and India was the US attempt at creating an artificial parity between India and Pakistan, this writer told Dr. Kissinger. His response was categorical that Washington had given up that approach, and that it now recognized that India was the major country in the sub-continent. Yet as soon as he reached the shores of the US, Washington announced a new arms aid package for Pakistan on the express plea to rectify the military imbalance between India and Pakistan.

Nothing substantial seemed to have changed in the history of the last three decades between USA and the sub-continent. Just as the United States embraced Zia-ul-Haq to train and arm the Taliban and Osama bin Laden's Al Qaeda in Afghanistan to be used against the Soviet Union, thus disturbing the delicate relationship between India and Pakistan, now also the United States chose to embrace General Musharraf in the fight against Osama bin Laden and the Taliban in Afghanistan, but once again threatening to disturb the critical stage of relationship between New Delhi and Islamabad. Surprisingly, and perhaps not so surprisingly, there has hardly been a squeak from New Delhi. The government failed to make any noise about it. There was only a modest expression of regret that India was not given any advance information. The Security Adviser, Mr. Brijesh Mishra, was reported to have telephoned his counterpart in Washington, Condeleeza Rice, but it is not known how strongly he expressed India's displeasure. In any case, the United States has again embarked upon a new policy towards the sub-continent which could have long-term adverse consequences. Expressing strong dissent in the country's own national interests cannot be regarded as tantamount to adoption of a hostile approach towards a big power. India would have to protect its own interests; it should not expect others to do it for her.

Russia's relations with India and Pakistan have had a different dimension so far. Russia supported the war against terrorism and declared Gen. Musharraf's commitment to counter terrorism within Pakistan and on the borders with Afghanistan. Russia also believed to be in its interests to make an opening towards Pakistan but so far has not tried to adopt a so-called even-handed policy. Putin has reasoned that by engaging General Musharraf, he has a better chance to influence Pakistan's policies in Afghanistan and Kashmir in a constructive direction than by just denouncing Islamabad. Russia also has its own agenda with Pakistan. Islamabad's policy towards former Soviet Central Asia has a far more immediate and important bearing on Russia than on India. Russia also has tangible economic interest in Pakistan. It would like to open the Pakistani market for Russian industrial goods, modernize Pakistani factories built by the erstwhile Soviet Union and help develop the Pakistani infrastructure. Russian experts do not rule out that Russia could even supply dual-purpose hardware to Pakistan, such as heavy-duty trucks or transport helicopters of the type Russia sold to Pakistan last year.[12]

General Musharraf paid a three-day visit to Moscow in early February 2003. Putin's understanding of India's sensitivities was evident from his telephone call to Mr. Vajpayee a day before Musharraf's visit commenced and from the fact that Moscow put out this news immediately. The press statement read, "as part of the maintenance of a continual confidential dialogue at the highest level, the leaders of the two countries (India and Russia) touched upon certain aspects of bilateral cooperation, and exchanged views with regard to the situation in South Asia, including on ways for normalizing relations between India and Pakistan. As reported earlier, a meeting was scheduled for February 5 between the President of the Russian Federation, Vladimir Putin, and the Pakistani President Pervez Musharraf. This telephone conversation (of Putin with Vajpayee) may be regarded as a "checking of the watches" of the leaders of Russia and India on the eve of Russia-Pakistani talks.[13] He followed this up with another telephone call less than 24 hours after Musharraf's departure from Moscow.

Reportedly Mr. Putin was unmoved by Musharraf's complaints against India and had told the General that he wished all success to him in implementation of pledges to tackle terrorists outfits and the menace of terrorism.

The joint statement issued at the end of the visit more or less echoed the same line with a slight difference. Pakistan and Russia stressed the need for "continuous sincere efforts by the parties concerned of South Asia to create conditions for resuming the dialogue between Pakistan and India in order to resolve all outstanding issues between them on the basis of equity and justice". More important, it said talks should be on the basis of the Shimla Accord and the Lahore Declaration.

General Musharraf in the past had said both the accords did not address the issue of Kashmir adequately.

The close contact with Russia was continued with the Foreign Minister Mr. Yashwant Sinha's visit to Moscow 13-18 May 2003. Yashwant Sinha was quite upbeat about his visit as, accordingly to him, Mr. Putin had shared with him the details of his talks with the Pakistani President. He also expressed his satisfaction at the outcome of these talks and at Russia's approach to the problem.[14] Russia welcomed President Musharraf's willingness to be a part of the fight against terrorism and to that extent Russia believed that Musharraf was an ally in this fight. But Russia was unequivocal that President Musharraf and the Pakistani government must do much more to halt all terrorist acts in Kashmir and other parts of India sponsored from the Pakistani territory. First of all, Russia believed that there was terrorism carried on from the Pakistani territory against India and secondly that Pakistan could do much more to stop it. There lay the difference in the Russian and the American approach to the issue. To that extent, Russia's forthright attitude was of strategic importance to India. There was no double talk or double speak about it.

Nevertheless, this writer must emphasise that we should neither take another country's friendship for granted nor should we allow our friendship to be taken for granted by another country. India must remain vigilant and sensitive to any changes, however nuanced, in the attitude or policy of other countries towards this sub-continent.

Yashwant Sinha had visited Russia partly to lay the ground work for the forthcoming visit of the Prime Minister to Moscow. The Russians had described Putin's telephone call to the Prime Minister before and after Musharraf's visit as "the checking of watches" between the two countries. This checking of watches was continued when the Prime Minister visited Russia 11-13 November 2003. The visit was intended to further cement the "strategic partnership" and cooperation between Russia and India which was exemplified in the large-scale defence relationship between the two countries, in the establishment of Russian aided nuclear plants in India, and in the commonality of approaches between the two countries to virtually all international problems. This commonality transcended political alignments and governmental changes within India and was firmly anchored to the national interests of the two countries.

This commonality provided the secure foundation for the strategic relationship. It was, however, not intended to be a military alliance or a ganging up against any other country, including the United States. Such military alliances were neither relevant nor feasible in the new international situation. Equally, neither of the two countries had the military strength to establish any such alliance. It was a political relationship, buttressed by the supply of state-of-the-art military hardware by Russia to India and by close political cooperation between the two countries in the international arena. Both countries were trying to carve more breathing space for themselves in international affairs, mitigating the rigours of one-power domination and for the establishment of a more equitable international order. It is in this sense that the India-Russia relationship is of considerable strategic importance to India, and one should like to think, to Russia also.

References

1. *New York Times,* 5 September 2003.
2. Ivo H. Daaldar and James M. Lindsay, America Unbound: The Bush Revolution in Foreign Policy, Brookings Institution Press, Washington, 2003.
3. *New York Times,* 23 October 2003.
4. *Ibid*, 9 October 2003.
5. *The Guardian,* 16 October 2003.
6. *The Hindu,* 28 August 2003.
7. *Rosbalt RU*, 11 March 2004 (electronically).
8. *Reuters* from Washington 18 March 2004.
9. See Elena Panova in Rosbalt RU, 10 March 2004 (electronically).
10. *The Times of India,* 12 April 2003.
11. *The Hindu,* 12 January 2004.
12. Vladimir Raduyin from Moscow in *The Hindu*, 25 January 2003.
13. *The Asian Age,* 5 and 6 February 2003. Also *The Hindu*, 9 February 2003.
14. See Indian newspapers of 13-18 May 2003.

2

Indo-Russian Strategic Partnership : Bilateral and Global Challenges

Prof. R.R. Sharma

At all times, relations between India and Russia have been close and friendly. In fact, the relationship between the two countries was so close during the Soviet period, that it was looked upon with a great deal of suspicion by the western powers, and their followers elsewhere. However, it served the basic national interests of the two countries. The close friendship graduated into "strategic partnership" at the dawn of twenty-first century. The milestone declaration on strategic partnership was proclaimed by the leadership of two countries in October 2000. The declaration on strategic partnership included several dimensions. In the first place, it reaffirmed the close proximity of national interests, and, therefore, the relations between the two would grow on the basis of each other's interests and major concerns. The declaration also indicated the geopolitical priorities of the two countries, which would form the basis of action in the global arena. Both President Putin and Prime Minister Vajpayee gave ample indication that the ties between the two countries drew their intrinsic strength from equality, and, therefore, these would not be allowed to take the road of realpolitik pragmatism.

The strategic partnership has been marked by intensity of close interaction in a variety of matters of bilateral nature, though the same cannot be said with regard to international matters. Of course, there are regular contacts, and even summit meetings between the leadership of the two countries. Prime Minister Atal Behari Vajpayee's last visit to Russia in November 2003 was his second visit to that country in less than six months. This is, perhaps, a transparent index of the state of political relationship between the two countries. Over and above, there are regular meetings at all levels to promote constant dialogue on bilateral issues pertaining to military, technical, scientific, economic and cultural cooperation. At a joint Press Conference in December 2002, President Putin pointedly emphasized that in the "environment of complex international situation, our constant dialogue is of special importance." Obviously, the frequent contacts between the two countries are intended to strengthen the process of constant dialogue on bilateral and multilateral issues.

During President Putin's visit to India in December 2002, there were two important declarations. One was the "Declaration on the further consolidation of strategic partnership", and the joint "Declaration on strengthening and enhancing Economic, Scientific & Technological Cooperation" between the two countries. These declarations resolved to strengthen bilateral bonds, expand mutual cooperation and elevate the relations to qualitatively new level. Apparently, these endeavours have expanded considerably the partnership agenda, and given a fillip to the pace for the development of bilateral ties. Though the framework of partnership is in place, the outcome would largely depend on the greater use of the available potential. Obviously, there are some specialized areas in which the cooperation between the two countries has taken long strides. However, there are several other fields in which there is either no progress, or the progress is not commensurate with the political and military levels of partnership. In fact, it was President Putin who outlined practical steps required to improve interaction between the two countries. There are tangible opportunities for the two countries to participate in large-scale and well-funded long-term projects and joint ventures.

The bilateral context of partnership, however, is thus not only fairly satisfactory, but has the inbuilt potential to improve further in the years to come. This level of close interaction has been achieved in the face of heavy odds. There were influential political lobbies in both the countries, which offered different options. Emerging from the womb of Indo-Soviet relations, the new relations have been witness to numerous turning points in the political life of the two countries. These are discussed in the latter part of this paper. One important reason why these relations survived and grew from strength to strength lies in the basic fact that both the countries have needed each other, needing cooperation and close interaction to advance their somewhat identical national, strategic interests. To further these basic common interests, both India and Russia were able to create a functional mechanism of mutual cooperation and consultation. The mechanism is, of course, not fool-proof. It has a scope to improve and become more productive.

From Friendship to Strategic Partnership

The former Soviet Union always claimed that it was both a European as well as an Asian power. Being the core of the Eurasian Land mass, it would not agree to its exclusion from either Europe or Asia. In the aftermath of Soviet dissolution, Russia, which emerged as the most important "successor state", was more than inclined to underplay its geo-strategic location on the Eurasian landscape. It revised its priorities, which created the erroneous impression that it was a mere regional power. However, gradually the perception changed. It gave way to the old natural perception that Russian interests cover a vast area extending from central and northern Europe to Asia Minor, the Middle East and the Pacific region. The renewed emphasis on this by the Russians was a remarkable endorsement of the views held by such diverse personalities as Macinder and Lenin.

The re-emergence of this perception has several and serious implications for Russian foreign policy. From the Indian standpoint, this means that the two countries have put behind a cool period in their relations. The cool period (1991-93) was characterized by a visible credibility gap in Indo-Russian ties. The source of the credibility gap may be located, largely, in the Russian government's views regarding the future of Indo-Russian relations. The scope of Indo-Russian relations was defined on the eve of former President Boris Yeltsin's visit to India in December 1992. There was a wide-ranging discussion both in Russian Duma, as well as in the governing board of the Russian foreign ministry. The dominant view, put forth by the then Foreign Minister, Kozyrov and his team, was that there was no need to preserve the "special" relationship with India. In the Soviet era such a relationship did exist. The Soviet Union was not only very friendly to India, but was also its largest trading partner, and a key supplier of sophisticated military hardware. The new argument put forth by Kozyrov was that a special relationship with India was likely to undermine Russia's interaction with other countries in South Asia, and more particularly with Pakistan. Obviously, the era of "special relationships" should come to an end. In the Parliamentary (Duma) hearings on relations with India, the then Deputy Foreign Minister Georgy Kunadze freely articulated these views.

In fact, this was only a continuation of projections made in the working paper on Russia's foreign policy, which was finally adopted in late 1992. This became the foreign policy concept of the Russian Federation. The 58-page document devoted a large space to relations with the United States of America. It concluded that Russia needed and looked for US support in carrying out the complex economic and strategic tasks before its foreign policy. Therefore, it was necessary that Russia should strive to achieve "stable" relations with the US and the West on the basis of "strategic partnership". It also envisaged a long-term perspective of a "Union" with the West.

It is important to recall that the so-called "working paper" prepared by the Foreign Ministry made pointed and critical comments on India's stand on international issues and problems, primarily on nuclear non-proliferation. It pleaded that this should be taken note of while developing military and technical ties with India. Of course, this was not the sole point of view regarding the scope of Indo-Russian relations. There also existed within the Ministry an entirely different perspective regarding the course of these relations. It was argued on this side that the Russian relations with a major country like India cannot be, and should not be, reduced to the level of other countries of the South Asian region. Several members of Russian Duma openly articulated the view that "India was, is and should remain Russia's first priority". The leader of the Communist party in a lengthy article published in *Pravada* went on to forcefully argue that India has "a great strategic potential" in global affairs, and this will be "felt more and more as the years pass". It was therefore in the "vital interest of Russia to preserve its closer relationship" with countries like India. These views were shared by quite a few other well-known political actors of the period like Zhirinovsky, Burbolous, Lukianov (who was earlier Chairman of the Duma's Group on India) etc.

President Yeltsin during his visit to India in December 1992 declared that India could become a "strategic partner of Russia". Of course, he also emphasized that Russia would like to develop its ties with India "in a de-ideologised manner" so as to minimize the possibility of these being directed against "Third Party". He also endorsed India's stand on the Kashmir issue, and further assured that Russia will refrain from selling arms to Pakistan. The complicated Rupee-Rouble issue for re-estimating and the size of the past Soviet credits was satisfactorily solved. This removed a major irritant in the way of resumption of trade relations. An understanding was also reached to ensure smooth supply of defense spares. Likewise, a mutually acceptable solution was found with regard to the issue of supply of cryogenic engines.

It is, therefore, legitimate to infer that the visit of Boris Yeltsin marked an initial breakthrough in the Indo-Russian relations. One cannot but take note of the fact that he openly talked about an "*Asian tilt*" in the foreign policy of Russia. He also spoke of "Russia-China-India axis" for building durable peace in Asia. During this visit a new Treaty of Peace, Friendship and Cooperation was signed between the two countries. The new Treaty replaced the 1971 Soviet era Treaty of Peace, Friendship and Cooperation. The credibility gap thus in the Indo-Russian ties was considerably reduced.

Prime Minister Rao visited Moscow in June 1994. This visit further underscored the growing importance of Indo-Russian relations. The so-called "Moscow Declaration" signed by President Yeltsin and Prime Minister Rao was indeed a historic document. It tried to pinpoint the commitment of the two countries to their territorial integrity. At a conceptual level the Declaration highlighted the fact that the two countries were "variegated, multi-cultural, multiethnic, pluralistic states". Such as, they faced a variety of common challenges to their territorial integrity. Moscow declaration gave a clear indication of the growing mutual understanding, and a realization to raise relationship to a strategic long-term level as demanded by the changed context. Moscow Declaration can also be viewed in the context of global politics. It sought to project the interests of multinational states. For the first time, it called world attention to the fact that the unity, territorial integrity of countries is a precondition for global and regional stability. It was a historic blueprint for global cooperation in preventing and dealing with the emerging phenomenon of conflict and terrorism.

Prime Minister Mr Chernomyrdin's visit to India in December 1994 went a long way in clearing the lingering doubts. He categorically assured that Russia was neither supplying any military equipment to Pakistan, nor it intended to do so in the future. He put an end to all speculations to sell sophisticated military hardware to Pakistan. He castigated Pakistan for lending its support to the extremists in Chechnya. He also disclosed that mercenaries from Pakistan have been captured alongwith others. During the visit, a number of vital agreements concerning cooperation in defense, space research, etc. were signed. Likewise, issues pertaining to merchant shipping, promotion of air traffic were discussed, and agreed upon.

At this point, it is necessary to point out that the continued relevance of a strong and healthy Indo-Russian relationship in the changed global environment was a point of dispute among a section of influential political opinion in India also. There was no dearth of skeptics who doubt the wisdom of re-energizing Indian ties with Russia in view of the economic and military weakness of Russia. They also invariably pointed to the political instability prevailing there. The argument was that India's requirements of economic and technological restructuring can only be met by the US and Europe. These skeptics forget that Russia's geo-strategic location on the Eurasian landscape; its advanced nuclear and human resources make it difficult for that country to reconcile itself for long to the status of a mere regional power. It was bound to regain its status as a powerful actor in international politics, and more particularly in Asia.

In the following period, it became increasingly obvious that Russia's foreign policy was undergoing a major face-lift, because the earlier policy had neither the strategic depth nor the vision. In the intervening period, the U.S. and NATO had also administered several pinpricks to the Russian interests in East Europe, Trans Caucasia and Central Asia. This led to the growing realization that Russia was conceding far too much to the U.S. The earlier tilt towards the US thus gradually yielded place to the concept of diversification. There was an open effort to upgrade its relations with countries like India to a strategic level. The new foreign minister of Russia Yevgeny

Primakov asserted that "Russian foreign policy today should uphold national interests more energetically than before". Obviously, the Russian diplomacy assumed a well-defined foreign policy concept under his perceptive leadership. Prior to that in the Russian academic circles, it was often pointed out that Russia continues to be lost in its "search for a true place between the East and the West, the North and the South".

Soon after taking over as the new Foreign Minister Primakov spelled out the parameters of Russian foreign policy in great detail in the new context. He averred that Russia's foreign policy suffered from "imbalances", which must be "overcome". He further argued that the "development of relations with the US as a state having considerable weight and influence in the world" was only one among the priority tasks of Russian foreign policy. He repeatedly underlined the need to "diversify" Russia's international ties. "Of great importance for us is the development of relations with.... the European Community as a whole, as well as China, India, Japan and the Asia Pacific countries", he clarified. With tongue in cheek, he suggested that the idea of "normalizing relations with our former cold war opponents" was "overdone too strongly". He stressed the imperative need to "counterbalance" the negative trends in international politics. This was so because "not all power centres of the multipolar would have been formed". Both Russia and India cannot but take into consideration the new geo-political realities. Russia has a point when it says that its relations with CIS, and particularly with Central Asia, are of "prime importance" for a variety of reasons. Foremost of these, as Primakov said, it is a "way for Russia to become aware of itself as a great power". Primakov's vision and projections were incorporated as an integral part of Russian national security doctrine of 1997 and 2001.

Likewise, India too has deep strategic interests in Central Asia. It may be argued that these interests—Russian and Indian—do not exclude each other in any major way. The projected "strategic partnership" between Russia and India has this, and several other concerns, to promote, and benefit from them. From a historical standpoint, there has always been a certain convergence of Russian and Indian interests in peace and stability of the Eurasian landmass, separated from India by a chain of mountains. It was indeed useful from the standpoint of India that Russia cogently redefined its priorities, foreign policy goals and its national interests. Under the leadership of Primakov, Russia, in fact, presented an alternative vision of not only Russian foreign policy, but also of global politics of multi-polarity and multilateralism.

In the year 2000, President Putin and the Prime Minister Vajpayee took the final and the decisive step and transformed the much talked about vision of "strategic partnership" into a historic agreement. It vividly projected the basic vision of democratisation of international relations, a multi-polar and a multilateral world order as against the unipolar world order. Soon thereafter, President Putin was forthright in arguing that the project of "creating a new architecture for international security, building a safer world has become particularly important after the two-polar world ceased to exist. We are in favour of improving the existing mechanism of the United Nations, mechanisms of improving international peace and security".

On the issue of trilateral cooperation between India, China and Russia, which was for the first time mooted by Primakov, President Putin asserted: "We are convinced of the need for positive development of relations between Russia and India, Russia and China, and China and India. I think that all the parties within this triangle are interested in this development. At the same time, I think we shouldn't get ahead of time, or move ahead without proper preparation." Both the countries are making serious endeavour to move in the desired direction.

The new vision in Moscow's foreign policy basically stemmed from the growing realisation to elevate its relationship with India to a strategic long-term level. Their so-called 'strategic partnership' has the necessary potential to counterbalance all those negative trends, which may be discerned in the current international politics. It is also necessary to come to an understanding that the two countries have geo-political interests dictating long-term mutual active cooperation, particularly in Central Asia. Moreover, this relationship can go a long way in perfecting the process of the formation of different power centres of the emerging world order, which will, of course, take quite some time to crystalize in view of the hegemonic agenda of the U.S. based on the policy of unilateralism and political doctrine of preemption.

More significantly, one of the major problems is to overcome the usual snags and bottlenecks in the implementation of various agreements. Invariably, there hangs this perennial question as to what extent various bilateral accords and agreements are likely to be fulfilled. There are already over eighty bilateral agreements within the framework of strategic partnership. Obviously, there is a crying need to activize various institutional structures, as also devise a more workable and productive mechanism for better coordination between the concerned bodies, establishments, and the bureaucracy in the two countries.

While hosting a banquet in honour of the visiting Russian President in October 2000,the then President of India, K.R. Narayanan, had cogently pointed out that the "multifaceted relationship between India and the Russian Federation is substantive in content and extensive in scope. As we consolidate our cooperation, the main challenge before us is economic development in order to meet the aspirations of our people." President Narayanan perhaps had also in his mind the state of Indo-Russian bilateral economic relationship, which had grown fragile after the demise of the Soviet Union. While major global and bilateral issues like terrorism, defence, space and technology cooperation etc. have been adequately addressed, bilateral trade and economic relations between the two countries have stagnated. Bilateral trade between the two countries had more or less disappeared in early nineties after the demise of USSR. It gradually picked up in the following years, but the two way trade is abysmal 1.5 billion dollors now. It is worth recalling that the former Soviet Union was India's largest trade partner.

The composition of bilateral trade has not changed much over the years. It is largely confined to such items as pharmaceuticals, tea, coffee, spices and tobacco. However, the volume of trade in respect of these items has plummeted sharply. The export of Indian tea, which enjoyed monopoly position in the former Soviet Union, has sharply declined to less than 50,000 tons from 100,000 tons a year. It compares poorly with the export of Sri Lankan tea which has shot up to over fifty thousand tons a year in less than a decade. Likewise, traditional Indian export items to Russia such as leather goods, garments and jewellery have become almost extinct. In the meantime, the consumption boom in Russia has attracted businessmen not only from the U.S. and E.U., but also many other small countries, including Taiwan, Philippines and Turkey. India has not taken any advantage of these new opportunities, which were so inviting to other countries and who have taken a huge advantage of them.

It is obvious that both the countries–particularly India–should impart dynamic impulse to their economic cooperation in order to sustain their strategic partnership. The main task in the new context is to devise a feasible mechanism for ensuring quantum jump in bilateral economic and trade ties. Apparently, an entourage of over 80 Indian businessmen, which accompanied the Prime Minister Vajpayee during his recent visit to Russia, was meant to remedy the situation. It may possibly generate the requisite economic impulse for building a fairly productive economic and trading partnership with Russia. The best route available to the Indian businessmen is the route of investment in Russian industry. The investment route is also likely to facilitate their entry into the wider markets of CIS, including Central Asia. Like Russia, India also had a strategic interest in Central Asia. We have already lost out to other nations in building our economic and trade relations with the Central Asian republics.

Obviously, both the countries regard the relations with each other as of "utmost importance". Both the countries view each other as a "major international partner". Putin goes even further in claiming that "we have not this level and quality of cooperation with other countries, as we have achieved with India". Both the countries are consequently engaged in joint development and production of high-tech, very complex and very promising weapon system. Bilateral cooperation in the area of defence has shown, as Prime Minister Vajpayee put it during his more recent visit in November 2003, "great versatility", and it is advancing so rapidly that it is set to reach new heights. The joint development of BrahMos supersonic cruise missile is an obvious indicator of productive defence cooperation between the two countries. They have a number of other ongoing projects in a variety of other areas, including energy. This level of cooperation would not have been possible without the existing base, which had come into being decades ago as a consequence of political vision and political understanding between the two countries. It is now required to deepen that understanding to meet the "global challenges and threats to world security and stability."

Strategic Partnership and Politics of Global Hegemony

As mentioned briefly earlier, the strategic partnership between India and Russia is struggling to find an adequate response to the emerging global politics of hegemonism and unilateralism. Of course, in their numerous joint declarations, both the countries have opposed the politics of unilateral solutions of major problems in global politics. They have invariably advocated the foremost principle that each nation is sovereign and has the right to decide its own destiny, its economic path of development. And both the countries have shown equal concern regarding the upsurge of political and religious terrorism, which poses a great threat particularly to the interests of multinational and multicultural societies. This, however, does not take us very far in restraining the super-hegemonism of the U.S., which is menacingly prancing over the weaker nations, who are in a "state of political torpidity" after the collapse of balanced bipolar system of international relations.

Evgeny Primakov had the vision to foresee in 1997 that the global politics for some time was bound to be dominated by one super power. But in order to prevent its total hegemony, it has to be countered by "multiple poles", which should emerge as independent centres of political and economic power. And Russia, therefore, should say categorical "no" to American unipolar idea. The unipolar concept has, however, developed deeper roots in the U.S. in the recent years without much opposition from the outside world. The global politics has turned upside down in the aftermath of September 11, 2001.

U.S. Doctrines of Hegemony

Throughout the recent history of international relations, the U.S. has played broadly three different kind of strategic roles: Limited Partner, Security Manager, Hegemon. Of these what role should the U.S. play invariably depended on its perception of national interests in a region or a country. The U.S. took a conscious decision at the dawn of 21st Century to shift U.S. security policy away from the collective security order to a unilateral policy, which apparently is focused on a more bellicose military posture. Evidently, unilateralism has its roots in, what an American analyst calls, "a strain of political thinking best labelled hegemonist". The hegemonist strain of thinking had always argued that "America's immense power and the willingness to wield it ... is the key to securing America's interests in the world. Hegemonist arguments were updated in early 1990s after the collapse of the Soviet Union. Dick Cheney and Paul Wolfowitz have forcefully argued that the US security policy after the Cold War should seek to "transform the unipolar moment into a unipolar era" by precluding the emergence of any political future global competitor.

The U.S. policy of hegemony rests on a few major assumptions. The foremost is that power, especially military power matters. If "power matters, great powers matter most of all". Therefore, the U.S. primacy was "both real and usable". Condoleeza Rice argues with passion that the power must be "exercised solely in terms of American interests. Another disturbing assumption underlying the new hegemonist worldview states that multilateral agreements and institutions are neither essential nor necessarily conducive to American interests. It is worthwhile to mention that the 1992 draft Pentagon planning document argued that the U.S. "should be postured to act independently", because "future coalitions would be *ad hoc* assemblies often not lasting beyond the crises being confronted..." More significantly, the hegemonists in U.S. administration hold on to the belief that the U.S. is a "Unique power and others see it as such". And since the U.S. possessed unrivalled power, it, therefore, had the right to set the international agenda.

The point being argued is because of a major paradigm shift in the U.S. foreign policy, the global politics and relations are in imminent danger of becoming more unstable. And since the U.S. is actually the most influential power in the world politics, its policies are adversely impacting the strategic environment. The U.S. strategy implies the use of power not only against terrorists and tyrants, who are determined to seek technologies of mass destruction, but also to use force to remove "obstacles and threats to liberty and freedom that existed throughout the world." Therefore, the U.S. has the right as well as the power to "change the *status quo*". This may be achieved by bringing about, if required, a regime change in the so-called "rogue" or "undesirable" states. The U.S. policy of toppling other governments is, of course, not new.

The environment of global hegemony poses a formidable challenge to both Russia and India. The U.S. has utilized the events of 11 September 2001 to project its unilateralist and hegemonist agenda. It is proposed to both Russia and India to give up the alternative version of new world order, which was envisioned in their declaration of strategic partnership. Both have refrained from strongly reacting to the mounting threat from the forces of global hegemonism. President Bush softened his approach to Russia (and China) only after the events of 9/11. However, if we scan through his earlier statements, it becomes clear that both Russia and China were projected a great "threat to the West and to our European allies in particular".

Bush and his close associates were extremely critical of Clinton for "appeasing a rising China and indulging a corrupt Russia". In fact, the hegemonist arguments were updated in early 1990s after the collapse of the Soviet Union, as the U.S. was no longer checked by a rival superpower. The Vice-President Dick Cheney, and Paul Wolfowitz had played a leading role in arguing that the time was ripe to eliminate "any future competitor. Dick Cheney forcefully argued that the serious danger to the U.S. emanated from Russia, China, Iraq, North Korea, and terrorists. While toning down U.S. stance on both Russia and China, President Bush nevertheless pledged to ask the U.S. Congress to increase substantially "our assistance to dismantle as many Russian weapons as possible, as quickly as possible." Before that, U.S. Defence Secretary Donald Rumsfeld and his Deputy Wolfowitz had publicly accused Russia of being "an active proliferator." This was a ludicrous accusation, which was heatedly denied by the junior Russian officials. Obviously, this was not a befitting response.

One obvious problem was that the U.S. kept quiet about the biggest proliferator, namely Pakistan. The audacious Pakistani nuclear transfer to the "rogue" states, or the so-called "axis of evil" was well-known and this is fully exposed now. Like the U.S. war on terror, the fight against proliferation has been reduced to a kind of ideological battle against such states which do not fit into the America's worldview. Both proliferation and terrorism are indeed the two leading issues in global politics. And the U.S. has used these issues to deploy its armed forces to a large number of nations, particularly in Asia. It has become obvious to other nations that by using these issues, the U.S. is only advancing its immediate strategic interests. The U.S.-led war on terror has thus fractured the global consensus.

The declared strategic partnership of Russia and India has had little impact so far on the global politics. Russia and China have entered into a similar partnership. This has hardly fared better. The three countries, or rather the three Eurasian powers, can be more effective if they form the Eurasian strategic triangle. The eastward expansion of NATO is a clear indication that an atmosphere of hostility is being created around Russia. Russia is also being accused of violating democratic rights, and a nursery of anti-Semitism. Russia, a long-term foe of the U.S., is, therefore an obvious target. The soft talk about Russia being a strategic partner is totally misleading. Russia will never be trusted as an equal partner. Likewise, China is always regarded as a "strategic competitor" which must be dealt with "without illusions".

In fact, in more recent times, the U.S. has openly articulated its disapproval of Russia's assertive policies in a variety of areas. It is particularly unhappy with President Putin's foreign policy reach, which has been redesigned to rebuild Russia's global role. The U.S. Secretary of State, Colin Powell, during his visit to Russia in February 2004 identified "four clouds" that were "threatening to darken" U.S.-Russian relations. These included human rights abuse, and Russia's "expansionist policy" in former Soviet States. Writing in Izvestia, Powell blasted the Russian political system for lack of democracy: "Political power is not yet tethered to the law. Key aspects of civil society .... Have not yet attained independent reality". Apparently, the U.S. is worried about President Putin's policies, which seek to consolidate his power inside Russia. And it is equally keen to thwart resurgent Russia's efforts to expand its power base in the CIS countries. Russian Defence Minister, Sergei Ivanov, while explaining Moscow's new defence policy, asserted: "The CIS is an extremely important security zone for Russia. Russia retains the right to preventive use of military force, including the CIS countries". American anxiety is also related to its burning desire to control energy resources of Central Asia and Caucasus.

The strategic importance of the region grew manifold after September 11. Central Asia which was for some American analysts "a strategic quicksand" or a "mission too far" became mission immediate and urgent. To begin with, the US decided to be "Central Asia's security manager". However, Eugene Rumer ; makes a bold observation, which is at the heart of the issue. He says: "In the aftermath of September 11, though it would be shortsighted to define US interests in Central Asia merely in terms of operational counter terrorism requirements and ongoing military operations in Afghanistan. The tragedy of the terrorist attacks has given a new and very different meaning to the notion first articulated by US policy makers in 1990s.... the absence of geopolitical competition..."

This was officially confirmed by Elizabeth Jones, Assistant Secretary of State for Eurasian Affairs in a testimony before the US Senate Sub-Committee in December 2001. Jones testified that US had no intention of abandoning Central Asia after the Afghan War. She outlined four US priorities in the region: *Combating Terrorism, reform, the rule of law*, and *Caspian Sea energy resources.* Collin Powel also confirmed that Kazakhstan's oil was of "critical importance" to the US. Military presence is essential for the US to control Caspian Sea and Caspian energy resources. Apparently, this is a "sub-text of the war" in Afghanistan.

The US cannot however maintain its footprint in Central Asia without the active cooperation of most important regional powers, namely, Russia, China and Iran. Each of these nations has a huge stake in the region. These nations have offered their cooperation so far in the interest of regional stability and security. However, their concern for stability and security does not "outweigh fears of US preponderance". Tensions are bound to rise, and resolving the growing tensions obviously would be a formidable task. Russian Defense Minister, Sergei Ivanov, in fact, reminded the US that it had promised to close down military bases in Uzbekistan and Kyrgyzstan after the completion of its military operation in Afghanistan. "We did not object to the basis, but set a condition that they operate only as long as it takes to stabilise the situation in Afghanistan", Ivanov informed a NATO Conference in Colorado Springs. He went on to assert that the "CIS is an extremely important security zone for Russia ... we have boosted and will further boost our presence in the Commonwealth of Independent States." Russia is thus showing a new assertiveness towards the CIS as a part of a broader revision of its "defense doctrine post-9/11." There is thus a clear signal to the US to accept Russia's dominant role in Central Asia.

While sharply disagreeing with the US on its policy of unilateralism and a host of other issues, President Putin has been steadily expanding the cooperative agenda with the US. Therefore, he will have to walk the razor's edge in promoting Russia's national interests, particularly in Central Asia. He has thus come out with what apparently is useful concept of building an "arch of stability" stretching from Europe through the Caucasus and Central Asia to China and South East Asia. This is a kind of paradigm to counter "the arch of instability, which the US argued extends from the Caribbean Basin through Africa to South and Central Asia and across to North Korea. This justified the role of the US as a global hegemon. President Putin clarified that the arch of stability must be based on "entwined regional security arrangements" that should preclude domination either by the US or China. Russia has thus worked out both military alliances as well as bilateral and multilateral agreements with the Central Asian States and China. Russia is also actively pursuing the project of Moscow-Delhi-Beijing triangle, which in its perception could emerge as a pillar of stability in Asia. The three countries of the Eurasian triangle have the strategic potential to build a combined power to checkmate the U.S. policies of unilateralism and hegemonism.

References

1. Text of Joint Declarations and the Statements of Boris Yeltsin, Putin, and other Indian and Russian leaders have been quoted from the reports appearing in *The Hindu.* I have also used Vladimir Radyuhin's reports of 9 Jan. 2000, 4 November 2003 and 11 Feb. 2004 published in the *The Hindu.*
2. *Foreign Policy Concept of Russia,* 28 June, 2000.
3. *Russian National Security Doctrine,* Jan. 2000, CDSP, Vol. 52, No. 44, 1995, and No. 4 (Vol. 52).
4. Mahavir Singh and Victor Krassilchikov, *Eurasian Vision,* Anamika Publishers, Delhi, 2003.
5. I.H. Daalder & James M. Lindsay, *America Unbound,* Brookings Institution Press, Washington, 2003.

3

Global Developments in the Twenty-First Century and Indo-Russian Strategic Partnership

V.D. Chopra

Any objective estimate of international significance of Indo-Russian strategic partnership cannot be delinked from some of the ominous developments in the beginning of the twentyfirst century. The recent North Atlantic Treaty Organisation's (NATO's) Eastward expansion is one such development, which has a far-reaching importance than what appears on the surface. Let us examine this trend at the very outset of this study.

NATO's Eastward Expansion

NATO's eastward expansion is a real threat to India, China and Russia's security, both political and economic.

It may be recapitulated that NATO was set up in 1949 to 'defend' Europe from the communists. There were 12 founding members. Greece and Turkey were added in 1952, Germany in 1955 and Spain in 1982. Later Poland, Hungary and the Czech Republic joined after the disintegration of the Soviet Union. In the beginning of the 2004, Bulgaria, Estonia, Latvia, Lithuania, Romania, Slovakia and Slovenia have joined the NATO. Now it has a total strength of 26 members, in addition to Pakistan and Kuwait, which have been given the status of 'major non-NATO allies'. This brings into sharp focus how NATO has already assumed the character of military instrument of transnationals. It will be appropriate to assess its implications for India.

The estimate of a senior Democratic lawmaker of America as reported in the press, granting of special status to Pakistan in NATO would give a setback to emerging ties between India and Pakistan. He did not leave at that. He said that naming Pakistan a 'major non-NATO ally' is completely inconsistent with U.S. policies. "Pakistan is not a democratic nation, Pakistan supports terrorism in Kashmir and Pakistan has emerged as a nuclear power. It has recently pardoned the key scientist who aided covert nuclear programmes in rogue nations". He underlined that the results of this new designation will be devastating. He further said that the most immediate concern of the designation is the rapid and large-scale supply of military equipment from the United States to Pakistan, including possible F-16s. This was cause for concern because US military supplies that were given to Pakistan for use against Russia and China have been historically used against India. It may be mentioned here that Pakistan has already been allocated US $ 3 billion assistance –50 per cent at which for military equipment - for its assistance in the war against terrorism. American experts have pointed out that Pakistan has a history of abusing military and nuclear equipment and yet USA has allowed Pakistan to have access to depleted uranium ammunition, special privilege in bidding for certain US government contracts, radar systems, attack helicopters and airborne early warning systems.

It is also relevant to mention that the Russian response to this development. Needless to say, Moscow is not happy with the enlargement of NATO because it feels that it is a dangerous and historic mistake. Russian experts point out that European history convincingly shows that as soon as the balance of forces is upset on the continent, the result is instability, conflict and wars. Gennady Zynganov, a leader of the Communist Party has called it the "biggest mistake in post-war history" and Russia's Foreign Ministry has said, it was a "tragedy" that "will inevitably lead to emergence of new dividing lines". Former Prime Minister, Yevgeny Primakov has promoted the idea of a Russian-Chinese-Indian alliance as a counterweight to NATO expansion.

Unmollified by a consultative role and a "partnership for peace" with the Western alliance, Moscow had drawn a redline beyond that NATO should not include the erstwhile states of Soviet Union including Ukraine and Baltic Republics. It is precisely this line of demarcation, which Washington has crossed.

Significantly, the Russian parliament has warned that Moscow could increase nuclear arsenals and pull out of arms control pacts if NATO fails to heed Russian concerns over the eastward enlargement of the alliance. Peace loving European people have expressed, the apprehension that the enlargement of NATO and taking it right upto the Russian border will make Europe more unstable by needlessly antagonising the Russians when they no longer pose a threat. There are others who argue that behind the recent moves to expand NATO is the fact that in the post-Boris Yeltsin period, Russia has once again begun to re-emerge as a great power. It has now a democratic system and the hallmark of which is that it has registered the highest growth rate and is engaged in restructuring its economy through its own model of mixed economy-combination of public sector and private sector. The standard of living of the Russian people is rising. The inflation is well under control. Seen in this context now America and other Western powers are engaged in deflecting it from this path of development. Above all, Russia is developing and deepening its political, military and economic relations with two Asian giants, China and India. In this sense, NATO's expansion is directed not only against Russia but also against China and India. How far this assessment is correct, it is difficult to predict at this stage. There is yet another aspect of this development, which can be aptly described as economic motive behind NATO's expansion.

After the collapse of the Soviet Union, which represented an alternative path to economic and social development with all its negative features, the transnationals have become a key factor in all spheres–political, economic and military. It is the transnationals, which control politics and economy in various parts of the globe. This has led to the emergence of transnational elite. We may define the 'transnational elite' as the elite, which draws its power (economic, political or generally social power) by operating at the transnational level. This elite does not express solely the interests of a particular nation-state, although one may expect that in case most of its members come from a particular nation-state, which happens also to be today's sole military superpower, the views of that part of the transnational elite which is dominant will prevail in achieving common objectives of the transnational elite in general, according to some social scientists in West Europe. The transnational elite consist of:

- the transnational economic elite whose members control the internationalised market economy (corporate directors, major shareholders, TNC executives etc.) and play the dominant role within the transnational elite as a whole given the predominance of economic factors in a market economy;
- the transnational political elite whose members control the political dimension of the New World Order (NOW) (globalising bureaucrats and politicians based either in major international organisations or in the state machines of the major market economies); and
- the transnational professional elite whose members control the scientific/ideological dimension of the New World Order (important academics and researchers in the various international foundations, members of think tanks and research departments of major international universities, mass-media executives etc.

This hypothesis is emphasised to understand the current situation in India and the stand of a section of political elite on American policies and their military instrument NATO.

The four 'wars' launched by the transnational elite in the last ten years since its emergence after the collapse of 'actually existing socialism', (i.e., the Gulf war, the war in Kosovo, the war on Iraq and the on-going 'war on terrorism') are cases substantiating the existence of an informal system of transnational governance, a political globalisation presided over by a transnational elite. This political globalisation is characterised by some as the latest form of imperialism. Nial Ferguson, a professor of history at Oxford University, for instance, describes in his article *'Welcome the New Imperialism'* as follows:—

Political globalisation is a fancy word for imperialism, imposing your values and institutions on others. However you may dress it up, whatever rhetoric you may use, it is not very different in practice to what Great Britain did in the 18th and 19th centuries. We already have precedents: the new imperialism is already in operation in Bosnia, Kosovo, East Timor and now in Iraq.

As far as the argument about surroundings of Russia is concerned, the present Russian elite, committed to integrating market economy, presents no serious problem to the West. However, its emergence as a great power is seen as a new challenge to America because the cooperation and integration between Russia and China can pose a serious threat to hegemony of Washington.

There is yet another aspect of it. The expansion and the use of NATO war machine are directed to consolidate and strengthen US hegemony over the world. The political and military hegemony in the institutional framework of an internationalised market economy is not an end in itself but is rather important only as a means for the protection of this institutional framework. This shows that domination over the world market is the main objective of the American political elite. NATO therefore has a dialectical linkage with expansion of NATO and setting up of military bases in the various parts of the world. In this sense, NATO should not be seen merely as an instrument in the war against international terrorism. This is only a tip of the iceberg. The basic motivation is to create a New World Order under the hegemony of the US—political, economic and military.

It is pertinent to mention here that political elite in India including left of the centre and centrist forces have not fully grasped the specific characteristics of the ambition of the American political elite to establish its political and economic hegemony over the world. Through various instruments it has established economic, political and ideological linkages with the new emerging elite connected with multinationals and transnationals. The fight against the American hegemony in India has its own characteristics.

Now let us briefly examine the new emerging American policy in the Middle East.

New American Policy in the Middle East

As a result of recurrent political crises in the area during the recent past including US-UK military occupation of Iraq, the installation of a new government in Baghdad and above all Saudi Arabia's elite commandos ended a 25 hour hostage drama by storming a residential complex in the oil city of Al Khobar on 30th May 2004, it becomes abundantly clear that this region is in a state of turmoil. As a matter of fact it would be politically naive to ignore that United States' pro-Israel policy and its occupation of Iraq have unleashed a new political upsurge in the entire Arab world, for that matter in the entire Muslim world. India cannot remain immune from this development because it has the largest Muslim population in the world after Indonesia. This in itself brings into sharp focus that a fresh look should be given to the developments in the Middle East situation from state-to-state.

Before any such attempt is made, it will be relevant to underline three basic facts.

Firstly, as has been reported in the press that Bush administration has acknowledged that the war, which has so far cost the lives of nearly 900 US troops and thousands of Iraqis, was motivated by Washington's desire to defend the Jewish state, i.e., Israel. "The Bush administration is surrounded by staunch pro-Israel, neo-conservative hawks, which is currently fighting an extensive campaign to ward off accusation that it derailed the 'war on terrorism' it launched after 9/11 by taking a detour to Iraq, which appears to have posed no direct threat to the US. Israel is Washington's biggest ally in the Middle East, receiving annual direct aid of US $ 3.4 billion". It may also be mentioned here that Iraq was one of the few states, which gave Palestinians right of citizenship and liberally financed Palestinian liberation struggle. To choke the Palestinian liberation struggle it was considered necessary by American policy makers to change the Iraqi regime. More and more telling evidence is coming out to prove that Iraq did not possess any Weapons of Mass Destruction (WMD) and it destroyed its stockpiles of WMD in the early 90s.

Secondly, America's much publicised 'alliance' has been almost shattered. This is confirmed by the fact that "the military units contributed by these so-called allies were either too small or too ill-trained to be effective. For instance, Kazakhstan's talked about contingent is not being replaced. The Italian and Japanese governments are under pressure from their people. Even the United Kingdom has finally voiced and officially expressed the opinion that the resistance is more broad-based than the US is willing to acknowledge. There is something more to it than meets the eye. The conservative pro-American regimes in the oil rich countries of the Middle East are facing popular pressure, mainly from the new emerging middle classes for democratisation of their political system. Thus, the pro-American ruling elite in the Arab world is feeling shaky, if one goes by the media reports from these countries.

Thirdly, Palestine liberation movement has always been a major political ferment in the Arab world, particularly in Iraq, Syria, Egypt, Lebanon and Jordan. For more than five decades Palestinian people have been struggling for their homeland. Even in the beginning of the present century as one writer has put it, "Israel wants to confine the Palestinians to small, economically depressed, enclaves or ghettos and keep them out of Israeli controlled, areas and subject them to extreme harassment, obstruction and economic punishment so that their will breaks. Israel has established 760 checkpoints to prevent people's movement throughout the West Bank and Gaza. It is demolishing their homes to uproot them and impose ethnic segregation. Over the past three years, Israel stepped up house demolitions - to fight 'terrorism'. Over 4,000 houses were destroyed and 15,000 damaged. Besides lakhs of olive trees were uprooted and hundreds of water wells closed. That's where the 700 km long 'Apartheid Wall' comes in Israel unilaterally started building this fence inside Palestinian territory to shield its settlements and bring them geographically into Israel". The neo-colonial policy of Israel, which is backed by the US, politically, economically, militarily and morally symbolises how colonialism has already begun to manifest itself and Palestinian people's struggle has become a source of inspiration for the entire Arab world. This has posed a new challenge to new imperialism. It has, therefore, begun to restructure its Middle East Policy. It seems to have decided to prop up pro-American regimes in the entire region and now is advocating that 'democratisation of the entire Arab world' has come on the immediate agenda. This implies growing American interference through various instruments–financial, political, military and media in the entire Middle East, which has been now redefined from 'Morocco to Pakistan'. This indeed is a very dangerous development.

The prevailing concept of the Middle East, whether as a geographical, cultural or political entity, would undoubtedly include the United Arab Republic, Israel and the Arab states of southwest Asia; yet now the American scholars have extended it to include countries as far apart as Morocco, Afghanistan and Pakistan. Prior to World War II, the Middle East Command over the British Royal Air Force even included Kenya within its sphere of operation. Confusion over the specific geographical or territorial limits that should be used to identify the region appears to stem from a failure to distinguish among the concepts of the Islamic or Muslim world, the Arab world and the Middle East.

Stretching from the Atlantic Ocean in the west to the Toros Daglari and Zagros mountains in the east, the Arab world forms part of the larger Islamic world. Like the Islamic world, the Arab world cannot be defined in terms of political groupings, but it includes those areas that were most profoundly affected by the Arab conquests of the seventh and eighth centuries. Not since the Mongol invasions of the mid-thirteenth century has the Arab world had any claim to unity, except in so far as it formed an enclave within the Ottoman Empire, but the impact of a common history and a common culture has been enduring.

It is the inheritance of a common language and a common experience that gives substance to the concept of an Arab nation and to the collective consciousness of the Arabs today. Arabic is spoken by perhaps as many as 120 million persons in Africa and Asia, although numerous local variations exist. With the spread of education and literacy, however, modern literary Arabic increasingly serves as a *lingua franca.* Islam is the religion of the majority of Arabs, but there are religious minorities that also identify themselves as Arabs. It was among the Christian communities in Lebanon and Syria, for example, that the ideas of Arab nationalism were first formulated. As Professor Bernard Lewis has noted in his book 'The Middle East and the West', "Arabism as a political movement, as a belief that the speakers of Arabic form a nation with national rights and aspirations.... dates only from the late nineteenth century and it was for a long time confined to small and unrepresentative groups, most of them Christian". Within the Arab world, there are communities, such as the Kurds of Iraq and Berbers of Northwest Africa that have resisted assimilation and have retained their own language or religion or both.

American new emerging Middle East policy cannot be delinked from the oil resources of the region, quite apart from its geo-political and geo-strategic location. The Middle East is the world's largest oil producing area and Saudi Arabia, Iran, Iraq, United Arab Emirates (UAE) and Kuwait are among the top half dozen or so oil producing countries in the world. It is relevant to mention here that proven oil reserves of Saudi Arabia are 260 billion of barrels, of Iran 130 billion of barrels, of Iraq are 112 billion barrels, of UAE are 98 billion barrels, and of Kuwait are 96 billion barrels. This in itself underlines geo-economic importance of this region for the USA, which is world's largest consumer of oil. This shows how link exists between geo-economic, geo-strategic and geo-political location of this region with the military and political policies of the United States. This is the harsh reality with which the world community is confronted today.

In this context it will be pertinent to make an objective assessment of the new US policy towards Pakistan.

US Policy Towards Pakistan

There are no two opinions that in the recent past a process of normalisation between India and Pakistan has begun to unfold itself. Whatever may be the claim of American establishment that it is the 'facilitator' of this trend, President of Pakistan, General Parvez Musharraf is again harping that Jammu and Kashmir dispute between India and Pakistan is the core issue. Therefore, a realistic and objective estimate about this new trend in the subcontinent should be made. While it will be naive to ignore this trend, it will be equally wrong to dismiss lightly the role, which the American policy makers have assigned to Pakistan. Apart from the fact that Pakistan has been given the special status of 'non-member NATO ally' as already mentioned in this article with all its strategic significance, there are some other dangerous developments.

The US, using diplomatic channels, has been giving a concentrated support to Pakistan in its attempts of getting a status of a "full dialogue partner" of the ASEAN and joining the ASEAN Regional Forum. This policy is in conflict with the Indian position and its national interests. The US State Department through its diplomatic missions in the South-Eastern Asian countries in the end of March 2004 brought it to the notice of the regional states "the US Administration's insistent request" to consent on giving to Islamabad a partner status. It supported Pakistan's desire to join the ASEAN

Regional Forum. Taking into account a consensus character of admission to the ASEAN Regional Forum, the US has been dealing individually with each member-country to persuade them to give their support to Pakistan.

The US has been exercising diplomatic pressure on the Association. It has been planning to lift all barriers preventing Islamabad from getting the status of a full partner of the ASEAN. This obviously is a major development in this region and runs counter to the national interests of India.

According to some Western European analysts, in spite of a slight shift in American policy towards India, Washington actually is not interested in strengthening Indian influence both in the regional level and globally. This shows the Americans regard Pakistan as a powerful counterbalance capable to effectively prevent spreading, what they call, "Indian hegemonism". As a matter of fact they are keeping alive all the contradictions existing in relations between India and Pakistan.

European observers believe that, besides the measures directed on strengthening political, economic and defence positions of the President Musharraf's regime, Washington will take steps aimed at encouraging smaller countries of the region, particularly Bangladesh, for initiating bilateral relations with Islamabad in order to raise its role in international arena, and in perspective - to turn Pakistan into a regional leader in the field of war against terrorism. It is in this context that the status of 'non-member NATO ally' by the USA should be seen. There is something more to it.

Pakistan has already pardoned three nuclear scientists who aided covert nuclear programmes to some nations as mentioned earlier. This stands as a complete contrast in its policy towards Iraq, where it has not been able to locate any stockpiles of weapons of mass destruction. Is this not a double standard? Above all, large-scale supply of military equipment by the United States to Pakistan, including possible F-16s in itself a significant development. Will these weapons be not used against India? Significantly, Pakistan has already been allocated $ 3 billion assistance –50 per cent of which for military equipment as mentioned earlier.

Promoting peace in Asia, Southwest Asia and South Asia may seem to be a simple proposition. The recent "peace offensive" of

Pakistan for what it calls the "normalisation of relations with India" sounds plausible on the face of it. But the scale and the speed at which it is building and modernising Pakistan's military strength including nuclear capability, raise doubts about the real intentions of the military rulers of Pakistan. The peace 'offensive' could just be a camouflage.

There seem to be, in fact, several grades and varieties of *raison de guerrilla* that overlie one another like so many geologic strata, the softer raisons lying at the surface, and the harder, the stronger ones, below it. So we must do some strip-mining, peel away the firmer underlying layers of ideology that give this propaganda its ground base and purpose. That is the objective here: to move the analytic focal point past the white lies of warfare politics of Islamabad into the ideological substratum where less pious and more dubious reasons are embedded for this unprecedented military build up. If some political leaders and a section of the mass-media in India pretend to be convinced by the arguments of Islamabad, not so the intelligent and objective observer who refuses to be deliberately naive.

Hostility between India and Pakistan has endured for so long that it has become a cliche of international politics. A general belief exists that the conflict originated in the clash over the Kashmir issue and that, as Pakistan is unwilling to give up its claims and India refuses to dilute its position (that Kashmir is a part of India and the illegal occupation of certain areas of Kashmir, both by Pakistan and China should be vacated), the rift has become permanent. Those with some knowledge of the history of the subcontinent would add that Pakistan had waged at least four wars against India–in 1947, 1965, 1971 and 1999 to occupy the whole of Kashmir. There is hardly any international forum where Pakistan has not raised the Kashmir issue.

It has now become an open secret that the Indo-Pakistan war of 1965 was started by Field Marshal Ayub Khan to "resolve the Kashmir question". The way this war was conducted has been debated in Pakistan after the publication of a book by Ayub, *My Version*: *Indo-Pakistan War 1965.* Here is one of the comments on this book: "what had been even more difficult to understand was why a crucial strategic operation for the final resolution of Kashmir dispute had to be launched at the other end of the spectrum in the wasteland of the Rann of Kutch—an area of very little tactical and no strategic value to Pakistan".

However, this argument of "permanence of bone of contention" over the Kashmir question between India and Pakistan does not explain the relationship, which has been developing between Pakistan and America. In fact, in American strategy, Pakistan has always been assigned a special role. This is a fact of history. In the 21st century, when the Soviet Union has already disintegrated, Pakistan still occupies a key position in the American strategy for whole region. On the contrary, India under the leadership of Jawaharlal Nehru, Indira Gandhi and Rajiv Gandhi have been consistently following an independent foreign policy. That being the position, Pakistan has been assigned the role to pressurise India to deflect from its independent foreign policy and the so-called dispute on Kashmir is used to subvert India's sovereignty and independence. To say this, however, does not mean that dialogue between India and Pakistan to resolve this conflict peacefully should not take place. What the strategic experts have to understand is the special role, which the American policy makers have assigned to Pakistan. This is the crux of the problem.

It is pertinent to overcall Jawaharlal Nehru's vision of India's independent foreign policy because it is relevant even today. As the first Prime Minister of independent India he was a strong opponent of imperialism and supported anti-colonial movements. The basis of this foreign policy was laid during the freedom struggle and after independence he gave concrete content to this policy. It is really unfortunate that a section of political elite does not refer to this basic concept even when according to some Western scholars, new imperialism has begun to emerge. Nehru nursed a deep distrust of Western powers and supported unequivocally the liberation struggle of subject nations against their colonial rulers; the Truman Doctrine was an "open-ended commitment to contain revolutions wherever they developed". Nehru gave moral support to struggles against colonial powers; Truman supported counterinsurgency in Greece, Vietnam and elsewhere; Nehru was opposed to the division of the world into blocs - the capitalist bloc of free countries and the socialist bloc.

Truman and his aides actively canvassed support for the free world led by the US. According to American administration and press, those countries that were not with them were against them; non-socialist states, which were not with them were against them; non-socialist states which did not join the free bloc were supposed "overtly or covertly to reinforce the objectives of the socialist bloc". This view was popularised both by American officials and important newspapers like the *New York Times.* In the great struggle of ideologies, John F Dulles regarded India's refusal to commit itself to the concept of free world as immoral. While Jawaharlal Nehru condemned military pacts, Truman created the NATO at a time when, according to George Kenan, "there was no need for the NATO build-up at all".

To pressurise India to play this role in Asia, both Washington and London wanted to use the 'Kashmir card'. But Nehru defended India's sovereignty and independence with determination. He stated publicly that his government had rejected the proposal for arbitration, which Truman and Attlee had pressed on him, and asserted that Indian troops would not be withdrawn from Kashmir unless the people of that state desire and the government of India was satisfied that the safety of Kashmir would not be endangered. He also rejected the advice of Mountbatten that India should make further concessions. So the Kashmir problem remained as insoluble as ever and perhaps there was more tension than ever before. For this, Nehru attributed considerable responsibility to what appeared to him to be the lack of fairness shown by the United States.

This shows how Indo-Pak conflict on Kashmir was used in the past to pressurise and blackmail India. In the new historic condition, a modified version of this policy has been evolved and Pakistan card is being wielded once again. This stands as a complete contrast to the policy of the Soviet Union and now of Russia on this sensitive issue. Seen in this context, Indo-Russian strategic partnership is both in the national interests of India and Russia. To say this however does not mean that various confidence building measures initiated by India and Pakistan should be ignored. In fact, the people of both India and Pakistan want a solution of Kashmir problem peacefully on the basis of balance of interests as visualised in the Shimla Agreement and some of recent developments.

It will be pertinent also to give a look at the changes, which are taking place between Sino-American relations.

Sino-US Equations Changing

In the Asia-Pacific region, an area, which continues to be of strategic significance, important changes are taking place in the relationship of the major powers. According to one estimate, though Beijing and Washington are interested in developing constructive cooperation, however, there are still areas of high conflict. China has been treating with suspicion the US policy in the Asia-Pacific region, especially towards China. The content of their concern is that the US would increase in the near future its attempts to use the Chinese domestic problems for destabilisation of the situation in the country. Washington's aim is to weaken Beijing, which has become an important factor capable of containing the US influence globally including in the Asia-Pacific region according to some experts.

Some Chinese experts point out that with a view to achieving its objectives, Washington has set its goal to impose the American values on China through mass-media, cultural links and so on in order to undermine the prestige of the Chinese leadership and to create the US-oriented opposition.

The Chinese are also worried that the Americans would encourage separatist tendencies in the Sinkiang-Uighur Autonomous Region and Tibet, separatist forces fighting for separation of national regions out of China, thus creating preconditions for split of the Peoples Republic of China (PRC).

Another area of concern of Chinese leadership is that the US attempts to 'westernisation' of China is directed to adjustment of the entire world to the American value system. Quite apart from this, American military force is being used to create a world order of the American value system. This will lead to negation of sovereignty, value system and social order, which each country is evolving for itself. This is the undercurrent of US-China conflict.

The dynamics of the Sino-American engagement should also be seen by the distinctive China-friendly tone of the remarks that the US President, George W. Bush made on the Taiwan issue in the presence of the Chinese Prime Minister, Wen Jiabao at the White House on December 9, 2003. Bush retained political space to manoeuvre as regards Taiwan. But this is half-truth. His administration has also indicated its intention to play tough to see Hong Kong emerge as a 'democracy' in future and to exert pressure on China on trade. These realities reflect the challenges which China faces in its dealings with the US, albeit in an improving political ambience overall. China knows that US is avidly seeking its cooperation to resolve the issues arising out of North Korea's nuclear weapons programme. This is the dual nature of Sino-American relations at the present stage, which can aptly be described as 'struggle and unity'.

Such crosscurrents have not yet assumed the proportions of a possible strategic conflict between China and the US as yet. For this not to happen, China has the choice of helping the US settle the North Korean nuclear question, while Washington holds the option of adopting a Beijing accommodative stance on three issues—Taiwan, Hong Kong and the Sino-American trade dispute.

President Bush has said he would "oppose any unilateral decision by either China or Taiwan to change the *status quo*". The sanctity of *status quo* implies that the US recognise three interrelated dimensions: Taiwan will become part of China under the 'one-China' principle at some stage in future; Taiwan is not at all a sovereign state and Taiwan today is also not an administrative part of the PRC. In the totality of *status quo,* Bush's specific message to Chen Shui-bian does not directly negate Beijing's 'one-China' doctrine given that it is accepted by the international community, including the US. For Chen, however, the *status quo* means, singularly, that Taiwan is a distinctive non-PRC entity. China does not want Washington to expand the proposed Theatre Missile Defence system (TMD) to cover Taiwan and embolden it to declare 'independence'. The authoritative Chinese sources see Bush's recent search for 'non-NATO allies' in East Asia as a move to meet asymmetrical security threats. This is yet another illustration of duality of Sino-American relations at the present stage.

If objectively examined, this duality of American policy towards China become clear on its policy on Taiwan.

Before we examine this let us see how American scholars look at China's role in the global fight against terrorism. According to them China is not an incredibly important player in the war on terrorism but that it has been relatively cooperative with the United States since 11th September 2002. On the other hand, their main focus is on military build-up of China including increase in its military expenditure as reflected in the recent figures.

The Peoples Liberation Army (PLA) is spending billions of dollars each year on its modernisation programme. However, this is debatable because of varying standards in accounting for military spending. What are long-term strategic goals of the PLA's modernisation? If we look at the broadest type of modernisation that is going on in China, the goals are relatively abstract in improving China's overall capability to project power from its shores and to match potential enemies decades in the future, according to Thomas Christensen, an American expert. He however, points out that China wants "to develop relatively quickly a coercive capacity against Taiwan involving various weapon systems and it is pouring quite a bit of money into that". "There seems to be a consensus among PLA watchers in Washington and Tokyo and elsewhere, that the tenor of the Chinese exercises has become much more serious and focused on real world scenarios relating to Taiwan with more actual training for combat". He does not leave at that. He underlines that China wants to build its sea power with a view to using blockades, including sea mines, 'to bring an unidentified opponent to agree on China's terms'. The submarines, the sea mines and to some degree even more accurate ballistic missiles and land attack cruise missiles could all be useful for blockades, as would anti-ship cruise missiles. China is working hard to develop more sophisticated anti-ship cruise missiles, including those that can be fired from submarines. That is a very tough task, but once China has that capability, it is very difficult for an opponent like Taiwan to counter. That capability could cause real damage if implemented. Taiwan is a very trade dependent economy, it is pointed out.

This brings into sharp focus, how the gulf between China and the United States about the future of Taiwan continues to be as wide as before. Washington's estimate is that later or sooner China will build military pressure on Taiwan to bend, which obviously is not in the American political, strategic and economic interests.

These contours in Sino-US relations in the second decade of the post-Cold War period should be examined within the framework of elevation of Sino-Russian relations on the one hand and the process of normalisation of relations between India and China on the other. This brings into the forefront that though slowly but steadily new challenges are emerging to unipolarism, the old alliance system seems to be breaking down.

It will be relevant to mention here to illustrate this point that while America's closest allies in Asia–Japan and South Korea–proved to be of little use in counter-terrorism efforts or the war in Iraq, the other US-led European alliance, the NATO, remained badly divided when Washington decided to dethrone Saddam Hussein. These developments, in turn, have given rise to an animated debate about the viability and relevance of alliance based policy either because of the lack of shared strategic interests or because the traditional allies of the US are simply helpless when it needs their support the most. This in itself shows how rapid changes are taking place on the global scale, in the Asia-Pacific region in particular, which, if develop, will challenge the American hegemony over the world.

In totality of the situation in the first decade of the 21st century correlation of the international forces is changing and challenges to imperialism–American hegemony—have begun to clearly emerge. In this background strategic partnership between India-Russia on one hand and China-India on the other, if of deepened, will set in motion new trends of multipolarism against unipolarism.

Neo Imperialism at Work

It will not be out of place to look at how neo imperialism has begun to reveal its fangs. This will throw light how neo imperialism has already begun to show its tentacles. This is graphically illustrated by the treatment meted out to Iraqi Prisoners of War (POWs). This indeed is an alarming development and has attracted the attention of the entire world including peace loving American people.

Day in and day out shocking facts have come to light about atrocities committed on Iraqi prisoners of war by American and British occupation forces, in Abu Gharaib jail on the road to Fallujah in particular. These blood-curdling atrocities are clear indications of neo-colonialism and have shocked the entire world including the American and British people. Anyone who has watched identical developments during the Second World War would inevitably come to the conclusion that neo-fascism has already appeared on the horizon in international politics. Let us not make any bones about it.

Even the Western scholars have underlined this new trend. What is happening in Iraq is not an isolated development. This is a continuation of the new trend in the US policy. The three wars launched by the transnational elite in the last fifteen years since its emergence after the collapse of 'actually existing socialism', i.e., the Gulf War, the war in Kosovo and the ongoing war on terrorism are cases substantiating the existence of an informal system of transnational governance, and a political globalisation presided over by a transnational elite. This political globalisation is characterised by some scholars as the latest form of imperialism. As mentioned earlier, political globalisation is a fancy word for imperialism, imposing your values and institutions on others. However, you may dress it up, whatever rhetoric you may use, it is not very different in practice to what Great Britain did in the 18th and 19th centuries. We already have precedents: the neo imperialism is already in operation in Bosnia, Kosovo, East Timor, Afghanistan and now in Iraq, according to some Western scholars.

This alone does not explain the whole situation. In the various universities of USA and Britain, a debate has begun on this crucial issue. As these scholars put it including Takis Fotopoulos, Editor, Democracy & Nature in his book 'Globalisation', "the term imperialism refers to a previous stage of market economy and has little relation to its present internationalised form. Imperialism was founded on national states and markets, whereas today's political globalisation is built on economic globalisation which, despite the untenable analysis of the reformist Left, is a new phenomenon and not controlled by any single national elite. The informal character of globalisation is needed not only in order to keep the facade of a well functioning representative democracy in which local elites are still supposed to take the important decisions but also in order to preserve the nation-state's internal monopoly of violence. The latter is necessary so that local elites are capable of controlling their populations in general and the movement of labour in particular, enhancing the free flow of capital and commodities. This form of political globalisation, given the uneven distribution of political/military power among members of the transnational elite, establishes the informal hegemony of the US elite. It is not, therefore, surprising that it has become part of the State Department's job to push deregulation and the dismantling of all barriers to trade and finance both with individual governments and in international negotiations on economic matters (WTO). The immediate aim of the transnational elite is to pull down "regulatory barriers" impeding free exchange of goods and services, initially between Europe and America and then between this huge trading block and the rest of the world. The ultimate aim is the formation of a vast single deregulated market, controlled by multinational companies, in which social controls over markets to protect labour or the environment will be minimised".

The kind of 'clash of civilisations' predicted by the ideologues of the New World Order, but rather the fact that the populations in countries like Afghanistan, Iran and Iraq, as well as Indonesia, Philippines and Malaysia have been the main victims of globalisation because of their geographical and economic position. After the collapse of socialism in general and Arab socialism in particular, it was natural for these populations to turn to Islamic fundamentalism.

George W. Bush went to great lengths to secure the political, economic and military backing of other members of the transnational elite, as well as various local elites, for its war in Afghanistan and Iraq. A kind of military division of labour within the transnational elite has emerged, with the US military machine used almost exclusively in the first stages of the transnational elite's 'wars' (involving the overwhelming use of air power in which US power is unrivalled) and the military machines of the other members mobilised at later stages for peace-keeping roles etc. It is in this background that the role of US-UK military occupation forces in the recent atrocities on the Iraqi POWs should be assessed. There is yet another aspect which needs to be examined.

After capture of Saddam Hussein, a major development has taken place in Iraq. It is significant to mention here that Shias, Sunnis and Christians have been organising demonstrations against the American occupation forces. Besides this, suicide squads are busy in violent activities. In fact, guerrilla warfare of the urban style has been going on after the overthrow of the Ba'ath Socialist Party regime. There are democratic and leftist forces, both Ba'athists and communists and a section of Kurdish people who want a constitution, which represents all ethnic-religious and political forces in the country. Recently, a meeting of twenty-one political parties was held to evolve a consensus on the future political set up of Iraq.

It is significant to mention here that the main objective of the U.S. during the next few months is to establish a credible Iraqi government over which it can exercise sufficient control. However, there is a limitation to it, primarily because of growing resistance to the occupation forces. This is a dilemma, which Washington is facing today.

The situation in Iraq is further complicated by new facts, which have come to light about weapons of mass destruction in Iraq. There is telling evidence, which shows that Iraq did not possess weapons of mass destruction, plea on the basis of which military action against Iraq was undertaken.

This shows that American occupation of Iraq has led to imbalance between political forces in the country. It has also resulted in sharp activisation of separatist tendencies, tension between Shias and Sunnis, Kurds and Arabs on the religious and ethnic bases. Administrative structures, which are being formed artificially by the Americans on the basis of loyalty to the USA, do not reflect an actual correlation of forces in the society.

The recent events in Iraq are just a prelude to what might happen to the country early this year, if the Americans do not display flexibility and continue to push forcible implementation of Mr. Bremen's plan which provides only limited sovereignty for Iraqi power structures. The situation could lead to a total war not only against the coalition forces in Iraq and terror against countries–members of the coalition, but it would result in rise of separatism and extremism in the Arab and Muslim world and in other countries including Syria, Jordan, Palestine, Turkey, Pakistan, India, China, etc.

This brings us to the conclusion that in the beginning of the 21st century the emergence of neo imperialism has become a harsh reality, though it may look to be too sweeping a statement. It is in this backdrop that global significance of Indo-Russian strategic partnership should be examined.

4

New Parameters of Strategic Partnership

Prof. K.R. Singh

India's security perceptions, like those of other states, are influenced by a set of three inter related variables; domestic, regional and global. Over the period, nature of these variables have kept on changing. These changes need to be kept in mind while evolving the framework of foreign policy that helps to buttress national security in the context of all those three variables. Indo-Russian strategic partnership will be examined in this framework.

Terrorism, use of unrestrained violence, primarily by non-state actors, has emerged as the major source of threat to domestic peace and security. Many governments are so challenged by groups that use violence as a part of their agenda to redress their perceived socio-economic and political grievances. India has the Naxalite movement and the People's War Group. These groups do not question the territorial integrity of the state. There are, however, other groups that question the territorial integrity. India has been facing that challenge almost since its independence.

Of late, this threat has taken a more formidable shape because of the impact of two additional factors; radical Islamic ideology or the so-called jahadism, as the prime motivating force, and the use of such groups, often mercenaries, by other states and organisations as instrument of low intensity conflict against India. Russia too is faced with this new threat which, in the post-Cold War era, has become a common denominator in defining their strategic partnership.

For India, Pakistan and China were two major security threats at the regional level. China was seen as a friend till the escalation of the border conflict in late fifties. It became an adversary after the armed conflict of 1962. It coincided with the Sino-Soviet rift. Pakistan was seen as a hostile power since 1947. Moscow's perception of Pakistan kept on changing. Till 1964 it was seen as a part of Western alliance system. Indo-Pak armed conflict of 1965 offered Moscow advantages. The West had ignored Pakistan and even imposed an arms embargo on both sides, which hurt Pakistan more. Moscow offered its good offices and the Tashkent summit helped India and Pakistan to politically resolve the after effects of the war.

Moscow sought to improve its relations with Pakistan even by offering it weapons. A few tanks, artillery pieces and helicopters were sold. Pakistan, however, preferred to revert to the West as also to strengthen its strategic ties with China and with several Arab-Islamic states after 1971 and more so following the Soviet military intervention in Afghanistan. Though Indo-Soviet relations did not directly affect the Afghan issue, yet India was clubbed together with USSR and was isolated *vis-a-vis* the West as also the Arab-Islamic states. Interestingly, during that period, the Organisation of Islamic Unity was gradually overshadowing the secular Non-Aligned Movement.

At the global level, India's independence had coincided with the beginning of the Cold War and the policy of alignment that was being imposed upon the newly independent states. India did not wish to surrender the autonomy of decision-making in external affairs by participating in these alliances and sought to pursue an independent policy. Thus, non-alignment became basic to India's policy during the Cold War era. Non-alignment was perceived as a hostile policy and was so condemned by the West. US Secretary of State, John Foster Dulles, reportedly called it immoral. India as well as other states like Egypt under President Gamal Abdel Nasser and Indonesia under President Sukarno became the targets.

While the West refused to accept the principle of sovereign right of a state to take its own decisions, by 1955 Moscow had given up the earlier antagonism towards states that wished to pursue a non-aligned policy. The Khrushchev era thus laid down the foundations of close relationship between many of the erstwhile colonies of the NATO members and the ideological and military adversary of the NATO. That infuriated the West further. This backdrop is essential to understand the bond of sustained friendly relations between Moscow and New Delhi despite changes of leadership over these years in both the capitals.

Framework of a country's foreign relations is formulated in the context of international environment prevailing at any given period, and the opportunity that it offers to promote the country's national interests. The end of the Cold War and more so the disintegration of the Soviet Union per se, has drastically altered the present world order. Hence, there is need to reassess India's broad framework of foreign policy *per se*. During the Cold War era compulsions of the bipolar system at global level forced the newly independent India to choose the policy of non-alignment as a means to retain an independent foreign policy. In the post-Cold War period it is necessary to reassess the changed as also the fast changing international environment to verify if the policy *per se,* as also basic structures of bilateral and multilateral relations need to be redefined or reformulated. It also needs to be noted that though India's domestic power structure did undergo a change and the country began to drift towards multiparty coalitions there was no basic restructuring of the society at domestic level.

Unlike India which had witnessed a gradual evolution during the post-Cold War period, USSR/Russia had gone through a revolutionary transformation. In the quest for *detente,* Moscow's leadership had given up the basic postulates of adversary relations like ideology as well as related socio-economic and political infrastructure before it could fashion an effective alternate model. This desire to imitate the West, so that Moscow could become acceptable to it, in a way, prompted the disintegration not only of the Warsaw Pact but also of the USSR itself. Centuries-old Czarist Empire disintegrated even without the emergence of an anti-imperialist movement leaving a truncated Russia to refashion a new role for itself and to rebuild a new state.

During the early years of the post-Cold War period, the new elite in Moscow favoured a look-West policy as also it associated political, military, social and economic orientation towards the West. Thus, the early years of the post-Cold War period saw a sharp refocusing of Moscow's domestic and foreign policies. It had its impact upon Moscow's attitude towards the countries of the South.

They were seen as a legacy of the Cold War era and an unnecessary burden.

The euphoria of 'look West' policy soon evaporated when the expected largess from the West failed to arrive. To top it, USA continued its Cold War policy of eroding Russia's influence in its immediate periphery in the Baltic, the Caucasus and the Caspian Sea regions. These were strategically sensitive areas. That, combined with the domestic chaos, forced Moscow to have a new look at its policy. The glimpse of the new approach was reflected in Russia's Military Doctrine of 1993 that spelled out Russia's special interest and peacekeeping role in the 'Near Abroad'.[1] Russia's disenchantment with the West, especially with the policies of USA, was reflected in Primakov's new approach to world order in which he advocated the need for a multipolar world order.[2] He also advocated a major role for the UN, particularly of the Security Council, in which other great powers could retain their influence. Primakov's views influenced the National Security Concept of December 1997. The Foreign Policy Concept of the Russian Federation of 28 June 2000 not only reiterated multilateral world order but also linked the threat arising from Islamic radicalism to Russian security.[3]

Period 1991-96 also witnessed a shift in the emerging world order. For a few years, soon after the end of the Cold War, the world had gone through what is termed as a unipolar system since USA was left as the sole Super Power. In fact, it was not a unipolar but a universalist model wherein major actors tried to find universal common denominators that would help them to regulate the events of the new era. Responses to the Kuwaiti crisis of 1990-91 were projected as a symbol of the new universalism.

The world was, however, not yet ready for such a universalist model. Many great powers had their own agenda that they wanted to impose upon others by force if necessary. By the middle of the nineties, universalist model gave way to two competing models; unilateralist model adopted by USA and multilateralist model favoured by others.

Though the NATO was retained, primarily as an instrument of American policy, the new trend was towards coalition in which ideology and programmes were set aside in favour of promoting short-term interests. These coalitions kept on changing. Hence, different types of coalitions were formed at international level. One was formed after 9-11 allegedly to wage war on terrorism. That included diverse states like USA, USSR, China, France, India, and Pakistan etc. But other coalitions were not so broadly constructed. The coalition formed for war on Iraq in March 2003 and for the subsequent occupation of Iraq reflected sharp differences among great powers as also regional powers.

Since the new world order represents the ethos of coalition rather than alliance, it should prompt India to reevaluate the formulates even of its policy of non-alignment. It is this new ethos that will also determine and shape Indian policy *vis-a-vis* great powers like USA, Russia, China, France as also middle powers. Hence, if we have to look ahead, we need to reformulate the basic postulates of bilateral relations between Moscow and New Delhi even outside the framework of four decades of Indo-Soviet relations during the Cold war period. This should take into account the new interests and aspirations of both the parties in the context of the new world order.

In that context, the term strategic partnership acquires a new significance. In the newly emerging world order alliances are being replaced by coalitions that are by nature short-lived and formed for specific purposes. Indo-Russian relations, therefore, cannot be based upon the foundation of coalition politics. Partnership, in turn, implies a long term and stable relationship based upon some commonly agreed denominators. Partnership also implies an awareness of equality among partners. While Russia is no longer a Super Power it is still the major great power. India too is no longer a weak developing country but a strong middle power aspiring to be a great power in the near future. That also sets the backdrop for strategic partnership between India and Russia.

Common Objectives

Common objectives at global and regional level help to strengthen this strategic partnership. Both the countries are faced with common challenges as well as are offered new opportunities. While threat from international terrorism that is largely sought to be justified on the basis of radical Islamic interpretation of jehad poses a new challenge to both the restructuring of the regional space between them since the breakup of the USSR has offered new opportunities for strategic cooperation to meet that challenge.

Threat from jehadi terrorism for India and Russia began long before the 9-11 episode. While India was facing the direct challenge in Jammu and Kashmir, Russia was confronting it not only in Chechenya but also in Central Asia. Radical Islamic groups based in Afghanistan posed threats to India via Pakistan and to Russia via Central Asian republics. The threat had intensified after the linkup between the Taliban and Al-Qaida. Afghanistan became an issue of common concern for India and Russia and a Joint Working Group on Afghanistan was formed following the visit of Putin to New Delhi in December 2000. The joint declaration during that visit said that the roots of terrorism which lay in their common neighbourhood posed threat to their security interests.[4]

Terrorism was one of the major issues for discussion during the Moscow visit of Prime Minister Vajpayee and led to the Moscow Declaration on International Terrorism that was issued on 6 November 2001. It stressed that whatever be the motive of their perpetration - political, ideological, philosophical, racial, ethnic, religious or any other, terrorist acts are unjustifiable. It added that in multi-ethnic and democratic countries, violent action being perpetrated under the slogan of self-determination in reality represents acts of terrorism, which in most cases have strong international links. Multiethnic and democratic societies are especially vulnerable to acts of terrorism, which are an attack against the values and freedoms enshrined in such societies.[5] Thus, an attempt was made to give an ideological thrust to their fight against terrorism of all kinds.

While the agenda of USA as also of the NATO on the question of international terrorism differed from that of India and Russia, events of 9-11 brought them closer; especially on the question of eliminating the stranglehold of the Taliban and Al-Qaida over Afghanistan. Events of 9-11 galvanized the world public opinion against jehadi terrorism and provided the pretext for US-led military action in Afghanistan. The coalition formed to launch Operation Enduring Freedom reflected active participation of NATO members who interpreted Article 5 of the NATO charter to legitimize their 'war on terrorism'. For the first time, NATO had extended its zone of operation to the heart of Asia. NATO continues to retain its presence under the UN resolution that provides for a multinational force to protect the newly formed government in Kabul.

Though the agenda of USA *vis-a-vis* terrorism as it affected India and Russia had differed from that of these affected parties, events of 9-11 had brought them closer. While India and Russia did not directly participate militarily in Operation Enduring Freedom and subsequent military operations of US-led coalition, yet their contribution was important for the defeat of the Taliban and Al-Qaeda. Russia's contribution, both political and military, was crucial for the successful operation of the forces of the Northern Alliance that, with direct air support provided by USA, succeeded in ousting Taliban and Al-Qaeda forces from their strongholds in Afghanistan.

Views on the future of Afghanistan were reflected in the joint statement, issued on 6 November 2001 during the visit of Vajpayee to Moscow. Both sides supported the need for a broad-based interim government comprising all ethnic groups. They also emphasised that there would be no place for elements belonging to the Taliban and Al-Qaeda in any future Afghan government.[6] In passing, it is worth noting that these bilateral declarations and statements did not refer to the event of 9-11.

Afghanistan is a major issue of common concern to India and Russia. *Jehadi* terrorism poses a major threat not only to India's security but also to security and stability in Central Asia. Putin, during his New Delhi visit of December 2000, had stressed Eurasian stability as a factor of global significance.[7] Thus, the new strategic partnership with the objective to combat international terrorism has led to the formation of an East-West axis that connects Moscow and New Delhi via Central Asia and Afghanistan.

The advantages of the East-West axis are further buttressed by the newly developing North-South axis formed by the sea-land route connecting India with Russia via Iran and the Caspian Sea and the inland river network of Russia. This axis not only emphasises the route of increased cooperation in future in trade and commerce but also enables India as also Iran to come closer to other regional powers of Central Asia and with Afghanistan. While the East-West axis is terrorism-specific, the North-South axis is of long-term significance since it helps to strengthen not only bilateral economic cooperation but also helps to integrate India, Russia and South-West Asia within the framework of growing economic interdependence. It also helps India as well as Russia to bypass the Economic Cooperation Organisation (ECO) from which both these countries have been isolated.

The new upswing in Indo-Russian relations since mid-nineties also witnessed the widening divide between the advocates of unilateralism and multilateralism. While to some groups in India, as also to some groups in Russia, joining the unilateralist camp seemed to offer new opportunities, by and large, regimes of both the countries preferred a multilateralist model of new world order. That policy was spelled out in the joint statement issued in Moscow on 6 November 2001 during the visit of Vajpayee. Both sides confirmed their commitment to promote the formation of an equitable multipolar world order based on the principles of rule of law and equality, territorial integrity and non-interference in domestic affairs of states. The joint statement also stressed the need for reform in UN that included expansion of the Security Council in which India would have a role.

Bilateral relations between New Delhi and Moscow had suffered a temporary setback during the early years of the post-Cold War period. During that period which lasted about four years, the new ruling elite in Moscow desired to pursue a 'look West' policy even at the cost of ignoring its long-standing ties with the countries of the South. According to Anita Inder Singh, South Asia was accorded seventh place in the order of ten priorities in the Concept of Russian Federation's Foreign Policy of January 1993.[8] That new perception also got reflected in Russia's overall policy towards South Asia, particularly towards Indo-Pak relations.

According to T. Shaumian, there were two sets of opinion on South Asia at that time. The one argued for keeping up the traditional relations with India and to accord priority to India even while developing relations with Pakistan. The other group advocated that the epoch of 'special relationship' with India should be ended, as it was adversely affecting Russia's relations with Pakistan. According to T. Shaumian, that was the dominant view at that time.[9] During that period Moscow had tilted more towards Rawalpindi. It supported Pakistan's position on the question of creating a 'Nuclear Weapon Free Zone' in South Asia as well as on the Kashmir question. Moscow probably hoped to turn a new leaf in its relations with Afghanistan and Pakistan in the context of Central Asia.

Russian Foreign Minister, Andrei Kozyrev, visited Pakistan during 6-8 April 1993. He said that his country wanted to do away with the foreign policy legacy of the former Soviet Union and desired to adopt a balanced foreign policy in the context of South Asia. Russia had also sought Pakistan's help in bridging differences between the Tajik government and the Islamic opposition that had been operating from Afghanistan.[10] During that period some Russian experts on South Asia also began writing articles supportive of the policy of Andrei Kozyrev. According to V. Moskolenko and T. Shaumian, for many years, Soviet leaders looked on the situation in South Asia largely through Indian eyes. It was argued that new political and strategic reality called for seeking opportunities for cooperation with other countries of the region, above all with Pakistan.[11]

However, ground realities as well as geopolitical compulsions both at global as also regional level forced decision-makers in Moscow to reassess the pattern of their relationship with South Asia. The change, though slow, was perceptible. It began with the state visit of President Yeltsin in January 1993. It was twice postponed in 1992. During that visit the two countries signed a new 20-year Treaty of Friendship and Cooperation. The previous treaty had lapsed. Though the new treaty excluded the security-related articles of the 1971 treaty, it did provide the semblence of continuity of the old pattern of close bilateral relationship between Moscow and New Delhi. Visit of Prime Minister Narasimha Rao to Moscow from 27 June to 2 July 1994 further cemented the ties. The Moscow Declaration on the Protection of Interests of Pluralistic States, not only reflected common identity of views of both states *vis-a-vis* multi-ethnic state system but also underlined their interests in promoting peace and stability in the borderland between Russia and India. It expressed concern of both the states in the context of religious extremism, inter-ethnic and inter-religious hatred, aggressive nationalism etc. According to Shipping Tang, Chinese point out with resentment that even as political factions within Russia debated whether China was friend or foe, none seemed to doubt that India is Russia's friend.[12]

Rise of the Taliban in Afghanistan in 1995 as also the appointment of Primakov as the new Foreign Minister of Russia in January 1996 paved the way for a deeper strategic partnership between India and Russia both in the context of regional as also global realignment of forces.

The Declaration of Strategic Partnership, issued during Putin's New Delhi visit in October 2000 underlined that the strategic partnership between the two countries was time tested and was marked by continuing trust and mutual understanding, and had elevated the multifaceted ties between the two countries to a qualitatively new and higher level, and had laid the foundation for further development in Indo-Russian relations.[13]

Three things can be identified as the cementing factors of Indo-Russian strategic partnership; improvement in bilateral economic relations, cooperation in science and technology, particularly in the field of space and energy, as also in military-related field.

Thriving bilateral economic ties of the Cold War era, that were based largely on government-to-government contracts and also upon their local currencies, suffered a setback due to three factors. The one was the decision to trade in hard currency. The other was privatisation of economy, including foreign trade. Finally, the large Soviet market itself collapsed following the disintegration of USSR. The combined effect of these factors is felt even now and it will take some time before the two countries are able to exploit the full potential of their bilateral and multilateral economic relations. Steps are being initiated towards that objective by governmental as also nongovernmental agencies of both the states.

Another field that can help to strengthen bilateral strategic partnership deals with cooperation in science and technology. Growth of technology in India owes a great deal to the contribution of Moscow even during the Cold War era. Now, both sides are able to benefit from this cooperation because India during the past five decades has also upgraded its own level of science and technology. Space and nuclear energy are two major areas in which the two countries have cooperated in the past. India's GSLV launch in April 2001 was possible because of Russian cryogenic engine that was needed for the final stage of manoeuvering. Also, Moscow is keen to collaborate in transfer of technology related to nuclear power. But future cooperation in both these areas is seriously handicapped because of restraints like Missile Technology Control Regime (MTCR) and other constraints on transfer of nuclear technology.

There is no doubt that ways will be found to overcome these constraints during the coming years. India is now capable of developing its own technology irrespective of these international constraints as it has succeeded in overcoming similar obstacles earlier. Lifting of sanctions will, however, help accelerate the pace of development of technology in India. It will also benefit Russia. These restraints by other powers, mostly of the West, have not dampened the spirit of long-term strategic cooperation between India and Russia. The two states have agreed to constitute a Joint Council for Implementation of the Integrated Long-Term Programme on Scientific and Technological Cooperation for the period 2000-2010.

New Delhi and Moscow have a long history of fruitful cooperation in the context of arms transfer and licence production of arms and other related equipment at least since late fifties. Over the years not only large number of equipment was acquired or produced under licence but the quality was also continuously upgraded and India began to receive the latest Soviet/Russian equipment. Tables dealing with the number of Soviet/Russian equipment used by the Army, Navy and Air Force of India in 1990, 1997 and 2003 show the extent of bilateral military related cooperation between the two countries.

Army: Soviet / Russian Weapons

Weapons	*1990*		*1997*		*2003*	
	Total	*Soviet/ Russian*	*Total*	*Soviet/ Russian*	*Total*	*Soviet/ Russian*
Main Battle Tank	3,150	1,500	3,314	2,100	3,898	2,724
Light Tank	100	100	90	90	90	90
Armoured Infantry Fighting Vehicle	800	800	1,350	1,350	1,600	1,600
Armoured Personnel Carrier	450	450	157	157	317	157
Artillery pieces	3,860	550	4,175	1,310	(n.a.)	1,700
Multi-barrel Rocket Launcher	80	80	150	150	150	150

These and subsequent tables are based upon data given in *Military Balance 1990-91*, IISS, London, 1991, *Military Balance 1997-98* London, 1997 and *Military Balance, 2003-2004* London, 2003.

Navy: Soviet/Russian Ships and Aircraft and Ships Built Using Soviet/Russian Equipment

	1990			1997			2003		
	Total	*Soviet/ Russian*	*Soviet/ Russian equipment*	*Total*	*Soviet/ Russian*	*Soviet/ Russian equipment*	*Total*	*Soviet/ Russian*	*Soviet/ Russian equipment*
Aircraft Carrier	1	-	-	1	-	-	1	-	-
Submarine Nuclear	1	1	-	-	-	-	-	-	-
Conventional	18	16	-	17	13	-	19	15	-
Destroyer	5	5	-	6	5	1	8	5	3
Frigate	()	8	5	(18)	4	8	7	1	6
Corvettes	3	3	-	3	3	-	7	3	4
OPVs (Missile)	5	5	-	12	6	6	12	6	6
OPV (ASW)	4	4	-	4	4	-	4	4	-
FAC (missile)	12	12	-	6	6	-	6	6	-
Minesweeper	20	18	-	20	18	-	18	18	-
Amphibious Ships and Air Craft	19	9	-	17	8	-	17	5	-
Maritime Reconnaissance Air Craft:									
Large	**8**	**8**	-	**13**	**13**	-	**17**	**17**	-
Medium	-	-	-	-	-	-	**35**	-	-

Air Force: Soviet Union/Russia, Purchased and Licence Production

Aircraft	1990 Total	1990 Soviet/ Russia	1997 Total	1997 Soviet/ Russia	2003 Total	2003 Soviet Russia
Fighter/Ground attack	400	252	368	280	539	435
Fighter/Interceptor	361	315	354	319	125	125
Attack helicopter	12	12	32	32	40	40
Transport aircraft, heavy	42	42	25	25	25	25
Medium	124	108	135	105	133	105
Air-refueling Air craft	-	-	-	-	6	6
Helicopters, heavy	10	10	10	10	10	10
medium	130	130	-	-	123	123

Most of the missiles used by India are of Soviet/Russian origin

As noted, quality of equipment also kept pace with the development of military technology in Soviet Union/Russia. In the Army, T-54/55 Main Battle Tanks (MBT) were replaced by T-72. Now T-90 tanks are being inducted. Old-fashioned APCs have been replaced by superior Armoured Infantry Fighting Vehicle (AIFV) like BMP-I/II. In the Navy, the Foxtrot-class submarines were replaced by the Kilo-class submarines. Now, some of these submarines have been reequipped to launch anti-ship missiles from their torpedo tubes. Indian-built Delhi-class destroyer has important Russian components. The Petya-class frigate is being replaced by modern Krivak-class frigates armed with the latest anti-ship missile. Old Osa-class missile boats were replaced by large OPVs of the Tarantula-class.

Indian Air Force also benefited from this modernisation. The first generation MiG-21 interceptor fighter was gradually modified to produce MiG-21 bis, which was in effect a multi-role combat aircraft. MiG-23 and MiG-29 were subsequently inducted as interceptor-fighters. Su-7 was replaced by more sophisticated MiG-23 and finally by MiG-27 for strike role. Indian Air Force has already started flying Su-30 aircraft that is the latest aircraft of Russia. India has also acquired Il-78 air-refueling tankers to enhance the combat range of these aircraft. In the transport sector, heavy-lift aircraft like An-12 was replaced by Il-76 while medium lift aircraft like Il-14 was replaced by An-32. Its helicopter fleet also acquired, over the years, Mi-4, Mi-

8, and Mi-17 medium lift helicopters as also better attack helicopters. Its missiles also kept pace with the requirement of new aircraft. Old air-to-air missiles like AA-2/3 were replaced by A 7/8/10/11. Thus, over the years, Indian armed forces have kept pace with rapidly changing weapons technology thanks to its sustained long-term military relationship with Soviet Union/Russia.

These developments have been favourably commented upon by many defence experts in India. Indian Air Force acquired its first Soviet aircraft in 1958 when a few Il-14 transport aircraft were handed over and were used for VIP squadron. Mi-4 helicopter and An-12 heavy transport aircraft arrived in 1960 and 1961 respectively. The MiG-21 deal was finalized in 1962 and the first squadron reached India by 1963. India acquired about 250 of MiG-21 versions from USSR and produced, under licence, about 500 more MiG-21s of different types. Subsequently, it also produced MiG-27 under licence. According to Air-Marshal B.D. Jayal (Retd.) by the end of the century between 80-85 per cent of the IAF equipment was from the erstwhile Soviet Union. Almost the entire fleet of medium and heavy transport aircraft, all SAMs, most of the medium and low level radar system and some high powered radars as also 32 of the 39 combat squadrons were of Soviet/Russian origin.[14] According to Air-Marshal Jayal, in spite of major changes in the international geopolitical arena and demise of the Soviet Union, Indo-Russian relations remain sound and on a healthy footing. To a large extent, credit must go to the healthy and mutually supportive military equipment partnership.[15]

Indian Navy was reared by UK but by 1964 UK began to ignore the requirements of the Indian Navy, especially on the issue of sale of submarines. India was thus forced to approach USSR. Under an agreement signed in September 1965, USSR agreed to transfer to India four Foxtrot-class submarines, five Petya-class frigates and a few tank-landing craft. Subsequently Osa-class missile boats were also sold to India. Indian Navy, that had developed under the British umbrella, realized the worth of Soviet equipment during 1971 operations. According to Vice-Admiral R.B. Suri (Red.), within the service, more confidence grew in the Soviet weapons and that resulted in the procurement of Soviet weapon system for future indigeneous shipbuilding programme, and their integration with Western and indigeneous systems. "Suffice to say that nearly 80 per cent of the force levels of ships, submarines and aircraft were of that origin."[16]

Soviet assistance was also important when India was designing indigenous ships like the Godavari-class frigate. Soviet experts were very cooperative and provided details of installations and related weapons and sensors. Designs were jointly made and that helped Indians to gain expertise in this area of ship construction. Over the years, greater confidence was possible due to continued reliability and operational capability of the missiles and gunnery systems supplied by Russia. That ensured that successive indigeneously built ships were fitted with improved variants in the eighties. The contribution of Admiral Gorshkov in this regard cannot be ignored. According to Vice-Admiral Suri, it must be stated that Soviet assistance under the guidance of such towering personalities as Admiral Gorshkov was largely responsible for the growth of the navy at a stage most needed.[17]

India-Pakistan conflict of 1965 stimulated Indian Army to search for new weapons, especially armour and artillery. USA had strengthened Pakistan's Army with new Patton tanks and better guns. According to Lt. General V.K. Singh, the 1965 conflict revealed that India's mechanized forces needed major refurbishing. Soviet Union stepped in with transfer of a large number of T-54/55 tanks, PT-76 light tanks, APCs and 130 mm guns. These were supposed to be a part of the stopgap arrangement till the Indian-built Vijayanta tank was made available. But the design of the Vijayanta, based on British technology, was of the fifties and sixties. While T-55 was improved by replacing its 100 mm gun with 105 mm gun with Soviet assistance, India needed a new modern tank. It settled for T-72 MBT. It was ordered in 1979. First batch arrived in India in 1981. India began to produce it under licence after 1984. Also, new BMP-I/II AIFVs were acquired/licence built. Indian Army acquired air defence equipment like SAMs and ZSU-23-4 SP system. According to Lt.General V.K. Singh, by mid-eighties, practically all the fighting elements of an Indian armoured division were equipped with weapon system acquired from Russia or other Warsaw Pact countries.[18]

Indo-Soviet military-related cooperation also benefited not only from the willingness of the Soviets to sell to India new technology but also on easy economic terms. Payment could be made in rupees. In the deal with the West, 90 per cent of the amount had to be paid on supply of the equipment or the commissioning of ship. In the case of Soviet Union, payment was on credit, which started two years after the delivery and was spread over the next twenty years. According to Vice-Admiral Suri, that was largely responsible for resource starved Navy to raise force levels, which otherwise would not have been possible.[19]

It is true that Indo-Soviet/Russian military-related cooperation suffered a setback in the early nineties. The breakdown of the entire state system disrupted Soviet Union's defence-related infrastructure including complexes where weapons and related equipment were produced. Indian Navy was probably the worst affected because some of its major warships like Delhi-class destroyers as well as corvettes, that were being built in India, had to wait for things to settle down before spares and fresh equipment could be made available. Also, now the payment was to be made in foreign exchange. Things have been streamlined now and bilateral military-related cooperation is back on track.

Conscious efforts are being made to look at this aspect from the long-term perspective. A bilateral defence cooperation agreement was signed for the period 1994-2000. In 1997 both states signed Military-Technology Cooperation Agreement and extended their bilateral defence cooperation till 2010. According to A. Kislov and A. Frolov, "Unlike China, arms trade with India is a successful example of relations with former Soviet client(!) that Russia can do business with a long-term basis. India's policy towards Russia contains a very large measure of continuity."[20] According to Biplob Gogoi, it was hinted at the time of the visit of Russia's Defence Minister Igor Rodionov to Delhi in October 1995 that the sale of Russian military equipment to India till 2000 could reach a figure of $8 bn.[21]

Indo-Russian bilateral cooperation at strategic level in military field is destined to continue for many more years for the following reasons. India already uses a very large percentage of Soviet/Russian equipment in its armed forces. More are being inducted. They will need a sustained flow of spares. Also they will be upgraded over the years. Already MiG-21 bis is undergoing major upgradation. There are proposals to upgrade MiG-27 strike aircraft. T-72 main battle tank will be upgraded soon. New missile systems will be gradually replacing old missile systems in the Indian Army, Navy and Air Force. India is also producing under licence Su-30 aircraft. According to Air-Marshal Jayal, about 140 Su-30 MKI (Indian version) would be produced at a cost of Rupees 37,000 crores at 2000 A.D. price. According to him it is the single largest defence deal signed by Russia with any foreign country.[22] Negotiations for the acquisition and refurbishing of aircraft carrier Gorshkov as also naval version of MiG-29 aircraft are being finalized.

More important than licence production and upgradation of weapons and other related equipment is the proposal for joint design and development of new and more advanced systems like the anti-ballistic missile system comparable to that of American Patriot and Israeli Arrow. There are proposals to jointly design a new fifth generation combat aircraft. India's experience in designing the light combat aircraft as also the software for the fly-by-wire technology incorporated in it will enable India to be an active collaborator in that field. Missile technology is another field for joint collaboration.

Yet another field for joint collaboration can target the new revolution in military affairs (RMA). It is in this field that India and Russia need to seek strategic cooperation because RMA is destined to dominate future battlefield. Russia, with its developed space programme as also successful application of precision-guidance technology, is well equipped to proceed in that direction. Moreover, RMA will strengthen Russia's security even with limited number of personnel in armed forces. India, unlike other developing states, is well ahead not only in the field of utilization of latest weapons and related technology but its trained manpower, particularly in the field of information technology, gives it a base to contribute towards RMA. Absence of any clash of strategic interest between the two states is also a major factor that should encourage bilateral cooperation in the sphere of RMA.

Another area for bilateral cooperation that is likely to further strengthen strategic partnership revolves around ways and means to combat terrorism-related low intensity conflict as also trans-border terrorism. Both states are facing similar threats. Both have their own experiences. They cannot only learn from each other but also help each other in combating the new threat that is increasingly being emphasised in their bilateral strategic partnership.

Conclusion

In the light of changing regional and global environment since the end of the Cold War, India needs to redefine the basic formulates of its foreign relations. Since the earlier rationale for pursuing the policy of non-alignment, conditioned by the bipolar world order of the Cold War era, is no longer valid in the post-Cold War era with its non-bipolar world order, India needs to stress multilateralism as the new and more appropriate basis for its policy in future. That will enable it to choose the path best suited to pursue its national interest without antagonizing other great powers. It will also help India to be on the safe side of the American policy of unilateralism.

By choosing a multilateral world order, relations with great powers like France, Germany, China and Russia will assume strategic significance for India. Also, such a policy dove-tails with India's emerging status. By all standards, India is emerging as a great power and must learn to project itself as one.

Since the right to choose one's policy and partners is basic to India's national policy, Indo-Russian relations will remain crucial in the context of India's policy in the post-Cold War period. It is, therefore, important that we start looking at relations between New Delhi and Moscow beyond the historical framework of relationship during the Cold War era and search for new rationale to further strengthen these relations which not only are of great benefit to both the sides in furthering bilateral political, economic and military-related ties but will also help stabilise and strengthen overall global world order.

Such a policy is more positive than the earlier policy of non-alignment, which by its logic had prevented India from pursuing its rightful role in world affairs and in the establishment of a stable world order. Policy of multilateralism, commensurate with its status as a potential great power, will be a right step in that direction. Strong Indo-Russian relations will contribute effectively in pursuing such a policy.

References

1. Bakshi, Jyotsna, "Russian National Security Concept and Military Doctrine", *Strategic Analysis*, 24(7), October 2000, pp. 1271-72.
2. Simon, Gerhard, "Russia's Identity and International Politics", *Aussenpolitik*, 48(1), 1997, p. 25.

3. Text, *Strategic Digest*, 30(9), September 2000, pp. 1247-56.
4. *Strategic Digest*, 30(12), December 2000, p. 1424.
5. Text, *Strategic Digest*, 31(11), November 2001, pp. 1474-75.
6. Ibid., p. 1475.
7. *Strategic Digest*, 30(12), December 2000, pp. 1428.
8. Singh, Anita Inder, "India's Relations with Russia and Central Asia", *International Affairs*, 71(1), 1995, p. 72.
9. Shaumian, T., "Russia's Eastern Diplomacy and India", *World Affairs*, December 1993, quoted in Bakshi, Jyotsna, "Russian Policy Towards South Asia", *Strategic Analysis*, 23(8), November 1999, p. 1375.
10. *Pakistan Horizon*, 46(3-4), July-October 1993, pp. 151, 153.
11. Moskolenko, V. and Shaumian, T., "Conflict Over Kashmir; Current Situation and Outlook: A New Geopolitical Concept", *Pakistan Horizon*, 48(3), July 1995, pp. 17-18.
12. Tang, Shipping, "Economic Integration in Central Asia: The Russian and Chinese Relationship", *Asian Survey*, 40(2), March-April 2000, p. 362.
13. *Strategic Digest,* 31(11), November 2001, p. 1475.
14. Jayal, Air-Marshal B.D., (Retd.), "Defence Procurement for Russia and Self-Reliance: An Aerospace Perspective', *Agni*, 7(1), May-August 2003, p. 46.
15. *Ibid.*, p. 46.
16. Suri, Vice-Admiral R.B., (Retd.), "Indo-Russian Cooperation in the Naval Field and Self-Reliance", *Agni*, 7(1), May-August 2003, p. 19.
17. *Ibid.,* pp. 19-20.
18. Singh, Lt. General V.K., (Retd.), "Indo-Russian Defence Cooperation and Self Reliance: An Army View Point", *Agni*, 7(1), May-August 2003, pp. 3-4.
19. Suri, Vice-Admiral R.B., (Retd.), *Agni*, 7(1), May-August 2003, p. 21.
20. Kislov, A. and Frolov, A., "Russia and the World Arms Market', *International Affairs* (Moscow), 49(4), 2003, p. 148.
21. Gogoi, Biplob, "Military-Technical Cooperation Between India and Russia: An Overview of the Post-Soviet Period", *India Quarterly*, 63(3-4), July-December 2003, p. 312.
22. Jayal, Air-Marshal B.D., (Retd.), *Agni*, 7(1), May-August 2003, p. 56.

5

Significance of Indo-Russian Strategic Partnership

Manohar Singh Batra

The historic visit of India's Prime Minister, Mr. Atal Behari Vajpayee to Russia in mid November 2003 became another landmark in the close and strategic relations between these two countries. Mr. Vajpayee and President Vladimir Putin signed 10 accords in the Kremlin after in-depth talks. They proposed a consistent and uncompromising approach in tackling the menace of terrorism and called for giving up double standards in dealing with the problem. In a declaration inked by Vajpayee and Putin, the two countries proposed a concrete and time-bound action plan to be adopted for the earliest restoration of Iraq's sovereignty under the aegis of the United Nations. Among the accords signed by the two leaders, one related to cooperation in space research, which would include Russian assistance in an Indian lunar mission. President Putin reiterated that cross border terrorism must end and the terrorist infrastructure in Pakistan must be dismantled as a prerequisite to peace in South Asia, which could follow a purposeful dialogue. There was complete agreement between the two leaders that international problems could be solved only through collective action on the part of the United Nations.

There was unanimity between Vajpayee and Putin that India-Russia defence cooperation has acquired great versatility and it encompasses a wide range of joint research, design, development and co-production. The fifth successful trial launch of the BrahMos missile a few days earlier was an example of this. Both leaders discussed other areas of defence production and cooperation. The two countries agreed to coordinate positions on key global issues, which were building blocks of the bilateral strategic partnership. They called for effective implementation of the UN Security Council Resolution 1373 which is aimed against those who support, fund or abet terrorists or provide them shelter or asylum to engage in cross-border terrorism. Vajpayee and Putin expressed strong belief that "Afghanistan should emerge as a peaceful, strong, prosperous, united and independent nation that would be free from external interference and living in peace and harmony with its neighbours." Both India and Russia affirmed that "the future international order based on multipolarity should be determined by collective and multilateral processes rather than unilateral ones." Russia called for lifting of sanctions against India on the supply of nuclear technologies. "It is high time to review bans on nuclear cooperation with India imposed in 1992 by the Nuclear Suppliers Group (NSG), the Russian Atomic Energy Ministry said. Noting that the Kudankulam deal between India and Russia was signed before Russia joined the NSG in 1992, a spokesman of the Atomic Energy Ministry said, "Besides the ongoing construction of two VVER-1000 MW light water reactors at the Kudankulam nuclear power plant, India wants four more such reactors for power generation, but Russia's hands are tied until NSG sanctions are eased."

Addressing the Russian Academy of Sciences in Moscow, Mr. Vajpayee stressed the interest of both the countries in the evolution of a multipolar world based on a "cooperative security order". "We are both opposed to unilateralism in international matters, Vajpayee said, highlighting that the Indo-Russian relations remained unaffected by the turbulent changes that had taken place in the world. The Indian Prime Minister visualised a bright future for bilateral relationship between the two countries, but, he emphasised that they should not rest on "past laurels", as this could lead to stagnation. They must strengthen the economic basis of their relationship. "Neither India nor Russia perceives a threat from the strength of the other. On the contrary, each sees a benefit for itself in the increased political and economic strength of the other," Mr. Vajpayee declared. He further said, "This is best illustrated by Russia's public and unambiguous support to India's permanent membership of the United Nations Security Council." The Indo-Russian "strategic partnership" is a strong factor in promoting peace, security and stability both in Asia and the world. "The fundamental factor behind the stability of Indo-Russian ties is the exemplary sensitivity both countries show to each other's concerns, including security concerns."

Mr. Vajpayee expressed deep concern about the phenomenon of global terrorism and appreciated Russia's consistent support to India's efforts in combating terrorism in this region. Pointing out that terrorism posed a threat to the entire civilised world, Mr. Vajpayee said, "Specifically, it is threatening the unity, territorial integrity and sovereignty of both India and Russia. President Putin minced no words in his address to the Indian Parliament three years ago, when he said the same individuals, the same terrorist and extremist organisations are involved in terrorist acts from the Phillipines to Kosovo, including in Kashmir, Afghanistan and Chechnya." He further said that the two countries had established a sound legal basis and a useful institutional mechanism for cooperation in the "struggle" against international terrorism.

Terrorism, in fact, has become a great source of concern for both India and Russia as for many other countries, as it impinges on their peace and security. No doubt India has been facing this menace since its independence. The jehadi mindset of the neighbouring country—Pakistan has been a major factor in posing this challenge to India. The low intensity conflict for the last decade and a half let loose against this country has been a source of great irritation and danger to peace and tranquility in this part of the world. Russia too has been under threat of extremists and fundamentalists, especially from Chechnya, which has alerted her to a new situation fraught with dangers of secessionist proportions.

Though Pakistan has been in direct conflict with India on many occasions, it has been adopting adversarial postures against the erstwhile Soviet Union and then Russia for the last five decades. Its membership of the South East Asian Treaty Organisation (SEATO) and Central Treaty Organisation (CENTO) in the 1950s, the granting of military bases to the USA in the 1960s and permitting U-2 spy planes from the Pakistani territory into the Russian space and then joining the western crusade against Russia in 1980s are potent examples of Pakistani hostility towards that second most powerful country of the world.

Moscow, on the other hand, has been benign and accommodative to Pakistan. It bailed Pakistan out at Tashkent after the Indo-Pak conflict of l965 and then has been trying to mollify it with offers of arms and equipment. With the changed world scenario, the present Russian leaders have been showing greater resilience and magnanimity to a country which overtly and covertly has been working against the interests of their nation and endangering it consistently. The present quasi-military regime in Pakistan under General Pervez Musharraf has been very keen on getting closer to Russia and seeking a new dispensation from Vladimir Putin, partially in the hope of neutralising the India-Russia close cooperation and friendship. The November 2003 visit of Musharraf to Moscow sent political observers all over the world in a tizzy. Many saw signs of shifting strategic partnerships for Pakistan and India. Christopher Langton, the head of defence analysis at the International Institute for Strategic Studies in London called it an unusual visit and really of great interest. Relations between Moscow and Islamabad have been uneasy since the Soviet intervention in Afghanistan in 1979. During the following decade, Pakistan became a staging area for the US-backed Afghan mujahideen guerillas. After the Soviet withdrawal from Afghanistan, the Inter-Services Intelligence of Pakistan rendered all help to the Taliban to occupy Afghanistan. Even after September 11, ISI has been actively helping the remnants of the Taliban regroup for cross-border attacks into southern and south-eastern Afghanistan. Though General Musharraf has taken on the stance of carrying out anti-Taliban and anti-Al Qaeda activities on the Pak-Afghan border in pursuit of fundamentalist leaders, he has failed to deliver on the arrest or extermination of the suspects of anti-US terrorism three years ago and subsequently.

According to Langton, the emergence of fundamentalist legislators in the North-Western frontier and Baluchistan provinces of Pakistan, both bordering Afghanistan, have cast a cloud over US-Pak relations. Irrespective of Russian overtures to Islamabad, the latter's support to the Afghan mujahideen has not tapered off. The persistence of Russia-India perception of the spread of militant Islam has brought these two countries closer. At one time Russia was flirting with the idea of equidistance between New Delhi and Islamabad. But Pakistan's fixation for jehad and its collusion with pan-Islamic crusaders would never allow moderation to set in. And for the very security and safe society of the secular world, cooperation to combat this phenomenon, between India and Russia has every chance of increasing.

In the initial post-Soviet period, certain Russian leaders expressed the view that there was no need to maintain the 'special relationship' with India, which existed in the Soviet era. On at least three occasions policy regarding South Asia was debated at special hearings in the Commission on International Affairs of the Supreme Soviet and the State Duma. Just before President Yeltsin's visit to India in January 1993, the representative of the Foreign Ministry, Andrey Kozyrev, expressed misgivings about Russia's special relationship with India. He explained that Russia needed the help of Pakistan in addressing the problem of Afghanistan. But Kozyrev's view was not supported by a majority of members. Several military experts, scientists and others insisted on the need to maintain the traditional ties with India. However, they pointed out that this relationship should pose no problem in Russia's reaching out to Pakistan for an understanding. Later hearings in the Commission on International Affairs of the Duma on relations with India, which took place in October 1994 and February 1997 were not controversial. Almost all participants supported the idea of special relations with India. The formula of 'strategic partnership' between Russia and India put forward in hearings in 1994 was included in the Commission's report of 1997. At the same time the need to improve relations with Pakistan was supported by a number of members. Former Russian Vice President Alexander Rutskoy visited Pakistan in December 1991. Then the Pakistani and Russian foreign ministers exchanged visits. Foreign trade operations between Russia and Pakistan started in the year 1992-93. But this cooperation did not make much headway. However, in 1998 parliamentary delegations exchanged visits.

During his 1993 visit to New Delhi, President Yeltsin boldly declared that India must continue to be a 'strategic partner of Russia', and that Russia would like to develop its ties with India 'in a de-ideologised manner'. He affirmed that Russia supported India's stand on Kashmir and that Russia would not sell arms to Pakistan. Russia and India amicably resolved the complicated Rupee-Rouble issue to settle the past Soviet credits. A major irritant in resuming trade relations between the two countries was thus removed. An understanding was reached for the smooth supply of defence spares. Thus a new life was injected into the hitherto stagnant bilateral relations between India and Russia. Yeltsin and Prime Minister, PV Narasimha Rao signed an agreement on defence cooperation. Both leaders agreed to promote defence cooperation through transfer of technology, production of weapons under licence and the sharing of experiences between the armed forces of the two nations. They also agreed on a joint venture in the aviation industry. Yeltsin reassured Narasimha Rao that Russia would not brook any external pressure on the question of transfer of cryogenic rocket engines to this country. But, unfortunately, Russia came under the US pressure in the matter of transferring cryogenic rocket engine technology to this country.

Narasimha Rao visited Russia in June 1994. In his meeting with Yeltsin, he emphasized the need for restructuring bilateral defence agreements and of launching strategic relations to accelerate cooperation in the economic and trade initiatives. They made it quite clear that their military cooperation was not targeted against any third country. Yeltsin and Rao successfully laid the foundation for a better strategic understanding between the two countries. This was followed by high level visits of other dignitaries to each other's country. The Russian Defence Minister, Igor Radionov visited New Delhi in October 1996 and signed an agreement on military technology cooperation with India's Defence Minister, Mulayam Singh Yadav.

In December 1994 Russian Premier Chernomyrdin visited India, when he reassured that his country had no plans to sell armaments to Pakistan. He was critical of the latter for lending its support to the Chechnyan separatists. During his visit eight agreements were signed, which covered military and technical cooperation from 1995 to 2000, merchant shipping and promotion and mutual protection of investments, trade and outer space cooperation. Political observers saw Chernomyrdin's visit as an occasion of returning to the earlier course of warm relations between Russia and India. In March 1995, both countries signed agreements aimed at suppressing illegal weapons smuggling and drug trafficking. And interestingly when Russian nationalist Vladimir V. Zhirinovsky visited India in March 1995, he declared that he would give India large quantities of arms and equipment if he were elected president of Russia.

In October 1997 Mulayam Singh Yadav visited Moscow and met the Russian Deputy Prime Minister and Economy Minister Yakov Yurison to work out modalities to establish a joint working group for defence production. They also discussed cooperation in land weapons like artillery, rockets, guns and tanks. This was the third meeting of the joint Indo-Russian Working group about defence production. Yeltsin assured Yadav that Russia was prepared to give everything that India needed for its defence and security apparatus. The Russian President also agreed to long-term defence cooperation with India until 2010. Russia delivered SU-30 fighter aircraft and other military hardware, including spare parts, to this country. To settle the deal, Yeltsin's top adviser on Defence and Foreign Policy matters, Boris N.Kuzyk had visited New Delhi in August 1996. He gave a personal message to Prime Minister, H.D. Deve Gowda from Yeltsin expressing the hope that Indo-Russian relations in all areas including that of defence would go ahead. The SU-30 planes delivered were meant to intercept targets moving at a speed of 120 km using medium range missiles. The SU-30 with a range of 3000 km with internal fuel with a special provisioning in the rear cockpit can be operated as a mini awacs operating in conjunction with up to four other similar fighters automatically controlling thom onto targets.

It was again declared by Russia's Deputy Prime Minister Oleg. D. Davydov on October 30, 1996 that Russia would not supply arms to any country inimical to India. In his discussions with the Prime Minister Deve Gowda, both leaders agreed that concrete steps should be taken to increase Indo-Russian economic cooperation. During this visit it was also agreed that the supplement to the agreement of November l988 on cooperation regarding construction of a nuclear power station in Kudankulam should be finalised. The value added norms for exports from India to Russia and exports to third countries of the goods under the rupee debt repayment fund were also discussed. The landmark visit to the Russian Federation undertaken by Prime Minister, Deve Gowda provided a new impetus to the traditionally close and amicable ties between India and Russia. The Minister of External Affairs from India visited Russia from February 9 to February 13, 1997 to co-chair the Third Session of the Indo-Russian Inter-Governmental Commission on Trade, Economic, Scientific, Technological and Cultural Cooperation. In addition to the Protocal of the Third IGC session, an Agreement on the establishment of a joint Shipping Service between India and Russia and a Memorandum of Understanding on Certification in the field of Information Technology were signed during the visit.

The Russian Prime Minister Yevgeny Primakov visited New Delhi in December 1998. It resulted in the signing of seven agreements between the two countries. One of them, a long-term military cooperation pact uptill the year 2010 was of special importance. In March 1999, Russia's Defence Minister Igor D. Sergeyev and India's Defence Minister, George Fernandes signed an agreement on military cooperation for the training of Indian defence personnel in key Russian military academies. The long-term military technology cooperation covered new areas of mutual cooperation such as naval and nuclear technologies and anti-ballistic missile systems. It prepared the ground for enhancing joint research and development capabilities of India and Russia in the production of new weapon systems.

According to a SAND Net Weekly Update from May 3, 2000 India placed orders for the purchase of three Russian battleships under a 1-billion dollar contract. In June 2000, India's Minister of External Affairs Jaswant Singh visited Moscow to be followed by the Defence Minister George Fernandes in July 2000. This visit underscored the defence and strategic aspects of India-Russia relations. It focused on strengthening of bilateral strategic partnership, India's defence needs and concerns over cross-border terrorism in Jammu & Kashmir. These developments were considered as a crucially important shift in Russia's policy towards India. This was the result of Russia's resolve to adopt tough pragmatism, which was considered necessary for regaining great power status.

President Vladimir Putin's visit to India in October 2000 lent a new dynamism to India-Russia strategic relations. Putin and Atal Behari Vajpayee signed the Declaration on Strategic Partnership and 18 more agreements in various fields. The visit imparted a new content to the relations between the two countries, as the defence deals worth $ 3 billion were concluded. Russia agreed to transfer its aircraft carrier Admiral Gorshkov free of cost to be fitted with MiG-29K fighters and Kamov-31 and Kamov-28 helicopters for which payment was to be made by India. The Declaration on Strategic Partnership took cognisance of earlier treaties of 1971 and 1993 and the Moscow Declaration of 1994, but it did not contain the formulation to consult each other in case of any threat to the other side. The new Declaration carried the provision of non-participation in any alliance directed against the other side. The Declaration proclaimed the "establishment of relations of strategic partnership between them based on mutual understanding and long-term confidence in each other." It also envisaged the "elevation of their multifaceted ties to an even higher and qualitatively new level" while imparting them a "specially close and dynamic character both in the bilateral field and in the international arena". The preamble to the Declaration referred to the "conviction that it is necessary to build a multipolar global structure based on sovereign equality of all states and peoples." It also took note of the need of the "desire to jointly contribute to the strengthening of international peace and security as well as to the promotion of the establishment of a new, just and stable world order" in conformity with the "purpose and principles of the UN charter." It was declared that the "strategic partnership between the two sides is not directed against any other state or group of states and does not need to create a military political alliance."

President Putin underlined in one of his statements in New Delhi that Russia and India held separate views on nuclear proliferation. But unlike western countries Russia had not imposed economic sanctions against India, nor had it sermonised India on conducting nuclear tests. Putin simply expressed the hope that India would continue to move towards a non-proliferation regime "taking into account its national interests". It was abundantly clear that Putin's visit was to consolidate old ties between the two countries. Economic considerations were paramount in his policy. He described India as an "equal partner, long-term friend and an ally", which implied that India-Russia relations are based on the mutuality and equality of interests. As regards defence deals, both Russia and India were keen that those went through for their respective reasons. For Russians it was the biggest single defence deal at a time when their economy was in doldrums and for the Indian armed forces it was a windfall ending a decade-old drought due to a severe cash crunch. Russia was feeling disillusioned with the USA and other western countries, as apparently it was becoming progressively more dependent on them.

Russia badly needed the Indian market for its armaments. Its economy got a shot in the arm when India signed $ 1.28 billion defence deal for the purchase of 40 yet-to-be-developed SU 30 MKI aircraft with another $ 300 million for indigenous development and the import of avionic systems. Though the aircraft carrier Admiral Gorshkov was gifted free to India, we were to pay the refitting charges as also the cost of 45 MiG-29 Ks as part of the package deal. Admiral Gorshkov, the fourth in the series built by Russia was commissioned in their Navy in l987 and it was later damaged in a fire accident in 1994. The Russians clinched its deal with India in their own interest as well as that of this country.

Prime Minister Vajpayee's visit to Moscow in 2001 further strengthened relations between India and Russia. The two countries signed and endorsed 17 bilateral documents including the Moscow Declaration on international terrorism. It condemned the double standard approach towards acts of terrorism. The two countries also signed a contract for drawing up a technological project to built the Kudankulam nuclear power station comprising two units of 1000 megawatt each. The old 1988 agreement was reactivated, India was planning to increase its level of production of nuclear power from 2000 to 6000 megawatt by 2010 and subsequently to 20,000 megawatt by 2020.

India's Minister Jaswant Singh visited Russia in June 2001 to emphasise India's policy of upgrading its defence systems and to further strengthen defence cooperation with Russia. A protocal was signed between the two countries which, according to available reports, could be worth $ 10 billion. Both countries agreed to jointly develop the Il-214 military transport aircraft, known as the multi-role Transport Aircraft. The first flights of this aircraft are scheduled for 2007-2008. On June 12, 2001 India and Russia jointly tested a developed supersonic cruise missile from the Chandipur test range. After the successful co-production of the BrahMos supersonic cruise missile, India and Russia are determined to develop a fifth generation of fighter and multi-role transport aircraft. Russia's Deputy Prime Minister Ilya Klebenov visited New Delhi in October 2001, who declared that TU-22 class bombers would be provided to India on lease. This class of bombers would be inducted into the Indian Navy for maritime reconnaissance. Putin approved the proposal for a missile shield for India at the Commission meeting of Military-Technical cooperation held with foreign delegates at the end of October 2001.

In April 2002 India's Minister George Fernandes went to Moscow, where he said that India and Russia had "identical and close" stands on regional and global security issues. He emphasised the deep trust between the two nations which is evident from their "joint design and production of weapons." The same month Vladimir B. Roushailo, Secretary of the Security Council of Russia visiting New Delhi reiterated that India-Russia relations were "time tested" and immune to political vicissitudes.

In June 2002 Putin and Vajpayee met in Alma-Ata during the summit for cooperation and confidence-building measures in Asia. In early December 2002, Putin made a formal call on New Delhi on his return from such a visit to Beijing. Putin gave indications of pursuing the idea of a Russia-China-India Strategic Triangle, which was first mooted by Russia's Prime Minister Y. Primakov during his visit to New Delhi in 1998. Primakov during a TV interview in Moscow confirmed about the progress in shaping such a triangle during Putin's trip to China and India. He emphasised that such an alliance should not be taken as a military or political bloc. A close identity of views among Russia, China and India was visible on various international issues including terrorism, West Asia, the role of the United Nations and Afghanistan. During Putin's visit, India and Russia signed a New Delhi declaration for the further strengthening of strategic partnership between the two countries, a Joint Declaration for strengthening and expanding economic and scientific-technical cooperation, the Memorandum on mutual understanding and cooperation in the fight against terrorism and a number of other bilateral documents.

The Deputy Chairman of the Russian Federation, Ilya Klebanov visited India in February and November 2002. He co-chaired the 8th session of the Indo-Russian Inter-Governmental Commission on Trade, Economic, Scientific, Technological Cooperation on February 7, 2002. During this visit, he and Defence Minister George Fernandes co-chaired the second session of the Indo-Russian Inter Governmental Commission on Military-Technical Cooperation. In November 2002, Klebanov attended the Inter-Session Review Meeting of the IRIGC and the Minister of External Affairs.

In January 2003 Defence Minister George Fernandes signed a protocal in Moscow on Indo-Russian Military Technical Cooperation covering all major other issues of procurement and other matters of defence equipment. Fernandes disclosed that the protocal envisaged India's involvement in the Russian programme for development of a fifth generation combat aircraft and plans to set up joint ventures in defence industry on the pattern of the Indo-Russian BrahMos Company for production of supersonic cruise missiles.

Putin and Vajpayee met on May 31, 2003 at the celebrations of the 300th anniversary of St. Petersburg and on September 25, 2003 at the 58th session of the UN General Assembly. On November 11-13, 2003 Vajpayee paid an official visit to Russia, which proved another landmark in close relationship between the two countries. Both countries gave a call for giving up of double standards in the war against terrorism and they proposed a consistent and uncompromising approach in tackling the menace. They signed a joint declaration calling for a concrete and time-bound action plan under the aegis of the United Nations for the earliest restoration of Iraq's sovereignty. Among the 10 accords signed in the Kremlin after detailed talks between the two leaders, one related to cooperation in space research, which included Russian assistance in an Indian lunar mission.

During Vajpayee's visit, Russia backed the Indian position on Pakistan. It reiterated the demand for ending cross-border terrorism and the dismantling of the terrorist infrastructure in Pakistan, which was a pre-requisite for a purposeful dialogue. Putin praised Vajpayee's initiatives to improve relations with Pakistan and declared that Indian and Russian approaches to international matters practically coincided. They confirmed that collective action on the part of the United Nations was needed for resolving, international problems. Mr. Vajpayee announced that India and Russia had agreed to increase the frequency of air connections between the two countries. Indo-Russian defence cooperation has acquired great versatility and encompasses a wide range of joint research, design, development and co-production. The two countries issued a detailed Declaration on Global Challenges and Threats to World Security and Stability, in which they agreed to coordinate positions on key global issues. Defence, space and science and technology were described as the building- blocks of bilateral strategic partnership.

During Vajpayee's visit, both countries called for promotion of confidence among members of the anti-terrorist coalition by giving due consideration to the interests of each one of them and ensuring that the fight against terrorism was based on rules of international law and the UN charter. Both countries favoured the effective implementation of the UN Security Council Resolution 1373 aimed against those who support, fund or abet terrorists or provide them shelter or asylum to engage in cross-border terrorism. On Israeli-Palestinian conflict, Vajpayee and Putin called for the prevention of the failure of the roadmap to settle the problem. Both leaders reiterated that "India and the Russian Federation strongly believe that Afghanistan should emerge as a peaceful, strong, prosperous, united and independent nation that would be free from external interference and living in peace and harmony with its neighbours." They also favoured the efforts of the "countries concerned" and the international community for a peaceful settlement of the nuclear issue on the Korean peninsula and maintaining its non-nuclear status. India and Russia also affirmed that the future international order based on multipolarity should be determined by collective and multilateral processes rather than unilateral ones.

Addressing the Russian Academy of Sciences in Moscow, Atal Behari Vajpayee lauded Russia's support for India's permanent membership of the UN Security Council. Going further in his appreciation of Russia, Vajpayee said: "The Indo-Russian strategic partnership was a reliable factor in promoting peace, security and stability both in Asia and the world. "The fundamental factor behind the stability of Indo-Russian ties is the exemplary sensitivity both countries show to each other's concerns, including security concerns." Vajpayee found India and Russia putting up a strong fight against terrorism, as this phenomenon was posing a grave threat to the entire civilised world. He said: "Specifically, it is threatening the unity, territorial integrity and sovereignty of both India and Russia. " Calling for a synergy between scientific endeavours and business enterprises of the two nations, Vajpayee recalled that India's pharmaceutical industry, recognised the world over today, was established "largely through our bilateral cooperation with Russia several decades ago."

Mr. Vajpayee said the Integrated Long Term Programme (ILTP) in science and technology was one of the most elaborate programmes in the world over 2,500 scientific exchanges had taken place during its 15 year existence. "Keeping the challenges of modern times, our scientific cooperation now extends to frontier areas of scientific research including bio-technology, informatics, environmental protection, drugs and development of new materials. This is in addition to the traditional areas of cooperation in space, atomic energy and defence technologies," he said. "One thing is certain. The tree of our friendship does not have its roots in the thin top soil of politics and ideology. For it has continued to grow in spite of the political upheavals and structural changes in our two countries," Vajpayee concluded.

The Russian envoy to India, Alexander M Kadakin did not lag behind the Indian leaders in eulogising the Indo-Russian close relations based on their fundamental national interests and described India as Russia's closest and most reliable friend and partner. "The intensity of political dialogue has been on a steady rise embracing ever new challenges and issues emerging in the context of a rapidly changing situation in the world," he wrote. About the situation in Afghanistan and Iraq, Kadakin thought that the views of India and Russia are in consonance with the assessments of our diplomacy. The centrality of the role of the United Nations is consistently being upheld by both India and Russia. In Moscow, Putin and Vajpayee stated that their talks "emphasised the need for Pakistan to implement in full its assurances to prevent infiltration of terrorists across the LOC in Jammu & Kashmir and at other points across the border, and to dismantle the terrorist infrastructure in Pakistan and Pakistan-controlled territory as a prerequisite for a purposeful dialogue between the two nations to resolve all outstanding issues in a bilateral framework as envisaged in the Simla Agreement of 1972 and the Lahore Declaration of 1999.

India and Russia have been showing apprehensions about the prospect of nuclear weapons falling into the hands of terrorists and that it is not a theoretical threat. Fairly powerful extremist groupings operate on Pakistani territory. Such factors prompted Russia to forward a draft convention to the UN on preventing terrorists from using nuclear weapons. India joined the Shanghai Cooperation

Organisation with its anti-terrorist centre based in Bishkek. There is also the CIS anti-terrorist centre, which was set up to coordinate cooperation between CIS law enforcement agencies and security services. The centre performs the crucial function of conducting cross-border searches for wanted criminals.

In the post-Soviet era while the Russian Federation is still consolidating its political and economic structure, it has been facing enormous problems of terrorism and secessionism. Though its strong economic recovery has given it enormous self-confidence , in international political field it has to contend with unilateral self-assertion by the USA. However, with all the aggressive US moves, President Putin remains unflappable and he is of the opinion that "not a single serious global or inter-regional problem can be solved without Russia's active and equitable participation."

References

1. *India's Relations with Russia & China—A new Phase* Edited by M. Rasgotra and V.D.Chopra
2. *Indo-Russian Relations-Prospects, Problems and Russia Today* Edited by V.D. Chopra
3. *Russia and Asia-The 'Emerging Security Agenda* Edited by Gennady Chufrin.
4. *New Trends in Indo-Russian Relations* Edited by V.D. Chopra.
5. New Theme-Russia and India Together in the Fight (October-December 2003).
6. India and Russia: Reassessing the Time-Tested Ties by B.M. Jain *Pacific Affairs*: Volume 76 No.3-Fall 2003.
7. Indo-Russian Defence Deals-Beyond Buyer & Seller Relationship by R.S. Bedi,*The Tribune* of November 13, 2000.
8. Rebuilding Russia's Global Role by Vladimir Radyuhin. *The Hindu* of July 26, 2003
9. Beijing-Moscow-New Delhi trialogue by K.K. Katyal,*The Hindu* of September 22, 2003.
10. *The Hindu* of November 12 & 13, 2003.
11. *The Tribune* of November 12, 2003.
12. *The Times of India* of November 12, 2003.
13. Russian Revelations-Once More with Feeling in Moscow by Alexander M Kadakin,*Times of India* of November 13, 2003.

14. *The Indian Express*, November 14, 2003.
15. Moscow on the line by J.N. Dixit, *The Hindu* April 22, 2004.
16. *The Tribune,* May 27, 2004.
17. Russia, India in New Convergence by Bunn Nagara in www. SouthReview.com
18. Vajpayee says India, Russia have common goals by Vinay Shukla in Moscow November 12, 2003.
19. Ivanov visit to revive Russia-India-China cooperation by P. Jayaram February 3, 2002.
20. Geopolitical Geometry-The Eurasian heavyweight by Stanislav Menshikov Moscow *Tribune*-December 9, 2002.
21. Russia/India: Both Sides Happy as Defense Deal is Signed by Radio Free Europe/Radio Liberty-January 28, 2004.
22. Strategic Partnership with India, China by V.P.Dutt—World Focus, Volume 18.
23. India and Russia agree protocal on defence cooperation—*Strategic Digest,* Volume 31.
24. *The Hindu*-editorial, December 7, 2002.
25. *The Hindu*-editorial, November 9, 2001.
26. India, Russia to discuss n-issues by C. Raja Mohan—The Hindu of October 3, 2000.
27. *Strategic Digest* 30(12), December 2000.
28. *Strategic Digest* 31(11), November 2001.

6
Importance of Indo-Russian Strategic Partnership

Maj. Gen. (Retd.) Afsir Karim

India and Russia recently took a significant step forward to reaffirm their general agreement on important international issues. Both the countries stressed the desirability of multipolarity in international affairs during Putin-Vajpayee summit in November 2003 in Russia. It was clearly enunciated by both the leaders that war on terrorism has to be based on well-established laws and the United Nations charter. Both the leaders indicated they would not support the hegemonic ambitions of the US on the pretext of combating terrorism.

Combating terrorism is one important aspect on which strategic cooperation between India-Russia is essential in addition to the strategic consensus that has survived despite the tremendous upheavals that have taken place in the post 9/11 environments. Linkages and cooperation in the field of defence alone, can no longer be a basis of future relationship between Russia and India, the relationship between the two countries has to take a new direction in view of the changing world order, Russia and India must focus on the issues of expansionist US policies and the rising tide of Jihadi terrorism.

During his visit in 2002 President Putin had reaffirmed Russia's plans of long-term cooperation with India in the nuclear field. India and Russia have since then moved towards close cooperation in nuclear and missile technologies. Russia has accepted India's status as a nuclear weapon power and has been advocating that there is no reason to deny advanced technologies to India. Moreover, Russia had made a clear distinction regarding nuclear status of India and

Pakistan although Russia has been making efforts to improve its relationship with Pakistan. In the present environments neither India nor Russia can afford an adversarial relationship with the US, nevertheless they have to play a significant role to keep American hegemonic designs in check. The Central Asian region, an area of great importance to Russia and India and China, rich in oil, gas and minerals, is not only under threat from fundamentalist Islamic groups based in Afghanistan and Pakistan but is a target of the US hegemonic design. It is important for regional countries to ensure that American designs are kept within limits and moderate Islamic culture of this region is not subverted. This can only be ensured with close cooperation of Russia, China and India. These countries can jointly provide military, economic and technological assistance for building up strong economic and industrial infrastructure in this region. It will not be in the interest of peace if any kind of rivalry develops between countries operating in the region. In this context Russia can help in building bridges between China and India and thereby ensure the safety and security of the Central Asian region from economic exploitation or fundamentalist aggression.

India and Russia should establish a strategic partnership, which promotes multidimensional ties without a narrow focus. India's private sector should be encouraged to explore the Russian market. However, Indian goods will have to compete for recognition because unlike the past, Soviet era, India will face many contenders in this field. For the past few years, people to people contact between Russia and India has reduced greatly. An attempt to restore old links is now necessary. Indians and Russians have become somewhat distant since India has improved its relations with the US. This trend must be curbed because our orientation to the west should not be at the cost of our relationship with Russia. The declared policy of Russia and India basing relationship on the principle of sovereignty, equality and territorial integrity of states, mutual respect and mutual benefit between countries must be translated into reality and not remain merely notional.

A new relationship in which India and Russia are equal partners should emerge and the supplier-client relationship of the past era should no longer form the basis of their relationship. If India hesitates to forge a strategic alliance with Russia because of various constraints, it may miss an opportunity of playing a meaningful role in the changing global order. Russia may move away into self-imposed isolation or move towards European Union, if it is unable to get adequate support in Asia. Russia already has a close relationship with China, and India should not hesitate to form a possible triangular strategic partnership that can play a significant role in keeping the US hegemonic ambitions in check. Things must not be allowed to drift because American bases and the NATO forces are already well entrenched and are in a better position to influence events in Afghanistan, Pakistan and Central Asia than India or Russia. Russia has, however, established a well-equipped air base in Kyrgyztan only 30 miles away from a US air base in this region.

India and Russia need to join forces to fight international terrorism as Russian-Indian alliance and cooperation can keep international Jehadi subversive groups in check in South and Central Asia that are presently anchored in Pakistan. India should try and join the multilateral Shanghai Cooperation Group that was established to settle territorial disputes in the region, demilitarise borders and for cooperation in counter-terrorism and regional trade.

Russia may not be able to openly oppose US hegemonic designs because of its present economic and political difficulties, but there are signs of change and Russia has once again started reasserting itself and has revived its defence relations with Central Asian States. The deliberate low key reactions to the increasing military presence of the US and NATO in Central Asian states in the past is now gradually changing under the new Putin Doctrine which reiterates Russia's strategic interests in Central Asian region and contiguous areas. Russia has started exercising its right to oversee the energy policies of gas-oil and mineral rich regions. It has made it clear that nuclear weapons will continue to be a key strategic asset in Russia's defence policies. It has also indicated that it would not hesitate from launching preemptive strikes in case its vital interests or interests of its allies are threatened.

Russia has started modernisation of its strategic forces including work on production of new missile systems. The 'Triumph' system that is in an advance stage of development can effectively take on any enemy strategic ballistic missile. Use of tactical nuclear weapons of low yield is also being configured for possible use in regional conflicts or counter-terrorists operations. The reemergence of Russia bodes well for India-Russia strategic partnership and cooperation in joint armament programmes.

The basic question is what direction Indo-Russian relationship would eventually take? It is not possible to develop a long-term strategic relationship without a common strategic vision and common goals for cooperating in combating American imperialist tendencies and Islamic fundamentalism. The areas for cooperation and action at the UN and other international forums have to be determined with greater care by the two countries in the present circumstances.

If Sino-Indo-Russian relationship develops in the right direction it could lead to a meaningful triangular relationship for mutual benefit of all the three. This process will promote multi-polarism, and mutual cooperation, with its focus on economic, cultural and technological ties between the three Asian giants. It will lead to rapid development of the entire region from Central Asia to Asia-Pacific. This strategic arrangement will ensure peace and stability and curb confrontation between various Asian nations. Sino-Russian strategic cooperation is already significant and both countries have close economic ties, and are cooperating in development of defence-related technologies. India can hope to be a part of this alliance as the Sino- Indian relations have been lately on the mend and both countries have given up confrontational approach in their border dispute. Islamic militancy and growing concern of US unilaterism may bring India and China closer sooner than expected. Better management of the border issue at various levels has already opened new avenues for border trade and closer economic ties. Separatism that breeds terrorism has been their common problem but with the advent of global Jehadi-terrorism there is a greater urgency for cooperation between the two giant neighbours.

In view of the fact that the US seems determined to follow its aggressive policies unilaterally, promotion of multilatlism has become a strategic necessity for China, India and Russia. The US-led invasion of Iraq and subsequent ham-handed policy to get hold of the oil resources of the region has increased the urgency for a triangular partnership. As Russia, China and India have a common goal of fighting global terrorism, and restoring a multipolar global system, the triangular strategic concept may take a concrete shape rapidly and this would lead to long-term strategic agreements among the three countries jointly or bilaterally.

India and Russia have lately revived interest in upgrading cultural relations. Recently Indian and Russian film industries have held film festivals in each other's country. Many Indian classics have been translated in Russian. However, we do not see many of modern Russian literature which have been translated in Indian languages. Similarly exchange of students has lagged behind and Russian language courses are not run in many Indian Centres; Indo-Russian seminars and exhibitions have also become rare. Arrangements in these spheres need to be improved.

In the post 9/11 environments India and Russia must establish a long-term strategic understanding to strengthen the hands of all the regional countries to withstand external threats, which may arise from international terrorism or hegemonic designs of the US. Their common interest in stability of Central Asia, Afghanistan and the Indian Ocean region which have a great potential for economic development, should provide an incentive to fight against the rising tide of Islamic fundamentalism and the economic chaos that follows in its wake. In peaceful conditions Central Asia and littoral regions can provide facilities for extended trade network in the Indian Ocean region both to Russia and India. The North-South trade corridor that was envisaged under a treaty signed at St. Petersburg between India, Iraq and Russia has to be developed to the required level with the close cooperation of Iran, Russia and India. If both China and Afghanistan can be taken on board this process can be expedited. The US would continue to play a key role in this area, and it would not allow any arrangement if its interests are jeopardized. Presence of US military bases in Central Asia and Afghanistan can create problems for Russia and Iran as they may obstruct the functioning of the North-South trade corridor.

The Indo-Russian relationship got a boost in the recent months after the Indian Prime Minister's visit to Moscow. Putin and Atal Behari Vajpayee reaffirmed the desire of both the countries for closer cooperation because of sensitivities of the two countries to each other's security concerns. Besides pledges for mutual support for combating terrorism, which threatens the secular culture of both countries, cooperation in defence and space issues were upgraded.

A protocol was signed for creation of infrastructure for joint ventures in development and sharing of new technologies related to new weapons systems for export. The signing of a MoU between the Russian Space Agency and ISRO (India) for cooperation and assistance for India's ambitious Moon-mission and space probes is a significant development. Russia has also indicated its willingness to supply enriched uranium for India's nuclear power stations, besides a proposal to provide floating Nuclear Plants to meet India's energy requirements, this arrangement may be able to initially provide electricity and thermal energy to more than 50,000 people and fresh water for a million people.

India and Russia require doing much more to widen their strategic and economic cooperation to enhance bilateral economic ties. India has to ensure that its past Soviet rupee-rouble debt to Russia is liquidated expeditiously, so that the two countries can finalise the plans to phase out the rupee-rouble trade and use the balance for investing in new joint ventures. A large business delegation that had accompanied the Indian Prime Minister to Moscow is understood to have discussed ways and means to expedite implementation of various trade agreements with the Russian authorities. By all indications an overall improvement of relationship and strengthening of strategic ties between Russia and India and a new Asian arrangement is very much on the cards.

7

Continuing Strategic Partnership between Russia and India

Chandra B Khanduri

A Tour D'Horizon

If the 20th century saw the end of colonialism and the Soviet Union, it also saw the beginning of a new kind of imperialism, fragmentation of large but historically aggrieved states and above all a new kind of threat—the threat of terrorism and its hydra heads. There were reunifications too; the unification of two Germanys, for example, was the most unpredictable phenomenon of the century. The result, in sum was a metamorphosis and a changing of the atlas of the world. The mind-boggling events of the century left many lessons to learn; foremost among them being what the President of India, Dr Abdul Kalam enunciated after the 1998 Pokharan Nuclear Test, "Power respects power". The power-game, perhaps, is the fulcrum of all strategies that nation-states adopt. It also vindicates the time tested political philosophy attributed to Lord Henry John Temple Palmerston (1784-1865) of Great Britain, that 'nations have no permanent friends nor enemies but only the performance of their self interests'.

The rise and the fluctuations in Indo-Russian relations need to be seen in the light of the above rudiments of international relationship.

The Indo-Russian relations have bordered on the pattern of 'friendship' more than a formalised relationship, the overtures of which have been both supportive and friendly. Beginning from the 1947-49 J&K War, Russia (then Soviet Union) had helped India fight its battles in the UNO triumphantly. The unfaltering Russian support, however peaked as India and Russia signed on August 9th 1971 the historic 20 year "Treaty of Peace and Friendship", barely three months before the war. The friendship sustained and endured itself through the liberation of Bangladesh to late 1980s when the Cold War ended and the Soviet Union dissolved, which saw the historic devolution of East Germany, Poland, Romania, Czechoslovakia. It resurrected as soon as it picked its new threads. In between, it needs to be admitted that the rupee-rouble trade suffered as also the defence forces, virtually equipped with the Soviet equipment and arms. Modernisation of the Indian Armed Forces was stalled and the country was compelled to rely on expensive western sources.

Nonetheless, Russia rose virtually from its sphinx and is well on its way to recovery and so are the Indo-Russian relations and intercourses. The friendship endures while Russia reorganised its own position in the form of the Commonwealth of Independent States, the CIS, through its one-time allies-Uzbekistan, Kyrgyzstan, Tajikistan and Kazakastan.

A New Kind of Intimidation

The devolution following the Cold War, as it is, was bad but a new kind of threat has troubled Russia. The Muslim separatists of Chechnya have continuously waged a so-called jehad against the central authority in Moscow. But bigger threats have surfaced from external enemies: NATO and the USA, both perhaps rolled into one. The eastward expansion of NATO to the border of Russia encompassing littoral states of Estonia, Latvia, Lithuania, Slovenia, Slovakia and Romania poses a threat of the future.

Similarly, the American military presence in their bases in Uzbekistan, Kyrgyzstan, Tajikistan and Kazakastan (besides Afghanistan and Pakistan) pose no mean strategic intrusion. In both cases it would appear that the American covert effort aims at restricting the Russian strategic manoeuvrability vis a vis its own expansion in this hitherto unviolated sanctuary of Russia.

This geo strategic effect is equally visible in relation to China. The American presence in Central Asia combined with the situation in Taiwan, when seen in the larger context of the US deployments in Japan, South Korea and in the Pacific have larger ramifications both for Russia and China especially for the former.

The Russian Response

In consonance with new ground realities and probable strategic scenarios, Russia under Vladimir Putin has followed what some experts in foreign policy call, ' aggressive vectors of foreign policy'. While handling the controversial unilateral Anglo-American decision to invade Iraq on flimsy grounds (such as Iraq in possession of Weapons of mass destruction that could be activated in 45 minutes and its suspected link with Al Quaida) early 2003, he has maintained the line that any policing, peace keeping and restructuring work should only be done under the aegis of the UNO, which the aggressors had bypassed. And as the American presence in the Central Asian region became a reality, he signed not only the 'Shanghai Cooperation Organisation' with China besides co-opting most of the republics of the CIS. This strengthening of bilateral relations with China, supporting it in its 'One China' policy in so far as it relates to the unification of Taiwan with the mainland has created a new alliance. Sale of front line aircraft and ships also followed.

As part of this new axis of alliance, Russia has reassigned the CIS role into a 'Collective Security Arrangement' with added Russian military presence in the region and even muscle flexing.

With India, as we saw earlier, Russia has steadily improved its old relations and has been constantly striving for a 'Triangular' relations among the three Asian big powers. It has lauded the China-India trade rapprochement signed during PM Vajpayee's visit to China in June 2003. However, a stumbling block remains between China and India owing to the intractable boundary dispute in Ladakh and Arunachal. But if the growth of trade and even proforma progress of the border talks is the indicator of the future course of events, one views the concept with optimism and the 'triangle' may not be far off.

The post '9-11' events have made Russia acutely aware of developing its economy and strategic potential. Among these the export of its vast oil and gas resources figure prominently. It is said to be exporting some 10 pc of its oil to the USA; its new oil contracts are under the scanner to lay direct pipe lines to Japan and/or China from its oil reserves of Lake Baikal and further east in Siberia; its Caspian Sea oil reserves are to be siphoned off to European Union and the Indian Sub-Continent through Iran/ Afghanistan; and a large marketing possibility opens from the new finds in the Sakhalin-Kurile archipelago.

Because the areas of the Russian strategic interests are under threat, owing primarily to the insatiable American thirst for global domination and control, the Russian defense forces too have begun to receive the overdue attention for reorganisation and modernisation, they deserve. Secondly, Russia has begun to cultivate the Organisation of the Islamic Organisation (OIC) not only for oil and retention of the Russian influence in the Islamic world, but acquiring their support to handle the much-maligned Chechen issue. The presence in the 10th OIC meet in Kuala Lumpur during mid October 2003 of President Putin, deserves mention. Concurrently the Russian policy has been to develop fruitful relations with USA and its allies, including NATO and the EU.

Impetus to the Indo-Russian Relations

With growing stability at home in Russia, notwithstanding occasional disruptions, the recognition of economic improvement in India (and its enhanced prospects for the future), Russia has once again discovered India as a sturdy friend and ally. An Indo-Russian Joint Working Group established since 2000 has progressed agendas for common goals very satisfactorily. India continues to be benefited from the advanced defence equipment needs of the armed forces and Russia finds India a reliable market, as it did in the recent $ 4.4 billion defence contract. (This is inclusive of Admiral Gorshkov, the new aircraft carrier, that has been under negotiation for the past five years.)

There are several areas that India would benefit from Russia such as nuclear forces command, integrated defence staff, and so on. Similarly, Russia finds the Indian Information Technology profitable. There is an ever-increasing list of mutual reliance between the two nations, both grappling with their own problems determinedly.

8

Looking Beyond Indo-Russian Military-Strategic Partnership

Ravi M. Bakaya

The expression *strategic partnership* would suggest, at first sight, collaboration in the military field. However, it would be interesting to observe how the meaning of the word *strategy* has changed over the past few decades. If we look at its etymology, the word derives from Greek and Latin roots, meaning *generalship*. The 1958 edition of Webster's 2-Volume Dictionary defines *strategy* as 'the science of planning and directing large-scale military operations, specifically (as distinguished from *tactics*) of manoeuvring forces into the most advantageous position prior to actual engagement with the enemy".

However, in the 1987 edition of Webster's New Collegiate Dictionary we find the meaning of *strategy* modified radically as follows: 'the science and art of employing the political, economic, psychological and military forces of a nation or group of nations to afford the maximum support to adopted policies in peace or war'.

The Random House Dictionary (1969 edition) had already left out *'war'* altogether. It defined *strategy* as 'a plan, method or series of manoeuvres or stratagems for obtaining a specific goal or result'.

However, since we are talking about *Indo-Russian strategic partnership,* we must examine how the other partner, i.e. Russia, understands this phrase. We in India appear to have borrowed the phrase *strategic partnership* from Russia. It is hardly ever used by English-speaking countries. Let us examine the following quotations taken from bulletins issued by the principal news agency of Russia — *Novosti.*

1. St. Petersburg, May 30, 2003. The Indian Prime Minister noted that *strategic partnership* relations between India and Russia were developing very well. Russia is India's good friend, and we are counting on Russia. Vajpayee stressed. (Prime Minister Vajpayee was in Russia to attend the city's 300th anniversary. —*RMB.*)
2. Moscow, May 27, 2003. 'Relations between Russia and China have reached a record high level', announced Vladimir Putin, opening talks with China's Chairman Hu Jintao in the Kremlin today. 'The President said that the two countries had signed a *strategic partnership treaty.*" (The new Chinese Chairman Hu Jintao was paying his first visit abroad.—*RMB.*)
3. Moscow, June 30, 2003. 'Russia and Iran have good prospects for the development of cooperation in the atomic sphere', Iranian Vice-President Qolam Reza Aqazadeh-Khoi, the Chairman of the Iranian Atomic Energy Organisation, said at a meeting with Russian Foreign Minister Igor Ivanov. 'Russia is Iran's *strategic partner* and real friend', he noted. On his part, Russian Foreign Minister Igor Ivanov said that Moscow considers Iran an important *strategic partner.*
4. Kiev, June 30, 2003. Meeting today with Russian Defence Minister Sergei Ivanov, who is in Kiev on a three-day official visit, Ukrainian President Leonid Kuchma said that Russia and Ukraine were *strategic partners.* (Let us note that Ukraine, a former Soviet Republic, has been trying hard for membership of NATO. –RMB.)
5. London, June 26, 2003. Addressing a Russian-British energy conference in London today, Vladimir Putin referred to Britain as one of Russia's major partners in the energy industry, noting that bilateral cooperation in this field has reached the level of long-term *strategic partnership.* (The Russian President was in Britain on a state visit. –*RMB.*)
6. Moscow, May 30, 2003. Common strategic interests of Russia and the USA are more important than their tactical disagreements, Russian Foreign Minister Igor Ivanov believes. An article by Ivanov in *Nezavisimaya Gazeta* today says: "We have every," ground to say that the upcoming St. Petersburg and Evian summits between the Russian and US Presidents

> will allow our countries to reach a new level of *partnership* in terms of regional and global stability... Even at the most sensitive moments of Iraqi crisis our country proceeded from the conviction that Russian-US *strategic interests* were more important than their tactical disagreements concerning the Iraqi settlement.'

Official Russian spokesmen have said repeatedly that Russia's strategic interests are not directed against any other country. (We may note that the Chinese take the same view about *their* strategic interests. They too seem to have borrowed this phrase from Russia, just like we have.) In a message to the youth conference on 'Moscow International Model of UNO 2003' President Putin said on April 14, 2003:

'At the end of the 20th century mankind did away with the Cold War. The tasks of world historic importance were thus accomplished and the threat of global nuclear war was practically eliminated. At the same time, new global challenges—international terrorism, drugs trade, proliferation of weapons of mass destruction, financial economic crises, environmental catastrophes and mass epidemics have replaced this threat. Moreover, many regional conflicts have emerged. Russian foreign policy strategy is based on the idea of broad multilateral cooperation for combating the new threats.'

Addressing a press conference after talks with British Prime Minister Tony Blair, Vladimir Putin pointed out during his state visit to Britain in June 2003 that a revival of the Cold War was ruled out.

> 'The Cold War came out of antagonisms between two systems based on confrontational ideologies. Now the situation is different. Whatever Russia is doing or intends to do has nothing whatever to do with confrontation in view. On the contrary, Russia desires *partnership*. An internationally split community cannot cope with terrorism, proliferation of mass destruction weapons and other burning problems.'
>
> On June 27 President Putin, addressing students of Kaliningrad University said:
>
> 'Official ideological unity betokens a totalitarian state. Any country which hopes for progress needs clash of opinions. Russia is a free country now and that is its greatest achievement in recent years.'

All the above quotations show that the Russians perceive the expression *strategic partnership* in a much broader sense and use it for Russia's *long-term relations* with almost ALL countries and not exclusively with ANY ONE country.

All that has been said above does not at all mean that Indo-Russian relations are like Russia's relations with any of the other countries referred to above. The US and Britain were on the opposite side of Russia during the long Cold War years. China, in spite of having a communist government, had denounced the Soviet Union as its 'Enemy No. 1' during the years of the 'Cultural Revolution' and there were even serious armed clashes on the Soviet-Chinese borders during that period.

Indo-Russian relations, on the other hand (barring a brief period after the disintegration of the USSR, and an earlier aberration during 1948-53), have always been warm and cordial. In the early years after India gained political freedom but lacked economic independence, the USSR played a significant role in building the key sectors of the Indian economy, training hundreds of Indian scientists and engineers, building our nuclear power stations, helping India in space exploration and launching space satellites and being the chief supplier of arms and equipment for our armed forces. The Soviet Union gave political support to India at critical moments and even used its veto in the UN Security Council in our favour on various occasions. It supported the Non-Alignment movement and India's role in it as its most important member. Russia thus always had a special relationship with India. In India too there was a national consensus among the major political parties on this question and Indo-Soviet friendship was warmly supported at the grassroots level by Indian public opinion of all political shades. This cooperation extended to the educational, scientific and cultural fields as well.

The collapse of the USSR at the end of 1991 marked the greatest change in the international situation since World War II. The world entered a period characterized by increasing domination of a single world power, the USA.

In a brief paper we cannot go into the complex questions of the post-Soviet world. But it is clear that apart from ideological considerations, post-Soviet Russia is in no position to challenge US domination of the world either militarily or economically.

In recent years there has been a welcome stabilisation of political life in Russia, as also a marked revival of its economy. What should worry us, however, is the growing dependence of Russia's economy on arms production and exports. Dr. Tatiana Shaumian. Director of the Centre for Indian Studies in Moscow, says in an article published recently:

> 'Russia was the world's largest arms peddler, surpassing even the US in 2002, according to the prestigious Stockholm International Peace Research Institute. Russian weapons exports were about $5 billion, or 36 per cent of global total, a stunning post-Soviet record/ (*The Pioneer,* June 22, 2003.)

Dr. Shaumian reveals that India and China, the world's biggest arms importers in 2002, accounted for over 80 per cent of Russian weapons exports. (*The Pioneer,* July 6, 2003.)

Another Russian expert. Victor Litovkin, says:

> "There is only one country, linked to Russia by a long-term military-technological partnership programme to be valid up to 2010. That is India. The programme is estimated at US$ 8 to 10 billion or even more....An impressive 80 per cent of the Indian Army and Navy's present-day arsenals and technologies have come from Russia... .There is nothing of charity to either side in Russian-Indian military-technological partnership. Suffice it to say that India accounts for 50 per cent of Russian arms and military-technological exports revenues. The profits come in handy to keep Russian military industry afloat, and design pioneer arms for exports and the Russian Army alike.' (Theme, July-September 2003.)

It is well known that one of the reasons for the collapse of the Soviet Union at the end of 1991 was its excessive concentration on heavy industry and on arms exports and its neglect to produce consumer goods to meet the needs of its people. However, leaders of the ruling Communist Party enjoyed a privileged life. In Russia and in practically all the former republics of the USSR Communist Party leaders became the new rulers after the disintegration of the Soviet Union. A new class of oligarchs—practically all of them former Communist Party or Komsomol (Young Communist League) bosses at various levels—within a matter of less than half a decade—became multimillionaires. These oligarchs now control up to 70 per cent of Russia's industrial assets. Let us quote Tatiana Shaumian once again:

> 'These oligarchs built their vast empires during the wild and woolly 1990's, when men with muscle, strong nerves and tight Kremlin connections basically plundered the crown jewels of the former Soviet economy—and called it "reform". The big cash cows they tried to seize were oil, gas, minerals, forestry, smelting (steel and aluminium), fisheries, telecommunications and arms production. Only a couple of these sectors still remain largely in state hands today, but most were handed over for next to nothing to a handful of Kremlin cronies in an orgy of dubious "privatisation". (*The Pioneer,* July 22, 2003.)

Now that Duma (Russian parliament) elections have taken place in December 2003 and the presidential election has been held in March 2004, the oligarchs are making a desperate bid to capture political power. When Vladimir Putin assumed power over three years ago, he declared war on two powerful oligarchs, Boris Berezovsky and Vladimir Guzinsky, who had meddled heavily in politics and seemed prone to oppose the President. Both of them soon found themselves charged with crimes dating back to the 1990's and were stripped of their properties and hounded into exile.

> 'Putin called the other magnates to a Kremlin meeting and made a deal with them. Businessmen would stay out of politics and the authorities would forget about the sources of oligarchic wealth. The bargain held for almost three years. Much of the political stability and economic growth that Russia has enjoyed is founded upon it.' (*Ibid.*)

Early in July Russian police arrested Platon Lebedev, one of the chief executives of Yukos, Russia's second largest oil company. But the main target was Mikhail Khodorkovsky, Yukos' main owner and Russia's richest man. Now Khodorkovsky himself has been arrested and charged with fraud, embezzlement and tax evasion. His arrest led to a storm in Russia's stock market, wiping out more than $ 15 billion. A US national, Steven Theede took over as CEO of Yukos, following Khodorkovsky's arrest. Yukos' chief financial officer Bruce Misamore is also a US national. (Sergei Blagov in The Hindu, November 1, 2003). This led to a political upheaval of the first order, and Alexander Voloshin, chief of staff of the President and the second most powerful figure in the Kremlin, a key member of "The Family" (the group of business tycoons and politicians who wielded enormous power under the previous President, Yeltsin), has been sacked by President Putin. As a *de facto* No. 2 man in Russia, Alexander Voloshin has been the main spokesman of the powerful oligarchs who control nearly 70 per cent of the country's industrial assets. His arrest came hours after state prosecutors froze Khodorkovsky's controlling stake in Yukos. The shares freeze seemed to be aimed at preventing the sale of a strategic stake in Yukos to American companies. Sergei Markov, a political analyst close to the Kremlin, said: "We did not privatise state property so that it could be sold to the United States and Khodorkovsky would get the money." (Vladimir Radyuhin in **The Hindu**, Nov.1, 2003.)

The purpose of this rather long digression is to underline the perils of basing Indo-Russian relations chiefly on arms deals. India undoubtedly needs strong and well-equipped defence forces to face the challenges from our belligerent neighbour in the north-west. Pakistan has had close historical relations with China and still relies heavily on the support of the US and of China. General Musharraf has visited China to press for its support on his claims on Kashmir. A large part of Pak-occupied Kashmir has been gifted by Pakistan to China. Meanwhile, India-China relations are on the mend and the two countries have held a few rounds of talks on their border dispute.

India and Russia are large countries with a history of many decades of friendship and cooperation. Together they can play a constructive role in working for peace in our part of the world. While we must undoubtedly be militarily strong and well-prepared to defend our borders, we cannot afford to engage in an arms race and base our relations with Russia mainly on arms trade. Our long-term (strategic) interests lie in peace in the sub-continent and in the world. People today in most countries yearn for peace. Repeated demonstrations in Washington against the occupation of Iraq by the US shows that the American people too are waking up once again to the need for peace.

If *strategic partnership* between India and Russia is understood as *partnership for peace* and against proliferation of weapons of mass destruction, then our two countries can play a very positive role in international politics. But engaging ourselves in an armaments race, subjecting our by no means strong economies to competition in producing and exporting arms, can lead to ruinous consequences. Neither India nor Russia can afford sustaining militarised economies.

Should we not then look beyond military strategy and work jointly for a strategy of peace?

POSTSCRIPT: This paper was written at the beginning of November 2003. Since then the Russian parliamentary elections have been held on 7th December. In the Russian election system half of the 450 Duma seats are allotted to political parties on the basis of their vote share, while the other half are filled in by direct election. The new elections have changed the face of the Duma. In the outgoing Duma the Communist Party led by Gennady Zyuganov had the largest number of seats. Commenting editorially. *The Hindu* appropriately sums up the significance of the Duma elections of December 7, 2003:

> '...United Russia Party, a party made up of Mr. Putin's loyalists, has obtained over 37 per cent of the vote and might get a majority on its own in the lower house of Parliament, the Russian Duma. Two other parties that broadly subscribe to the President's nationalist agenda, the Liberal Democratic Party and Rodina, together garnered another 20 per cent....About the only opposition the nationalists will face is from the Communist Party that will have less than half the 117 seats it had in the outgoing house after its share fell from 24 to 12.7 per cent. The two pro-Western parties, the Union of Right Forces and Yabloko. will have no parliamentary representation since they failed the qualifying mark of 5 per cent of the vote....The result appears to indicate that he (Putin) will easily win the second term when the presidential elections are held in March next year....
>
> '....Allegations that Kremlin advocates of a strong state rigged the polls need not be taken seriously. It was not as if the nationalists were pitted against the Russian masses. The deeper political struggle was between the nationalists and the handful of robber barons who took control of huge chunks of the Russian economy when the Soviet Union collapsed. In attempting to convert their economic clout into political power,

these oligarchs did not hesitate to subvert state institutions. They also provided the conduit by which the Western governments and financial interests were able to influence Russia's internal affairs during the term of President Boris Yeltsin. However, the heads of the Russian conglomerates will continue to have a powerful say in Parliament since they or their representatives figured on the list of candidates of all parties including the Communists...

'The resurgence of Russian nationalism should have a balancing impact on international affairs. It can contribute to the restoration of multi-polarity at a time when the sole superpower is straining to impose its unilaterist vision on the rest of the world...." (*The Hindu*, December 10, 2003.)

9
Russian-South Asian Relations

Kalim Bahadur

South Asia has occupied a prominent role in the foreign policy of the former Soviet Union and it continues to do so now in that of Russia. In this context it should be noted that Russia and India have a long history of friendship which goes back to almost seven decades. The Indian national movement was greatly inspired by the Soviet revolution and the Soviet Union in its turn supported India's freedom struggle. When India became independent, for some time the Soviet leaders did not accept the fact of Indian freedom. They believed that the Indian leadership was acting as agents of the former colonial powers. However, after the death of Stalin in 1953 the Soviet leaders came to realise that the Indian independence was genuine and thereafter India found a trusted friend in the former Soviet Union. Russia was also drawn to India because of India's first Prime Minister Jawaharlal Nehru's policy of non-alignment. One of the basic ingredients of non-alignment was that India would not join any military alliance and this was a great assurance to the Soviet Union that a large country like India would not join the emerging American alliance against it. Relations between the two countries developed steadily in the post-Stalin period and by 1965 Russia had become the second largest contributor to India's development. The Soviet aid was extended to India on deferred payment and on long-term basis. It was in 1959 that the Soviet Union started supplying arms and defence equipment to India on deferred Rupee payment. This was a boon to India which at that time could not have afforded to make the payment in foreign currency. The major advantage in Soviet-India defence relationship was that the former did not impose any restriction on the Indian autonomy in foreign policy in return for its assistance in security relationship. The Soviet leadership also did not want any political concession from India like bases on its territory. The signing of the Treaty of Peace, Friendship and Cooperation between the two countries in August 1971 was an important milestone in strengthening their economic and security relationship and was of great help during the Bangladesh crisis. India on its part showed understanding for the sensitivities of the Soviet Union by abstaining from public criticism when it intervened in the civil war in Afghanistan in December 1979s although it did not agree with the Soviet policy. The former Soviet Union had also supported India in its dispute with Pakistan over the state of Jammu and Kashmir. The Soviet Union had recognized the Indian claim of the state's accession to India which was being challenged by Pakistan.

The break up of the Soviet Union has not resulted in any gulf between the two countries. On the contrary they have tried to broaden their relations after the end of the cold war. Russia-India relations are like earlier period, which continue to be marked by close cooperation in the field of defence and shared hopes to recreate the world which was passed out. The visit of President Yeltsin in January 1993 to India marked a new phase in India-Russia relations and signalled a new emphasis in economic cooperation. Russia agreed to extend help to India in its space programme. The new Russia has continued to affirm its support to India on Kashmir. The visit of President Yeltsin also reaffirmed continued defence cooperation and flow of latest arms to India. Joint production of defence equipment was also mooted. Both countries are attempting to give a fillip to economic relations which have considerably reduced over the years since the demise of the Soviet Union. Analysts point out that the Russian relations with India are influenced by strategic need of Moscow to neutralize the United States influence in Asia and the growing power of China. The close relations between Russia and India are reflected by two visits to India by President Putin within a short period of two years. In this perspective India Russia relations are central to Moscow's South Asia policy. The nuclear tests by India in 1998 did create problems with Russia. While the latter was a signatory to the Non-Proliferation Treaty, India has consistently resisted all pressure and has refused to sign the Treaty. Moscow's support to Pakistani sponsored move for South Asian Nuclear Free

Zone did create uneasinees in India. However, both Russia and India have common interests in fighting the rise of terrorism and Russia has been supporting India in its fight against Pakistan sponsored terrorism in the state of Jammu and Kashmir. Both Russia and India have sought to improve relations with Washington after the end of the cold war.

Russia's relations with Pakistan have been uneasy ever since independence. The world was divided in two camps—one led by the United States and the other by the Soviet Union. Both these powers were keen that the two newly independent countries-India and Pakistan should join their respective camps. In fact India and the Indian leaders were known throughout the world, whereas Pakistan and its leaders were hardly known abroad. The policies of the two great powers towards South Asia had been deeply influenced by India-Pakistan conflicts, tensions, and rivalries. It was in late forties that the first Prime Minister of India, Pandit Jawaharlal Nehru was invited by Washington. The then Prime Minister of Pakistan Liaquat Ali Khan was invited by Moscow for a state visit to the Soviet Union. Later, he was invited to Washington for a state visit to the United States. The Pakistan Prime Minister forgot about Moscow's invitation and visited the United States. It is to be noted that the first Pakistani head of government visited Moscow only in the sixties. This reflected the Pakistani perception of its interests. It was as early as the first few months of independece that Pakistan had sent its request for military and economic aid to Washington. Initially Washington rebuffed Pakistan's importunities. However, in the early fifties, at the height of the cold war, when the United States was cobbling a security ring round the Soviet Union, Washington realised the strategic importance of Pakistan so closely located near the soft under belly of the Soviet Union. Pakistan more than willingly joined the U.S. camp. Pakistan's adherence to the American military alliance was prompted by its vulnerability against India rather than a desire to join the crusade against communism. Pakistan's Prime Minister Zulfikar Ali Bhutto (1971-1977) attempted to mend fences with the Soviet Union but to no avail. Pakistan's close relations with China at a time when Sino Soviet relations had soured had also a negative effect on Pakistan's relations with the Soviet Union. In the late seventies the Soviet invasion of Afghanistan when Pakistan had become a frontline state could not bring the two closer and was a cause of strain in their relations.

Russia-Pakistan relations worsened in the eighties when Pakistan foreign policy was sponsoring Jehadis not only across the border in the Indian state of Jammu and Kashmir but also in Afghanistan. Pakistani trained Jehadis had spread out to many countries in West Asia, Chechnya, Dagestan, Uzbekistan and the other newly independent states of Central Asia. While Pakistan was committed to help first the Afghan Mujahideen and later the Taliban seized Afghanistan, Russia was helping the Northern Alliance to resist the Taliban.

However, in the post 9/11 world there has been some relaxation in the relationship between Russia and Pakistan. Both Pakistan and Russia have opposed the US invasion of Iraq and the threat of impending attack on Syria, yet both have supported the war against terrorism. Pakistani analysts point out that India's arms purchases in United States, Israel and other Western sources will force Russia to look elsewhere hinting at the possibility of Pakistan getting some weapons from it. However, this should not make one to conclude that Russia and Pakistan have always been estranged. In the sixties the former Soviet Union played a major role in bringing India and Pakistan together after the 1965 war when the two countries signed the famous Tashkent Declaration. Later in the late eighties the Soviet Union had agreed to supply a limited amount of arms to Pakistan as one time exception and which had annoyed India at the time. Pakistan has been making no secret of its keenness to secure Russian arms.In the nineties several Russian backed Muslim groups had challenged Moscow in the regions particularly in Chechnya, and the Central Asian Republics. The Russian President Putin on a visit to India had also expressed doubts about the security of the Pakistani nuclear arsenal which has turned out to be prophetic in view of the recent disclosure of the nuclear proliferation by Pakistani nuclear scientists.

The former Soviet Union had also had friendly relations with Bangladesh from the very first day of its independence. The Soviets had supported India during the Bangladesh crisis in 1971. The famous Indo-Soviet Treaty of 1971 had been of great consequence during that conflict. The Soviet Union was one of the first foreign powers to recognize Bangladesh. In the early years the Soviet Union contributed extensively in relief and rehabilitation in the war torn country. By 1989 Soviet Union ranked 14th among the donors in aid for Bangladesh. Russian assistance to Bangladesh is focused on power, natural gas, oil, and promotion of cultural relations between the two countries. Russia has financed the construction of the largest thermal power station, the Ghorasal, in the country. Russia had signed a deal with Dhaka for supply of US $ 129 million defence equipment which included supply of the Russian fighter jets Mig 29.The delivery of the Mig 29 aircraft had been completed by 1999.

Russian relations with Nepal have seen their ups and downs. Nepal had chosen non-alignment in a world which was divided in two camps. Nepal's strategic location of sharing a common border with China, a member of the Soviet camp in the late forties, in the north and with India in the south. However, Nepal desired to develop relations with the Soviet Union as a counterfoil to the Western camp while Moscow wanted Nepal not to tilt towards the western camp. Thus the interests of Nepal and that of the Soviet Union coincided on Nepal's policy of keeping equidistant from the two rival camps. It was King Mahendra who established diplomatic relations with the Soviet Union in 1956. Nepal-Soviet Economic and Technical Cooperation introduced a new dimension to developing public sector in Nepalese economy. Moscow advanced 30 million Roubles as aid to Kathmandu. However, Nepal could not escape the fallout of the growing rift between China and the Soviet Union in the early sixties. The situation was compounded by the Sino-Indian war of 1962. These developments strained Russia-Nepal relations and the Soviet aid dried up. After the fall of the Soviets Union a new situation has developed. There is great potential for trade and cheap technology from Russia for Nepal.

Sri Lanka was one of the founders of the non-aligned movement in the early fifties. Sri Lanka and Soviet Union had established diplomatic relations in 1957. Russia's relation's with Sri Lanka have been developing since then. The recent signing of a pact on military cooperation for Russian supply of hardware and exchange of expertise to Sri Lanka marks a new milestone in the relations between the two countries. This was a follow up of the setting up of the Sri Lanka Russia Business Council in December 2001 .The Sri Lankan armed forces already have Soviet tanks and aircraft.

Russia is now focused on the internal problems and is no longer a major player on the world scene. However, South Asia remains important for it because of the region's strategic location. South Asian countries have had close economic and defence relations with the former Soviet Union. Russia could still be a source of important technology and arms for the South Asian countries at competitive prices and on very convenient terms. One analyst has pointed out that three great powers that is United States, Russia and China's interests coincide in South Asia. They do not want an India-Pakistan war and that they want to block the Islamic terrorism spreading out of Pakistan-Afghanistan region. Both Russia and China would want to limit the expansion of American influence in the region.

10

US-Russian Relations: A New Phase

B. K. Shrivastava

After the cold war came to an end the Soviet Union began to draw closer to the United States. The high point of this phase was reached during the Gulf War. Most of the resolutions in the UN Security Council during the war were adopted either unanimously or with a few dissenting votes. The Soviet Union did not exercise its veto. The Soviet cooperation so pleased President George Bush that he concluded that the world had been reordered.[1] There was marked change in the Soviet behaviour. It did not use force to suppress demand for independence in the Baltic States. President Gorbachev tried persuasion that did not succeed. One important reason for taking this approach was the US opposition to the use of force. Eventually the Soviet Union disintegrated because ethnic upsurge could not be controlled. Fourteen republics broke away from the Soviet and became independent. But the Soviets did not grant independence to the Muslim majority autonomous republic of Chechnya. The Chechens resorted to terrorism to back up their demand for independence and the Soviet Union tried to suppress it by the massive use of force. For two years from 1992 to 1994 it waged a war in Chechnya. The human rights activists led an agitation in the United States and demanded that the United States should intervene in the conflict. The demand for adopting a tough approach was backed by conservative senators and congressmen. Undoubtedly there were genuine supporters of human rights among this motley crowd but there were also elements that used this as pretext for exerting pressure on Russia. They would have liked to see Chechnya become independent. Russia had other reasons to be unhappy with the United States. When it adopted policy of cooperation rather confrontation it expected that the United States and Western Europe would give generous economic aid and investment would be made. But that did not happen. On the other hand it received a lot of advice from the United States as to how it could restructure its economy. This led to a great deal of frustration and resentment among the Russian policy elite.

Russia began to move away from the United States. When the events leading to the disintegration of Yugoslavia began to unfold, Serbia expected that Russia would come to its assistance. The Slavs have been historic allies of the Serbs. And indeed, Russia opposed the use of force and argued in favour of political settlement of the Bosnian crisis. But when Milosevic did not heed President Yeltsin's advice to agree to the compromise proposal Russia eventually supported the use of force by the United States and Western Europe. Four years later in 1999 Russia remained opposed to the use of force in Kosovo till the end. It declared that it would veto any resolution that would be brought before the UN Security Council legitimizing the use of force. US Secretary of State, Madeleine Albright therefore decided that she would not approach the Security Council for that very reason. The United States bypassed the United Nations. It was NATO that was used to force the Milosevic government to agree to the condition laid down earlier in a Security Council resolution.[2] After the end of the war when the UN Stabilization force was occupying Kosovo, Russia wanted to have an area marked for its control. In a dramatic move, the Russian forces moved fast and occupied the airport. The crisis was resolved but Kosovo showed how far Russia had moved away from the United States by the end of the decade in contrast with its position during the Gulf War in 1991. The stand off during the Yugoslav crises did not, however, result in rupturing Russia's relations with the United States.

The Al Qaeda's attack on the United States on September 11, 2001 shocked the international community. It became aware of the great threat that international terrorism posed to the peace and security of the entire world. The international community offered its sympathy to the United States and promised to extend its cooperation in the war that the United States had declared on international terrorism. It was obvious that the United States could not fight Al Qaeda whose operation cells existed in more than sixty countries, without cooperation from other countries.

Russia had been fighting against the terrorism of the Chechen extremists since 1991. It was the first country to condemn the terrorist attack and offered all possible support to the United States. As the main theater of action was going to be in Afghanistan, where the Al Qaeda leader Osama Bin Laden had been living in exile, cooperation from Pakistan and Russia was of the utmost importance. Pakistan was one of the three countries that had recognized the Taliban government in Afghanistan. It agreed to cooperate with the United States under the threat that it would be declared a terrorist state if it would not cooperate. However, it was not willing to openly allow the American forces to invade Afghanistan from its territory. Therefore, the US could not carry out its southern strategy. Russia permitted US to lease air bases in Khanbad and Kakaida in Uzbekistan and Dushanbe and Kulyab in Tajikistan and in Manas in Kyrgzstan. It permitted the use of its air space to ferry troops to these bases. It stated that it did not offer troops because they were not needed. From the Russian point of view one positive outcome of the contingency was that the rhetoric on human rights violations of the Chechens and expressions of American concern for the plight of the refugees of the war was toned down. The Central Asian Republics facing the threat of destabilization from Islamic fundamentalism had entered in to security agreements with Russia and without its concurrence the bases could not be offered to the United States.

Russia not only extended cooperation in the conduct of operation in Afghanistan but after the rout of the Taliban regime it helped in reaching an agreement at the Bonn Conference. It persuaded the Northern Alliance over which it had considerable influence to accept the provisional arrangement and agree to be part of the Karzai government. The American and Russian interests partially converged on Afghanistan. Both of them wanted to see the end of the flow of the extremists in to neighbouring Central Asian Republics and spread their brand of Islamic fundamentalism and destabilize the governments there. American interest in oil and gas deposits of the Central Asian Republics could be served only if there was peace and stability in the region.

As the war in Afghanistan neared its end the Bush Administration decided that the time for removing Saddam Hussein had arrived. For a decade since the Gulf War ended economic sanctions against Iraq and the bombing of targets in Iraq by Britain and the United States had considerably weakened the defense capability of Iraq. But the Bush Administration on the basis of manipulated intelligence claimed that Iraq's weapons of mass destruction posed an imminent threat to the United States and the world. It also tried to link up Iraq with Al Qaeda. To these charges it added that Iraq had defied the resolutions of the UN Security Council for ten years and had tortured its opponents and used lethal chemical weapons against its own citizens. The task had become urgent because Iraq could get its nuclear weapons ready for the launch within a very short-period of time, as short as 45 minutes. The majority of American public supported their government's decision to go to war against Iraq because 9/11 had scared them. When the United States wanted endorsement of its plan to attack Iraq the Security Council declined to adopt the US sponsored resolution. France opposed it and asserted that it would veto the resolution. It opposed war and argued that the UN inspectors could find the alleged NMD and eliminate them without going to war. Germany, Russia, and China agreed with France. Even the effort of the United States to get a resolution adopted by majority of nine votes did not succeed. The American media did not fail to point out that Saddam Hussein's Iraq owed nearly eight billion to Russia and in addition Russia had secured a number of oil concessions and therefore had vested interest in wanting Saddam Hussein to continue in office. What Russia opposed was American decision to intervene in Iraq unilaterally. It repeatedly stressed its support for multilateralism in international politics especially where decision was to intervene in a sovereign state. However, neither its rhetoric nor its action was as strident as that of France. Both Russia and China spoke in mild language expressing their preference rather than their strong protest. Nor did they ever say that they would veto the US sponsored resolution. Russia did not want any confrontation. The critics of the Bush Administration's policy on Iraq pointed out that the war against international terrorism was not over. Osama bin Laden had neither been arrested nor killed. On the other hand the Taliban had resurfaced and reorganized itself in Afghanistan. Opening another front against Iraq would only blur the focus of attention of the war on terrorism. The Administration had already made its decision and no amount of criticism could make it change it.

The military operation of the coalition forces led by the US barely lasted a few weeks. The Iraqi army did not want to fight. President Bush officially declared the war to be over on May 1. Russia picked up business where it was before the war. It resumed its cooperation with the United States and Britain. In the last week of June 2003 President Putin was in London for the signing of an agreement on oil. At the press conference attended by both President Putin and Prime Minister Blair, the former declared that they have put their differences over Iraq behind them. He pointed to the energy deal that would make Britain the world's largest foreign investor in Russia. The British Petroleum agreed to invest $6.15 billion to create a new oil company-TNK-BP. [3]

In the last few years of the decade the Russian economy had turned the corner. It's economy had stabilized and growth rate had picked up.[4] Oil money and strong economic growth pushed Russia to a position where other countries including the United States sought better relations with it. American search for energy security created a new area of convergence of interest with Russia. The recent blackout in a large part of the eastern part of the United States extending up to Canada showed its vulnerability on this score and highlighted the urgency of ensuring energy security. Russia has one of the largest deposits of oil and gas in the world. Thus far the United states had relied on Saudi Arabia for controlling the international oil market. But after its experience in the wake of 9/11 it considers the Saudis as undependable. Russia is also outside the OPEC and can help the US in keeping the price of oil at the desired level. Other areas of mutual interest also emerged as the result of changes in world economy. *The Business Week* noted in an article in March 2003 that big American corporations are "aiming at China, Russia and India." Undoubtedly the western markets are far larger but they are barely expanding. Russia is no longer a supplicant for aid and investment either from the United States or Europe. It is bargaining for better terms. It still has veto in the UN Security Council and can prevent a consensus shaping in America's favour. It also has huge stockpile of nuclear weapons and capability to deliver them. Russia has been part of international nuclear establishment and has abided by relevant nuclear and missile technology regimes. It did not transfer either nuclear or missile technology to a third country. When the United States pressured Russia not to assist Iran's nuclear programme, Russia stood its ground claiming that it was providing assistance to Iran only for the development of nuclear energy. It did not agree when the US wanted to take the issue of Iran's nuclear programme to the UN Security Council for imposing economic sanctions against Iran. The US had to reconcile with the position being taken by France, Russia and Germany on the issue.

One sensitive issue after the end of the cold war for the Soviet Union was inclusion of former communist countries of Eastern Europe in to NATO. The expansion would have brought NATO to the very border of the Soviet Union. The United States reasoned that NATO was no longer only a military organisation but in the changed context of the post cold war it was an organisation for the development of peace and cooperation in Europe. In 1991 North Atlantic Cooperation Council was established for consultation. Two years later Partnership for Peace was begun. Although Russia opposed the membership of former Warsaw Pact countries and threatened to abstain from Partnership for Peace, it eventually joined it. In 1999 Russia broke all its relations with NATO after the bombing of Kosovo. But after the war in Kosovo was over it again agreed to become a limited partner as a member of NATO-Russian Council in 2002. In the same year NATO invited the three Baltic States (Latvia, Lithuania, and Estonia) alongwith Slovenia (a splinter of Yugoslavia) Bulgaria, Romania, and Slovakia. In 2003 NATO took the historic decision that its role would no longer be confined to Europe but would extend to rest of the world. After this decision NATO forces began serving as Peace keeping force in Afghanistan in tandem with the forces of the United States. Presently there are 5,500 NATO forces and 11,700 American forces serving in Afghanistan. The creation of NATO- Russian Council gave Russia an opportunity to take part in the discussions about NATO decisions but without a binding vote. Most important decisions like expansion were confined only to the Council of Ministers.[5] Thus, Russia not only gave up its objection to expansion of NATO but also accepted a limited role in it. But as the 1999 Kosovo decision showed, Russian objection was not enough to deter NATO from taking action that was being opposed by Russia.

As recent developments have shown Russia is not willing to accept the expansion of American influence in newly independent states that were formerly part of Soviet Union. In February 2001, National Security Advisor Condoleeza Rice told Izvestia in Moscow that the United States had recognized the newly independent Central Asian Republics. It wanted to establish economic and political contacts with them but not military relations. She assured that the United States had no plans to oust Russia from the region. But the war on terrorism after 9/11 opened new a window of opportunity to establish its military presence in the region.

These Republics so close to Russia presented to the US strategy planners an alluring prospect in view of rich oil and gas deposits. These Republics live under the shadow of their giant neighbour. There is substantial Russian minority in all the Central Asian Republics. The majority, belonging to a different ethnic group, looks upon the Russian minority with suspicion as inclined to look up to Russia. Having lived under the Russian rule for several decades, the majority considers American economic and political and now even military presence in the region as a guarantee of their own independence. There is a paradox. They also know that their security against the rise of Islamic fundamentalism can be ensured by Russia. Russia has signed security treaty with three of the Republics and Russian forces are on their territory in sizable numbers.

After 9/11 Russia agreed to Uzbekistan, Kyrgzstan and Tajikstan providing base facilities to the United States for carrying war in Afghanistan. The bases were given to the US on lease and are not permanent. Russia is now engaged in strengthening its own military presence in this region. On October 24, 2003 President Putin opened its first air base in Central Asia in Kyrgzstan near its capital Bishkek. Just a few kilometers away are the American base in Manas near Khanbad where 2000 American forces are stationed. At the opening ceremony of the base Putin said that while the base at Manas was for fighting the war against international terrorism, the base near Bishkek was for the security of the state. He said that Muslim militants just walked into the state in 2000-2001 as if it was their home. Putin did not say anything about countervailing American presence in the region that not too long ago were exclusive Russian preserves. The US led war against international terrorism was focused only on those areas where it threatened American interests. Russia had to take its own measures.

South Caucasus is second region where American interest is coming in conflict with Russia. The region is geopolitically important. Its border touches Russia, Turkey and the Caspian Sea. Since 1992 Russia has been fighting against the Chechen extremists who are not satisfied with anything less than independence. Since 1999 when the Russian forces moved in to Chechnya, extremists have launched terrorist attacks increasingly on targets in the heartland of Russia. More than 400 people lost their lives since then in these attacks. In the southern Caucasus there are four states, Georgia, Azerbaijan, Armenia and Moldova, these were part of former Soviet Union. In 2000 Chechen insurgents moved in to adjacent Pinkisi gorge in Georgia. Russia threatened to intervene if their activities from that hideout did not end. Georgia sought US assistance and the latter sent 500 of crack troops to Georgia in 2000 to assist it in fighting against the Chechens.

For the last eleven years President Shevardnandze governed Georgia. The government leaned towards the West and wanted Georgia to be integrated with Europe's military and civilian structures. Shevardnandze was the Foreign Minister of the Soviet Union before its disintegration and had developed amicable relations with many of the top leaders in the United States. His popularity at home was gradually declining. Parliamentary elections were held in which President's party won the election. But the united opposition claimed that the elections were rigged. After three weeks of hiatus there were massive demonstrations demanding cancellation of the results, holding reelection and more importantly, the resignation of the President. A massive demonstration on November 22 burst in and occupied the parliament's building. It was reported that the security forces joined the opposition and refused to use force to oust the demonstrators. Mikhail Saaskhvili, an American trained lawyer, led the massive protest. Under the circumstances President Shevardnandze was persuaded to resign. His plea that he would complete his term and then leave in 2005 was turned down. He resigned on November 23.

Russian leaders alleged that the United States was behind the opposition. It was alleged that the fund set up by George Soros, an American philanthropist; to support the civil society and the rule of law in the former Soviet Union was generously used to organise the opposition. Shevardnandze himself accused Soros and said that the United States betrayed him. Igor Ivanov, the Russian Foreign Minister, told an interviewer on TV: " I think there are enough facts proving what happened on those days wasn't spontaneous, it did not arise suddenly." The protest march was carefully planned and executed and the person who was supposed have carried out the plan was Richard Miles, the American Ambassador. As expected, the American officials denied these allegations. However, the fact remained that at the height of the crisis Washington sent former Secretary of State, James Baker, to Tiblisi. It was his persuasion that led Shevardnandze to give up. Ivanov remarked " I don't have documents or any information what the aim of the Baker mission was but it was to persuade Shevardnandze to resign." Ivanov was present in the meeting when Shevardnandze's decision was taken. He agreed because no other realistic option was available. But the fact that Americans had such a vital role rankled Russia. President Putin issued a veiled warning to the new leaders. He asked them not to repeat Shevardnandze's mistakes in taking his country towards the West and away from Russia. He added that Georgia's policy had been conducted without taking into consideration its deep cultural roots and geopolitical reality. [6]

Whether the US conspired to encourage opposition and forced the resignation of Shevardnandze or not, it was the first country to recognize the interim government headed by Ms Nino Burdzhenadze, former speaker of the parliament. Donald Rumsfeld, Secretary of Defense, visited Georgia in the first week of December, the first high-ranking American official to do so after more than a decade. He offered economic aid to the Georgian government. Burdzhenadze responded by declaring that relations with the US were of "main importance for us." She further said that "Georgia would continue its course of early integration in to European and Atlantic structures" while trying to maintain good relations with Russia.

The Georgian leadership has its grievances against Russia. It believes that some elements in Russia want to undermine its territorial integrity by encouraging and supporting secessionist movements in Abkhazia and south Ossetia. The conflicts with separatists, it contends, would have been resolved had they been not supported by these elements. Rumsfeld asked Russia to withdraw its troops from Georgia as it had been agreed upon in Istanbul agreement. To this Russia responded by pointing out the troops were to withdraw in ten years that no deadline had been set for their withdrawal. There is no doubt that the United States was consolidating its relations with Georgia.[7]

Before his visit to Georgia, Rumsfeld visited Azerbaijan, another former Russian Republic bordering on the Caspian Sea. The country elected a new President in October. As President Allyev succeeded his own father there was unlikely to be a sudden or a major shift in country's foreign policy. Rumsfeld ex~ressed American desire to expand defense cooperation between the two countries. The emphasis was to be on expanding military to military cooperation. Azerbaijan's defense minister stated that his country might host American forces in future. The United States gives $3 million dollars aid annually to Azerbaijan to train and modernize the army. Azerbaijan has reciprocated by extending support to the United States military adventures abroad. It sent a platoon of peacekeepers in Afghanistan and 125 troops to Iraq. This may have nothing more than symbolic value. But helps the US to claim that its policy in Iraq enjoys support of many countries in Europe. Azerbaijan has conflict with Iran and Turkmanestan over the right to offshore oil and gas of the Caspian Sea and hopes that the United States would support its claim and ensure its security.[8]

Besides consolidating its political and strategic interest in Caucasus by integrating both Georgia and Azerbaijan in to West European civil and military structures the United States has great interest in the Caspian Sea oil and gas. It has committed itself to construct an oil pipe line from Baku in Azerbaijan to Ceyhan on the Mediterranean coast of Turkey. The line passes through Georgia. It bypasses the alternative routes either through Iran or Russia. The 1,767 km line is expected to be completed by the end of 2004. The value of the project is $2.5 billion.

Till 1991 Moldova was part of the Soviet Union. When Soviet Union disintegrated Moldova was established as an independent republic. It joined the Commonwealth of Independent States (CIS) and became a member of the United Nations in 1992. In the southern part of Moldova there is Turkish majority and the northern part, the trans Deniester region has Slav majority who fear that Moldova would become part of Romania. In 1995 Deniester voted for independence that was declared illegal by Moldova. In 1997 an accord was signed between Deniester and Moldova that granted substantial autonomy to the former. The southern part, Gagauz area, was granted more limited autonomy. Russia that had earlier stationed its troops in the Deniester region agreed in 1999 to withdraw its troops from the region by 2001 but about 1500 troops still remain there.

Both Georgia and Moldova are eager to become part of the West, but are facing strong separatist movements within their own territories which would like to retain their relations with Russia to counterbalance the majority. It is against this background that Secretary of State Colin Powell in the meeting of Organisation for Security and Cooperation in Europe criticized President Putin for failing to meet commitments to withdraw troops from Georgia and Moldova. He went on to support what he termed the strategies of the two countries to oppose Russia's effort to meddle in the affairs of the two countries. A resolution was moved in the meeting that stated: "The international community should do everything possible to support Georgia's territorial integrity. No support should be given to break-away elements seeking to weaken Georia's territorial integrity." Russia blocked the adoption of the resolution. The United States had extended support to Shevardnandze all along. After his fall it switched its support to democratic opposition.[9]

Russia wants to keep the former Soviet Republics in Central Asia and Caucacus in its own sphere of influence. Initially it made several concessions to the United States. After resisting it for quite sometime it agreed to the expansion of NATO to the former Warsaw pact countries and even to the Baltic states that were formerly part of the Soviet Union. It agreed to the abrogation of the ABM treaty of 1972 signed by both the countries because of the insistence of the United States to pursue National Missiles Defense. It only expressed its dissent instead of opposing like France did the US led invasion of Iraq. It swallowed the bitter pill of seeing the disintegration of Yugoslavia. But politics does not leave a vacuum. If Russia withdrew, the United States occupied the space. But it is now resisting American effort to consolidate its position in the Central Asian Republics and Caucasus.

In the new millennium the context of American-Russian relations has drastically changed. The unipolar moment has passed. In absolute terms the United States is still the largest economy in the world, but in relative terms the economic growth of the Clinton years is missing. The report on the economy in the last quarter of this year showed that while the GDP attained the extraordinary growth rate of 8.2 per cent, the employment generation has not kept pace with the growth. The unemployment is still at 5.9 per cent. Several million jobs have been lost, as manufacturing industries have shrunk. Though of late the economy has shown some signs of recovery analysts are not certain that it would either be sufficient or last. Its armed forces are over stretched with additional commitments in Iraq, Bosnia, Kosovo, Afghanistan, Pakistan and the Central Asian republics. The global alliance that had emerged for the war against international terrorism after 9/11 is fractured. And its unilateral decision to go to war in Iraq has isolated it from the world public opinion. The occupation and reconstruction of Iraq has run into serious problem. It is not in a position to take additional confrontation. This was confirmed by the conciliatory policy it adopted towards North Korea that has defiantly declared that it has in its possession nuclear weapons and the missiles to deliver them. However, it does not mean that the US has given up its policy of expanding its influence wherever it can. Since 1991 when large number of Soviet republics became independent, it has shown keen interest in expanding its influence in the Central Asia and Caucasus. As Russia resists the American moves, analysts have suggested that a new era of "Great Game" has begun.

Russia wants to keep these states under its sphere of influence. There is substantial Russian population in many of the newly independent states, which have become independent. From the beginning Georgia and Azerbaijan have faced the problem of secessionist movements. Russia will stop backing these movements only if the governments in these countries would remain within its sphere of influence. The position of Russia in the later half of the nineties has been improving. Its economy has stabilized and the high prices of oil are spurring its growth. It certainly seeks trade and investment from the West. But it is not desperate. The strong economic growth has infused a sense of confidence in the Russian leadership. In a recently published article President Putin declared that "not a single serious global or inter regional problem can be solved without Russia's active and equitable participation."[10] In the past the Russian power was in retreat. But it may feel that it has retreated too far. And further retreat is not possible.

Russia is not going to return to a policy of confrontation with the United States. Nor would the United States resort to it. In the new millennium American Russian relations have become more complex. New tensions may have cropped up in the United States relations with Europe and the latter may be happy if Russia joins it but in situations where the United States is opposing Russia, Europe is more inclined to support the United States than Russia. In the new era each country is trying to maximize its interests. Therefore, there is neither complete convergence nor divergence. Foreign policy has become issue based. The US has committed itself to expand influence in the former Soviet republics to advance its economic and political interest but it seeks Russian cooperation for enhancing its own energy security, waging war against terrorism in Afghanistan, against drug trafficking, and for maintaining nuclear and missiles regimes. Shifting alliances on issues have become the dominant mode of global politics.

References

1. George Bush and Brent Scowcroft, *A World Transformed* (New York: Alfred A. Knopf, 1998).
2. Thomas W. Lippman, Madliene Albright: *New American Diplomacy* (Boulder: New Vista Press, 2000), p. 156.
3. *The New York Times* (On the Web), June 27, 2003.
4. Russian GDP is currently $308 billion and per capita income is $7800. It is a low middle income country. It is a transition economy and is likely to remain so for a long time. Its primary sources of imports are the United States and European Union. See: T. A. Bhaumik, "Window Shopping in Russia," *The Hindustan Times*, November 12, 2003.
5. "North Atlantic Teaty Organisation: Microsoft® Encarta® on Line Encyclopedia 2003.
6. Jeffrey Donavan, "Georgia clash of Interest Test US Russian Relations" Radio Free Europe, December 2003. Charlotte Keatley, "A Very Georgian Coup," *The Guardian*, December 6, 2003. The Hindu, November 25, 2003.

7. "Rumsfeld Visit Georgia's new leaders," *The New York Times*, December 5, 2003.
8. *The Hindu*, December 5, 2003.
9. *The Washington Post*, December 4, 2003.
10. Vladimir Putin, "Churning the Pacific," The Guardian. Republished in *The Hindustan Times*, October 15, 2003.

11
Significance of Indo Russian Strategic Partnership: Its Impact on Arab World

A K Pasha

The backdrop

Jawaharlal Nehru decided to follow non-aligned foreign policy for India during the height of Cold War. This was criticized by the USA, which called it immoral. Since then the USA has worked to undermine NAM and infact never understood Third World nationalism. After initial reservations, Moscow under the leadership of Khrushev and Bulganin at the 20th Congress of the CPSU in 1956 recognized that there were different paths to socialism besides the Soviet model and that the 'national bourgeoisie' could spearhead it. This realization was a significant shift in Soviet policy, which provided the ideological justification for closer ties with many third world countries.[1] Soon Moscow came to have close ties with India, Egypt, Iraq (since 1958), Syria and other Arab countries. India received political, economic and military support from Moscow. Gamal Abdel Nasser, Egypt's leader who was under pressure from Israel, US and the West in general sought Moscow's help during 1955 especially to counter the emerging threat from the Baghdad Pact. In this connection the Soviet statement read:

> ...the Soviet Union cannot be indifferent to the situation taking shape in the Middle East, since the formation of the blocs and the creation of foreign military bases on the territory of the countries of the Middle East having a direct bearing on the

> security of the USSR. The Soviet Government will take positive action towards any steps by the Governments of the Near and Middle Eastern countries to strengthen the national independence of their states and to promote peace and friendly cooperation among nations.[2]

Moscow gave not only weapons to India, Egypt and other Arab countries but supplied related technology. When the West attacked Moscow on this issue, Tass in a Communiqué on 1 October 1955 said:

> *The Soviet Government holds the view that every state has an integral right to take care of its defense and purchase weapons for its defense needs from other states on commercial terms and that no foreign power is entitled to interfere with the rights or interests of their states.*

Moscow's decision to come to the rescue of India and the Arab states, to help them resist Western pressures was a very shrewd decision and it marked the first bold thrust and an attempt to gain foothold in West and South Asia. Moscow continued to transfer sophisticated weapons to India and its allies in the Arab World despite objections from the West. Egypt suffered military defeat in the 1956 Suez war when Israel, France and Britain attacked Egypt and captured huge quantities of arms supplied by Moscow. Egypt and Syria also suffered defeat at the hands of Israel in the 1967 war. Nehru and Nasser had a personal liking and respect for each other and both saw Moscow as a close ally. Even though Nehru died in 1964, the close relationship between Cairo-Belgrade-Delhi and Moscow continued at least until Nasser's death in 1970. Just as Nehru never recovered from the 1962 Chinese attack on India, the 1967 defeat shattered Nasser. But India strengthened its ties with Moscow through the 1971 treaty and developed extensive ties with Arab countries like Iraq, Syria, Yemens, Algeria, Libya, Sudan, PLO and others. Egypt under Anwar Sadat moved away from Moscow to the US camp, especially after the 1973 October Arab Israeli Conflict. This led to Cairo's isolation in the Arab World mainly due to the 1974-75 Disengagement Agreements with Israel, Sadat's visit to Jerusalem in 1977, the Camp David Accord of 1978 and the bilateral peace treaty of 1979 between Egypt and Israel. Soon Egypt came to be seen as a client state of the US.[3]

Despite India's close ties with Moscow in the 1950's and 60's, the Indian leadership maintained fairly good ties with USA and the West. New Delhi could not ignore US allies in the Arab World like Saudi Arabia, Jordan, Morocco and other Gulf States. Infact, Nehru visited Saudi Arabia in 1956. But India established closer ties incidentally with such Arab countries as Iraq, Syria, Yemen, Libya, Algeria, PLO and others which also had close ties with Moscow. Mrs. Gandhi visited Iraq [and other Arab states] in January 1975 and Saddam Hussein came to India in March 1974. The 1973-74 oil price hikes propelled India to establish close ties with Iran and the Arab Gulf States like Kuwait, Saudi Arabia, UAE and others. But India balanced these relations with support to the PLO, Syria and other States in the region that had close ties with Moscow. India had modest defense ties with Iraq, Syria, Yemen and other Arab States who imported similar arms from Moscow.

In the 1970's India came to establish close political and economic ties with Iraq. Both India and Iraq had signed Friendship treaties with Moscow in 1971 and 1972, [Egypt, Sudan, Somalia, Syria also signed treaties with Moscow] which had raised eyebrows in the West. The US expressed concern over Moscow's attempt to encircle Iran and Pakistan as India, Iraq and Afghanistan had close ties with Moscow. The US also suspected India and Iraq of providing base facilities to the Soviet Navy in the Gulf and Bay of Bengal. The upturn in Indo-Iraqi ties was also due to Egypt's' isolation over its separate peace with Israel which was condemned by Arab League summits held in Baghdad during 1978-79. Since then Iraq had assumed the mantle of Arab leadership. But soon the 1979 Iranian Revolution and the eight years Iran-Iraq war soured India's ties with both Iran and Iraq. Due to these developments the Seventh NAM Summit had to be shifted from Baghdad to New Delhi in 1983. Initially Mrs. Indira Gandhi and later Rajiv Gandhi tried to end the ruinons Iran-Iraq war bilaterally and through the NAM but that was disliked both by Iran and Iraq. The continuation of the Iran-Iraq war for eight years led to decline in Indo-Iraqi trade. Iraqi invasion of Kuwait in August 1990, and the US led war in January 1991 to liberate the oil rich Gulf State - Kuwait, UN sanctions on Iraq all led to decline in Indo-Iraqi political and economic ties.

Iraq - a close ally of India and Moscow suffered unprecedented destruction at the hands of US led coalition over the Kuwait crisis in 1991. It is precisely around this time the USSR disintegrated and the cold war came to an end. Many saw the emergence of Pax Americana not only in the Gulf region but globally. The weak Indian governments under V.P. Singh and Chandrasekhar could not manage India's mounting economic problems as revealed by growing dependence on IMF and World Bank for loans. India had to choose between moving closer to US (which meant choosing the path of economic liberalisation-privatisation) or risk being isolated in the global affairs.

Russia under Boris Yelstin and the new elites were themselves keen on pursuing a "look West" policy especially working for closer ties with USA. India and Arab states that had friendly ties with Moscow like Iraq, Syria, Libya, Algeria, Yemen, PLO and others felt ignored by Russia. Ever since the Egyptian President Sadat excluded the Soviet Union from the Arab Israeli Peace Process, Moscow has been losing ground in the Arab world. Israeli invasion of Lebanon in 1982 and the expulsion of PLO from Beirut restricted Moscow's allies to Syria, Libya and Yemen. Yasser Arafat under Egyptian influence gradually switched over to diplomacy, eventually accepting UNSCR 242, recognizing Israel and renouncing violence. The eight year Iran-Iraq war and Saddam Hussein's ties with GCC states as also indirectly with the US and West in general made Moscow rethink on Iraq as a dependable ally. The eccentric and often contradictory policies pursued by Libya's Gaddafi were very often an embarrassment to Moscow. The only consistent ally was Syria under Hafez al Assad but he also was preoccupied with Lebanon where substantial Syrian troops were maintained and the no war no peace with Israel was intolerable. So the eighties was a period, in which Soviet Union was gradually getting marginalized in the Arab World due to the policies of Reagan administration, growing Israeli power in the region, the fratricidal war between Iraq and Iran and the US dual containment policies. In addition, the Soviet leaders Gorbachov and others were preoccupied with *Glasnost and Perestroika*. Coupled with this, the military and economic aid component declined in Soviet interaction with Arab countries.

India under Mrs. Indira Gandhi and later Rajiv Gandhi took the initiative to revive close ties with Egypt, Iraq, Libya, Sudan, Syria,

South Yemen, PLO and other countries. But there was no major breakthrough. India had to lower its sights and the result was renewed focus on the Gulf states obviously due to the oil factor, Indian migrant workers, trade, investment and concerns over security and stability in the Gulf region. It was the economic factor which was crucial and the previous heavy dose of ideological content in which Moscow also prominently figured began to recede in the 1980s.

Since the collapse of the Soviet Union, its implications on the WANA region could be seen from two angles: Soviet military, economic, political support to a number of Arab countries was an established fact. The Arab states like Syria, Libya, Yemen, PLO who have close ties with India came under pressure from the US/ West. The impact of this event on India's relations with pro-Moscow Arab states was substantial as cooperation with these states suffered. It was similar to the Egyptian example i.e. once Egypt moved away from close ties with Moscow to the US camp under President Sadat, Indo-Egyptian ties also sharply declined. This has become a pattern which is being repeated as India itself worked hard to get closer to the US.

The second major fall out from disintegration of the Soviet Union has been the emergence of the Central Asian Republics as independent states all dominated by Muslims. These countries have become members of international and regional institutions to enhance their legitimacy and gain wider recognition. No doubt India maintains fairly good ties with all of them but China, Russia, Turkey, Iran, Pakistan and Israel are working hard to extend their influence. Saudi Arabia with its financial clout and Islamic credentials is also seeking influence in this strategically crucial area. Under these circumstances this region is witnessing intense competition. Iran has sought India's expertise for the development of these states and India is willing to take part in the development efforts. Thus both India and Iran are working closely in Central Asia. Due to developments in Kashmir, Afghanistan, Iran, Iraq and in Central Asia itself our interaction must be sustained. Since some of the Central Asian States are oil/gas rich we should go in for barter trade in which our industrial technology and manpower could be traded for oil/gas.

Even though Iraq was a close ally of Moscow [since both signed friendship treaty in April 1972], certain steps taken by Saddam

Hussein since he became President in 1979 made the Soviet Union become lukewarm towards Baghdad. The Iran-Iraq war, Iraq's ties with the US and the West in general, especially the visit of Donald Rumsfield during the Iran-Iraq war, Saddam Hussein's invasion of Kuwait are significant. When the US attacked Iraq in January 1991, the Soviet Union was heading towards disintegration. The Gulf crisis over Kuwait when Iraq marched into the oil rich Emirate on 2 August 1990 posed India a major challenge. Due to India's close political and economic ties with Iraq, an impression was created in the initial stages of the crisis that New Delhi tended to support Baghdad. This led to a misunderstanding between India and the GCC states. To be correct India strongly disapproved of Iraqi invasion of Kuwait and called it illegal and said it should be vacated but stopped short of condemning it. Since India did not openly take sides, Kuwait and other GCC states assumed India's sympathies lay with Iraq.

The Kuwait crisis affected India in many ways. New Delhi mainly due to domestic turmoil displayed no apparent enthusiasm to resolve the crisis. The minority government of VP Singh appeared to be primarily concerned with the evacuation of more than one lakh Indian citizens from Kuwait and about 25,000 from Iraq. Public pressure and the decision of MP's from Kerala to sit on a day long fast at the Parliament House on 16 August 1990 to protest against the "inaction of the government regarding the plight of Indians" in both the Gulf States also forced the government to accord the safe evacuation of Indians top priority. This partly explains India's decision not to condemn the Iraqi invasion as it could have jeopardized the repatriation of Indians from the Gulf. India was also faced with the loss of crude oil supplies from both Kuwait and Iraq, which compelled New Delhi to look for alternative supplies. During 1990, Kuwait had agreed to sell India about 1.5 million tones of oil and Iraq 6.25 million tones, which included about 4.5 million tones that Iraq was transferring to India on behalf of the Soviet Union against rupee payment. Before the crisis began India had received only half the oil from the total of about 7.75 million tones and it was difficult for India to procure the rest. Moreover, increase in oil prices in the spot market from about $16-17 per barrel in July 1990 to $35 per barrel upset India's budget and economy. In addition, India lost nearly $ 3 billion (US) in foreign exchange alone due to the crisis. All of these economic compulsions pushed India to seek IMF loan where US support was crucial. The Indian government partly shared the fear of the West and in particular the US, that Saddam Hussein would control fifty per cent of the world's oil reserves, if he were not pushed out of Kuwait. No wonder India allowed the refueling of US military planes and went alongwith the sole superpower at the UN. It became very clear that India was not inclined to annoy the US or other western powers given their determination and resolve to contain Saddam Hussein and cripple Iraq's military machine. The Indian government was unwilling even to criticize the US in view of the need to restructure India's policies to the harsh ground realities. No wonder India's former Foreign Secretary Muchkund Dubey states: "We will do what the UN wants us to do".[4]

Unlike Cuba, which opposed, Yemen and Ecuador, which abstained, India voted in favour of the "mother of resolutions" passed by the UN Security Council (687) on 3 April 1991. Many have criticized India's affirmative vote on the ground that it brushed aside the principle of respect to state sovereignty and imposed a series of humiliating terms for cease-fire, virtually turning Iraq into a demilitarized nation. India played a minor role in drafting and adopting the 21 page UNSC Resolution 687, the longest in UN's history, imposing very harsh conditions. It was due to India that the emphasis on bringing to an end the military presence in Iraq was included and adopted. Again at India's instance a paragraph was added whereby the Security Council decided that the UN Secretary General would take into account "the requirements of the people of Iraq and in particular their humanitarian needs, Iraq's payment capacity as assessed in conjunction with the international financial institutions, taking into consideration the external debt service and the needs of the Iraqi economy". India also played a role in getting the Security Council to adopt a measure whereby the prohibitions imposed against Iraq "shall not apply to foodstuffs, materials and supplies for essential civilian needs as identified in the report of the Secretary General, and in any further findings of humanitarian need by the Sanctions Committee established by the UNSC Resolution 661 of 1990". It must also be mentioned that India expressed serious reservations against "the right to interference" in the internal affairs of a member nation on humanitarian grounds, especially in the context of Kurds and Shias in Iraq. This was on UNSC Resolution 688 of 5 April 1991. Moreover, India is a member of the 35 nation UN Iraq-Kuwait Border Observer Mission [UNIKOM] to patrol the DMZ along the Iraq- Kuwait border. India is also associated in the monitoring commissions and teams meant to supervise Iraqi payment of compensation and elimination of weapons of mass destruction.[5]

Most of the above initiatives taken by India on the Iraq crisis had the support of the Soviet Union which was in fact pursuing very confused policy. Moscow was an ally of Iraq through the friendship treaty and had supplied huge quantities of weapons. They also maintained contacts with the Iraqi leadership at the highest level and had military and technical advisors in Iraq. On paper Moscow still supported Iraq and other Arab States against "Zionism and US imperialism". They intensified diplomatic negotiations and supported Arab efforts for a peaceful resolution of the Iraq-Kuwait Crisis . On the other side from the very outset the Soviet Union was critical of Iraq and its invasion of Kuwait. They called for an "immediate and unconditional withdrawal of Iraqi troops". They endorsed the UNSC Resolution 660, which demanded an unconditional withdrawal by the Iraqis from Kuwait. The Soviet foreign minister Edward Shevardnadze and the US Secretary of State James Baker signed a joint statement whereby they reiterated their respective positions on the issue but also appealed for an international arms embargo. Indirectly it gave support to US position. Since the Soviets knew about Iraqi military installations and capability they shared with the US. Marshal Akhromeyev discussed military issues with US representatives. They were unhappy with Saddam Hussein as they had not been consulted over Kuwait. Hence, Moscow considered that the friendship treaty had been contravened by the Iraqis. The Soviets in turn did not feel committed to the treaty.[6]

The Soviet Union it must be remembered itself needed US support on a number of issues and the joint statement was seen as the basis for US support to Moscow. Some diplomatic initiatives taken by the Soviets including appeals were rejected by the Iraqis. The Soviet Union supported UNSC resolutions 661, 664 and 665 which among other measures also imposed economic sanctions against Iraq. The USSR in a summit meeting at Helsinki also agreed to the January 15, 1991 deadline set by the Bush administration.

The mounting domestic crisis, threat of secession from the Baltic republics, resignation of Shevardnadze, fear of coup all added pressure on Gorbachev's tenuous control over Soviet power base. Although Gorbachev sent Primakov as his envoy to Iraq to get a settlement but the US was adamant with its ground offensive and Soviet attempts made no headway. In the end the Soviets did try to maintain their ties with West, Iraq and much of the Arab World.

Among the GCC states only Saudi Arabia and Bahrain had not established diplomatic ties with Moscow. Talks between Moscow and Riyadh had been going on for sometime in this direction but the Gulf crisis gave an impetus to early establishment of ties. Riyadh decided on September 17,1990 to restore diplomatic relations at ambassador level. The timing was excellent. Not only they were pleased with unprecedented Soviet support to Arab/Western stand against Saddam Hussein, they also wanted to drive a wedge between Moscow and Baghdad. Their presence in Moscow, Saudis perhaps thought, will further the isolation of Iraq. Saud al Faisal on a visit [September 17] to Moscow said Riyadh's wishes and intentions go much further than the establishment of mere normal diplomatic relations: "we want them to be much deeper". He was hopeful that intensive relations would develop in the political, economic and social spheres. More significantly he foresaw good relations in the "security sphere" especially in the context of Iraqi invasion, which he called "tragic". Finally he said both the countries realised the need to resolve the present crisis "by peaceful means". With this step Riyadh had come to establish balanced relations with all major powers. It had established ties with China in July 1990. Bahrain followed Riyadh in establishing ties with Moscow that was announced in New York on September 28 after talks between the two foreign ministers. It was projected as a balance for their heavy reliance on the western powers in the crisis.

It was reported that Saudi Arabia and other GCC states had given four billion US dollars to Moscow as loans during the crisis. Konstantin Katushev, Soviet Minister of Foreign Economic Relations visited Riyadh in November 1990 to strengthen economic relations. Almost all GCC states came to establish diplomatic relations with the East European countries and subsequently with the Baltic Republics as well. The GCC in the initial phase were apprehensive of Soviet reaction to the Iraqi take over of Kuwait in view of the 1972 USSR- Iraq treaty and the close relations between Moscow and Baghdad. The August 2 official Soviet statement removed GCC fears when Moscow described Iraqi action as "invasion" and called on Iraq to make an "unconditional withdrawal" of its troops from Kuwait. More important to the GCC states was the close coordination between USA and USSR during the crisis. On August 2, 1990 itself James Baker and Edward Shevardnadze issued a joint statement which condemned the "naked illegal aggression by the Iraqi forces against Kuwait". Soon the USSR stopped arms supplies to Iraq and began withdrawing its military and other advisers. In addition, the Soviet Union supported all the UN resolutions on the Kuwait crisis. But it expressed its concern over military buildup in the Gulf and the threat to use force. Even though President Gorbachev told Egyptian President Mubarak that Soviet stand was not anti- Iraq but they supported US initiatives. While they insisted on "sovereignty, national independence and territorial integrity of Kuwait to be fully restored and protected", Moscow warmly applauded the rapprochement between Iran and Iraq even as the GCC states watched with concern. Besides supporting an Arab solution to the crisis Moscow was skeptical of Saddam's August 12, 1990 linkage proposal. But later on Shevardnadze said on August 20, that despite the West's "negative reaction". Saddam's linkage proposal did contain "elements deserving serious attention". Meanwhile as US pressure mounted on Moscow over the continued presence of Soviet military specialists in Iraq, Gorbachev became very critical of the Iraqi stand and called it "unacceptable" since "the aggression was committed with the help of our weapons". But he added: " we are in favour of political methods being used to avert its escalation into a military confrontation on an even greater scale, an even more dangerous scale". Despite close cooperation with USA, Moscow was in favour of giving economic sanctions more time and certainly for the war to be UN sanctioned and UN operated war. During the ariel bombardment, there were hectic consultations between Iraq and the USSR and naturally this was noticed by the GCC states but the reaction to these talks was that it will not affect the military plans of the multinational forces working to liberate Kuwait. Saudi Defense Minister Prince Sultan Bin Abdul Aziz said:"these talks have effect only if they submit to what is right". When he was asked about those talks he said that actions are judged by their ends and to judge prematurely is undesirable. He emphasized that sincerity of intentions could not be manifested except through the implementation of the Arab, Islamic and international resolutions.

Soon after the war Moscow on 19 March 1991 came up with its views on the post crisis set up in the Gulf area. The Soviet Union in putting forward its ideas for the Gulf security noted that other approaches "either coincide with or run parallel to our own approaches". The following steps were suggested. [1] Besides giving key role to the regional countries in the promotion of security, the settlement should not be directed against anybody. Moreover it should promote the interaction of all the regional countries as well as of the states which are not directly linked with this area but which make important contribution to maintain peace and stability there; [2] practical steps to be taken to cut the arms race in the region; [3] foreign military presence not to exceed the levels which existed prior to Iraq's invasion; [4] the task of initiating comprehensive economic cooperation among the states of the region arises, primarily for the restoration of their war torn economies; [5] UN to be involved at all stages of the post- crisis settlement; and [6] efforts aimed at removing political causes of instability and conflicts to be given priority especially the early resolution of the Arab- Israeli conflict.

The statement ended with an offer from Moscow to make "its contribution with the aim of speediest advancement towards the settlement of the problems of the post-crisis set up in the Gulf area to discuss any constructive ideas to actively cooperate with all parties concerned". In other words, Moscow was available as a participant and was waiting to be invited. Like the West, the GCC states also ignored this statement because of the rapid disintegration and collapse of the Soviet Union.[7]

Soon after the liberation of Kuwait, the UN sanctions on Iraq continued and arms inspections were carried out under the guidance of Rolf Ekeus and later by Richard Butler. Most of the banned Iraqi WMD's were destroyed in the 1990s but UN sanctions continued. In view of mounting economic problems, deepening crisis in the military, Saddam Hussein had accepted UNSC resolution 715 which imposed additional conditions on Iraq including the installation of a very elaborate system for long-term monitoring of Iraq's arms industry. Considerable progress had been made over the implementation of paragraph 22 of the UNSCR 687 which stated that the oil embargo would have "no further force or effect" if Iraq were disarmed of its weapons of mass destruction and had no longer the capacity to make them again except with limited range. At one stage it was felt that UNSCOM chief was about to issue a favourable report to the UNSC on Iraqi's cooperation in destroying banned weapons. Iraq could have looked forward to an easing of economic sanctions at least in stages. Infact, Saddam Hussein could have been close to obtaining permission to resume oil exports which was being vigorously supported by Russia and to a certain extent by France, China and many non-permanent members of the UN Security Council. But Saddam Hussein committed the blunder of sending 80,000 troops near the Iraqi border with Kuwait and gave an opportunity which the US was too eager to seize and not to let the Iraqi leader "off the hook" in October 1994. The Iraqi leader overplayed his hand at a time when even the UN Security Council members especially Russia and France were beginning to campaign for an easing of the economic sanctions. In the face of Iraqi blunders and sustained pressure from the US, Russia virtually could do nothing to prevent US occupation of Iraq in 2003. The several lucrative oil deals and Iraqi debt of several billions of US dollars remains to be recovered. There was a lesson in this for India also.

The collapse of the USSR left the new leaders busy bringing order on the domestic front. Initially the new leaders focused their attention on improving ties with the West. They also tried to restore ties with the former Soviet republics, all of them now independent and trying to chart new direction and of course shedding the last vestiges of Soviet connections. The Arab world was not high on priority for the new Russian leadership. Moscow simply did not have the resources to compete with the USA in the Arab world besides numerous complex problems within Russia also prevented them from playing even a marginal role. The only notable role was in the 30 October 1991 Madrid Peace Conference and the subsequent Arab-Israeli Peace Process as cosponsors of Peace. Several meetings on arms control for the region were held in Moscow and of course nothing tangible came out of this process or conferences.

The only noteworthy feature was that for the first time India attended a meeting on 12 May 1991 alongwith delegations from thirteen West Asian countries as well as China, Japan, Turkey and EU. Syria, Lebanon and Mauritania declined invitations to attend. The fact that so many Arab delegations were attending meetings with the Israelis (and talking) was nothing unusual. That was already regarded as one of the major achievements of the Madrid Peace Process.

Russian leaders in the opposition like Vladimir Zhirinovsky, Alexander Rutskoi and some moderates in the Boris Yeltsin's government made statements to the effect that Russia remains a great power. This raised hopes for a revival of the old power and naturally some Arab leaders who looked to Moscow for political/diplomatic support and arms, thought Russia could re-emerge as a superpower if it is determined to play that role. But not only Russia faced severe problems at home but the worst crisis was the economic. Moscow stopped giving aid to Arab States like the Yemens. Infact, Russia itself needed economic help to tide over their own severe economic problems. The two Yemens which merged in May 1990 were the first in the Arab world to feel the effects of the collapse of USSR. Before the merger, USSR gave military and economic aid and the Yemens owed three billion (US) dollars to Russia. Moscow now in her state of severe crisis expected the Yemenis to repay this debt either in hard currency or through oil. Yemen which saw a civil war (some leaders of the South wanted to restore the Marxist state) soon after the merger felt there was no chance Russia would get back money, because Yemen was also experiencing acute economic crisis. But both sides remembered the past glorious days and hoped to return to that era, which only created bitterness given the present predicament.[8]

The Madrid Arab Israeli Peace Process did not move far. Although the multilateral talks in Canada, Russia and Oman had provided a forum for the parties to debate and discuss the several contentious issues like arms control, refugees, water so on, but the bilateral track made no headway especially the talks between Syria and Israel. The Jordanians had continued the process of negotiations which culminated in a peace treaty with Israel on 26 October 1994. It was the second treaty between Israel and an Arab state after Egypt and Israel signed the first treaty in March 1979.

Anwar Sadat of Egypt had kept Moscow out of the peace process in 1978-79 while Russia had no worthwhile role in the Jordan-Israeli Peace Process. The US kept Russia out of the process and called them only to join in the "commemorative photograph" - session. US monopoly of the peace process was paving the way for the emergence of US-Israeli domination of the Arab World. Some Arab countries like Iraq, Libya, Syria, Yemen and the PLO still looked to Moscow for help but it had become obvious to these so called radical Arab leaders that Russia was too preoccupied with domestic reconstruction with little time and resources for the Arab States.

It is in this background Israel and the Palestinians negotiated a secret deal which culminated in the Oslo Accords of 13 September 1993, whereby Israel recognized the PLO. Yasser Arafat who had supported Saddam Hussein in the 1991 Gulf War was anxious for a deal with the Israelis. The Madrid conference in 1991 was an important step on the road to peace as it involved direct, bilateral, public and official peace talks between Israelis and the Palestinians [who would be part of the joint Jordan-Palestinian delegation] which would be conducted in phases, beginning with talks on interim self-government arrangements. It was also agreed that these talks would be conducted within one year. Arrangements once agreed would last for five years. At the beginning of the third year talks will take place on permanent status. All these negotiations will take place on the basis of the UNSCR 242 and 338.

The Israelis under pressure from the Palestinian intifadah and also the victory of the labour party in the 1992 election under Shimon Peres and Yitzhak Rabin, together with the prospects of economic and other benefits pushed the Israelis to conduct secret negotiations with PLO. On the other side, Iraqi defeat in the 1991 Gulf War at the hands of the US led coalition together with the end of the cold war and collapse of the USSR led to the talk of a New World Order. The US came under mounting pressure especially from its Arab allies to work for Arab-Israeli Peace.

The Palestinians were also affected by such factors: like the disintegration of USSR, collapse of the Communist regimes in Eastern Europe, large influx of Jews from these states, accelerated construction of Jewish settlements in the occupied territories and by the mounting economic problems in West Bank/Gaza as intifadah appeared to have reached a dead end. PLO also came under fire from the GCC states leaders for its support to Iraq in war. Thus, Russia came to be marginalized in the Arab World both due to its own problems as also due to determined US efforts to monopolize the Arab-Israeli peace process. Moscow's allies were not sure of securing support from Russia as the latter was seeking help from the US/West for its mounting economic problems. PLO and Iraq although sought help from Russia but in the ultimate analysis realized that it would be foolhardy to bank on yesteryears and nostalgia alone.[9]

In October 1994 Iraq again provided an opportunity to the US and its allies to intervene in the Gulf affairs to highlight the UN sanctions on Iraq and its effects on its regime and people. Saddam Hussein mobilized Iraqi troops and massed them along the Kuwaiti border on 7 October 1994 to put pressure on Kuwait and other GCC states directly as also on their supporters i.e. USA and Britain to lift the UN sanctions on Iraq. Saddam Hussein thought Russia and other friends would come to the rescue but unfortunately the pressure from friends like Russia and also the US simply intensified. India also urged Iraq [like Russia to] comply with UN resolutions on the issue. One can see similarities in approach between Russia and India in their reaction to the Iraqi troop mobilization step.

Reacting to the Iraqi troops movement near the Kuwaiti border, the official spokesman of the Indian Ministry of External Affairs expressed concern over the situation in the Gulf region and hoped that "no posture will be adopted to threaten the territorial integrity of any state". He said: "India has been taking note of recent developments in the Gulf with concern". He also said that India has always believed that there should be no use or threat of use of force in international relations. This principle, he stated, applies to the present situation in Iraq and Kuwait. He added: "India supports the sovereignty, independence and territorial integrity of all the states in the Gulf". This should be seen in the context of the relevant UN resolutions on the subject and stressed the need for compliance with these resolutions. When Iraq decided to withdraw its forces amassed near the Kuwaiti border under US pressure, India welcomed Iraq's decision. In a statement, the External Affairs Minister, Dinesh Singh, hoped this would lead to full compliance by Iraq of the relevant UN resolutions for settlement of outstanding issues in the region.

India's options in the crisis were extremely limited given the insistence of the US-UK alliance - egged on by the GCC States to maintain economic sanctions on Iraq.[10]

During the Iraqi troops movement issue Russia condemned them and clearly said in a statement it issued that "the language of ultimatums addressed to Kuwait and other states is rejected". Russia had sent its foreign minister Andrei Kozyrev and the First Deputy Foreign Minister Igor Ivanov to Baghdad to resolve the crisis. This step should be seen as a turning point in Russian diplomacy in the Arab World as Moscow had sent high level team to the area to diffuse a crisis. Although it could not play the role as a super power, yut certainly a more assertive Russian policy could be discerned since then. It was clear that Russia had reestablished itself as a great power. Russia is now more concerned over developments in the Arab World precisely due to their security implications on the Caucasus and Central Asian Republics and from there on Russia proper itself. Russia's renewed interest in the region indicated its displeasure over US domination of the Gulf area and unilateral promotion of US security and economic interests. The fact that Russia was being gradualley displaced by the US in the region alerted the Russians to reactivate their diplomacy lest they be sidelined. Russia's concern for security and stability in the Gulf region and fear of instability spreading through Caucasus and Central Asian States to Russia itself especially through Chechenya, Dagestan and Osettia prompted Moscow to reactivate its diplomacy to help contain Iraqi threats to Kuwait in October 1994. Russia also played an active role in persuading Saddam Hussein to recognize Kuwait formally, thus paving the way for the removal of one major hurdle towards peace, security and stability in the Gulf region. Russia openly acknowledged that it had to exert pressure on Iraq to recognize Kuwait's independence and the new boundary drawn by UN between Iraq and Kuwait. Baghdad had refused to accept the new border as new areas near the port of Umm Qasr had been given to Kuwait thereby further reducing Iraq's narrow access to the Gulf waters. Russia's active role in defusing the crisis was said to be motivated by its desire to obtain its debt back from Iraq. But Victor Posuvalyuk, then Deputy Foreign Minister [although acknowledged the debt issue as significant] denied it was the sole factor. He was Soviet Union's first Ambassador to Oman in 1988, then became Ambassador to Iraq in 1990 and later headed the Middle East Section in the Russian Foreign Ministry and in November 1994 was made deputy foreign minister. He articulated Russian policy towards the Arab World in an article to the London based *al Hayat*. He wrote:

> I think, this was a superficial assumption (debt issue) regarding the motives that prompted the Russian leadership and the minister himself to undertake this extremely complex tour. The matter was much more delicate and sensitive. Russia is a big power that shoulders a responsibility for security in this volatile and geographically close area. It is not a remote area that makes it possible for us to disregard the political games that take place in it. It is an area close to our southern borders. The effects of what happens there are clearly felt in our political life, our domestic life. Therefore, our primary task was to safeguard security by shifting the efforts to the political sphere. I will go further and say that during our long talks in Baghdad, we did not discuss the debts issue, because more burning issues that demanded an immediate solution were on the agenda.

He acknowledged that Iraq's debt to Russia is a "matter of national interest. We are not disregarding it. We will try to ensure the necessary conditions to guarantee that Russia is paid back." He again reiterated that the debt recovery issue was not the primary motive at the moment. "The main motive is to ensure security and stability. The existence of a permanent smouldering or burning fire near our borders is damaging to us".[11]

At the UN Security Council, Russia repeatedly called for easing of economic sanctions imposed on Iraq, although its ally wanted an immediate end to the sanctions. Russia urged the UN to start a "test period". Once UNSCOM Chief Rolf Ekeus determines that Iraq had implemented UN resolutions on the elimination of WMDs then UN Security Council could review the decision to end oil embargo placed on Iraq. The Russians at no point urged the lifting of UN sanctions in total. They accepted that the "distance is still not small". Victor Posuvalyuk was candid in mentioning that Russia is "showing extreme interest in this area"(WANA) at all levels especially security and defense fields. Russia being the closest neighbour of this region, a big maritime state, and a permanent member of the UNSC, he said, is "increasingly interested in becoming one of the guarantors of security and stability in the Gulf area". He was keen that Iraq would become the most important component of this security system for the Gulf.

Soon after the Russian foreign minister Andrei Kozyrev's visit to Iraq and two other Gulf States during the Iraqi troops movement to Kuwaiti border in October 1994, the Russian Prime Minister Viktor Chernomyrdin visited Kuwait, Saudi Arabia, UAE and Oman in late November 1994. Most analysts saw the visit mainly in terms of economic in nature, that Moscow needed oil money to restore its economy. Some also saw in terms of Russian arms exports for hard currency. Many had also projected Russia as a weak country in the Arab World with dwindling influence in the wake of determined efforts by the USA to spread its influence. Many also concluded that Russia had no ability or willingness to challenge the overwhelming US influence in the WANA region. During the October 1994 crisis when Saddam moved troops to Kuwaiti border, the Russian foreign minister who was in the area was in constant touch with his counterparts of US, Britain, China and other major powers so as not to give the impression of unilateral steps by Russia. Iraq being an ally of Russia was subjected to severe economic, military and political pressure from US and its allies. Russia also largely went alongwith the US [instead of protecting Iraqi interests even if it meant challenging the US attempts to impose its hegemony in the Gulf region], thereby further discrediting Russia in the eyes of the Arab States.

Chernomyrdin's visit was the first by a Russian Prime Minister to an Arab State. He led a powerful delegation of political, military and economic affairs officers. It included the Speakers of the two houses of parliament (the Duma), the Presidents of the republics of Bashkiria and Kabardina - Balkaria, Deputy Prime Minister Oleg Davidoff, two ministers and several top military officers.

The Russian Prime Minister had a tough time in the four GCC States whose leaders - Saudi monarch King Fahd, Sheikh Jaber of Kuwait, Sultan Qaboos of Oman and Sheikh Zayed of UAE - are close allies of the US. All of these states have not only signed security treaties with the US (and other western states) but have also allowed the stationing of US troops and pre-positioning arms as well as given naval and air base facilities to the US on a long-term basis. These Gulf leaders also follow western advice in terms of oil production, pricing and trade, recycling of oil money and purchase of arms from the US. The Gulf leaders had been told that Russia is a weak country in all fields, i.e. it has lost its weight and it is futile to deal with a declining power. The press in the GCC states had written about Russian Mafia, crime, smuggling and other social ailments. The Russian leader apparently tried to present their role in October 1994 crisis between Iraq and Kuwait as a success for Russian diplomacy. They also tried to sell arms by saying that Russian planes and tanks "were no worse than others, and some of them were better".[12]

Although the pro-US Gulf leaders patiently listened to Chernomyrdin's lecture in which he said that Russia has "one of the most talented people, patient and benevolent and that it has begun to climb out of its economic nadir," and that it's showing signs of stability and its weapons technology is good. But obviously there were sharp differences in views on Bosnia, Iraq issue and so on. Apparently the Russians tried to convince the Gulf leaders that Moscow is against aggression and violence and that it supports Kuwait's sovereignty and is willing to guarantee its (Kuwait's) security. On the whole the visit did make a breakthrough in the sense, US monopoly was broken and Gulf leaders were given a realistic picture of Russia. Since the Gulf States had established ties with Moscow recently (except Kuwait) the visit itself was a success given Russian domestic constraints. The Russians also became aware how obstacles are being created for them in the Gulf by the US and Israel. The very fact that the GCC States were prepared to receive the Russian leader itself showed their growing interest in Russia. They also showed interest in Russian offer of technology in water desalination. Moscow said water could become a source of concern or even conflict in WANA in future. The Gulf leaders were also told about the enormous business opportunities in Russia. Although the Gulf businessmen were cool towards offers of incentives by Russia, Chernomyrdin reminded them of a Russian proverb. "better get there late than never". He urged them to invest in Russia's vast market by saying: "It would be better for you not to delay".

These were bold moves on the part of Russia in the Arab World especially the Gulf region, since the disintegration of USSR and the severe battering given by the US to its ally Iraq. But one should not conclude that these moves were anti-western or hostile to USA. As Victor Posuvalyuk noted in his concluding remarks:

> For seventy years, the USSR mobilized all its capabilities, which were not few, in a muscle-flexing competition with the West. Our people paid a high price for this. In other words, we have encountered that lesson and absorbed it in depth. This was one of the battlefields of the cold war, and we do not want to return to it or the logic of confrontation. We do, however, hope for a new political logic on our partners' part, and for a position that respects Russia's interests and needs.[13]

The USA decided to focus on Iraq due to the following facts: Russia had good ties with both Iran and Iraq, Moscow's desire to make the latter a major component of Gulf security, failure of dual containment policy of the US, Iraq's continued opposition to Arab Israeli peace settlement, possession of large military, industrial complex, highly nationalist Baath party rule and of course the huge oil resources. The US kept up its pressure on Iraq under President Clinton with daily bombings especially in the no fly zones in north and South of Iraq, UN weapons inspectors destroying much of Iraqi WMD capability, support to anti-Iraqi forces, engineering several coup attempts, all of it failed to dislodge Saddam and his regime. In October 1998 the US Congress enacted the Iraq Liberation Act to overthrow Saddam Hussein and a sum of $ 97 million was allocated for carrying out the task through covert means. In December 1998 the US carried out massive bombing of Iraq but couldn't bring down Saddam's regime. From the very outset it was clear that removal of UN sanctions was linked to the removal of Saddam by the US and all this to control Iraqi oil to implement the Cheney report i.e. US energy plan - which calls for a major increase in US engagement in the Gulf region in order to secure future oil supplies.

Securing Russian support alongwith other major powers became a priority for the new Bush (US) administration since it came to power in early 2001 in order to tackle Iraq. The neo-conservative group in US led by Dick Cheney, Paul Wolfowitz and others had brought out a document in September 2000 which called for the creation of a "Global Pax Americana" including an attack on Iraq to secure "regime change" even before Bush took power. The group also called for US global military supremacy and the use of pre-emptive military force to defeat any challenges to that supremacy. The September 11, 2001 attacks on WTC and the Pentagon enabled the Bush administration to declare war on international terrorism. The US concentrated on the worldwide anti-terrorist struggle as a matter of high priority to safeguard its security interests. Most of the leading countries in the world supported US approach towards fighting the menace of terrorism. The neo-conservatives were successful in bombing Afghanistan to overthrow the Taliban and Al Qaeda but failed to apprehend Osama bin Laden and other top leaders. Now they turned their attention to Iraq arguing that UN sanctions had failed to remove Saddam. They openly propagated a US invasion of Iraq as the panacea to international political terrorism after 9/11. The 'Axis of Evil' speech of Bush on January 29,2002 identifying Iran, Iraq and North Korea was a clear signal to Iraq about the impending focus on Iraqi WMD. With legal and moral principles abandoned, the debate focused on US "national interest" and its ability to use force to punish its enemies. So Saddam had to go and Iraq had to be occupied in April 2003 so as to implement US strategic goals.[14]

With the neo-conservatives dominating the US administration it soon became their main agenda after 9/11 i.e. to fight against global terrorism. Unable to catch Osama bin Laden in Afghan war or any other top Taliban or Al Qaeda leadership, soon the focus shifted to Iraq and especially to remove Saddam Hussein. The neo-conservatives openly propagated a US invasion of Iraq as the panacea to global political terrorism, after September 11, 2001. They also connected Iraq to the anthrax attacks in the US as well as Iraq's alleged links to an Islamic revivalist group in northern Iraq-*Ansar al Islam.* No wonder the US became more strident in its demands for the return of UN weapons inspectors to Iraq who had been withdrawn in December 1998 to facilitate US-UK air attacks. Due to persistent pressure and lobbying from the US, the UNSC resolution 1441 was passed in November 2002 allowing for strict time bound weapons inspection in Iraq. The UN inspectors under Hans Blix of UNMOVIC went to Iraq and no WMD's were found and this was reported to the UNSC. But the US continued to insist that Iraq was not in favor of giving the UN inspectors enough time to peacefully disarm Iraq.

Actually, Hans Blix and IAEA Chief Baradei wanted three more months to complete the inspections and to certify that if Iraq did not have WMD's - the UN sanctions could be lifted. By now the US and UK adopted the language of "regime change" in regard to Iraq. US Secretary of State Colin Powell confirmed that UN sanctions were aimed at wider political change in Iraq and not simply the securing of Iraqi disarmament: "Sanctions and the pressure of sanctions are part of a strategy of regime change (along with) support for the opposition, and reviewing additional options that might be available of a unilateral or multilateral nature". Thus, removal of sanctions was linked to the removal of Saddam Hussein and all this to control Iraqi oil and then re-order the region's political map as articulated by the neo-conservatives.

Russian inability to control events in Chechnya and the challenge posed by Chechen fighters both in Russia and outside together with 9/11 events in USA and inability of the Bush administration to nab Osama bin Laden and Al Qaeda's threat to US interests brought US and Russia on a common platform to fight global terrorism. Growing interaction with EU and NATO were additional factors which was a clear indication that Russia after a long period of over thousand years of indecision of whether it is part of Asia or Europe, had finally made up its resolve to become "part of the West", and to be a partner of the US just like Europe had become since the Second World War if not earlier.

It is in this background one should see the Bush-Putin summit in Moscow during May 2002 which ushered in a new global partnership between the US and Russia. Many felt the new *entente* between Russia and America can only weaken Moscow's role as a restraining influence on Washington in the WANA region, thus giving the US virtually a free hand to pursue its aggressive policies against Iraq, Iran and other states. It has given Israel also a free hand to impose its agenda on the Palestinians and pursue its vendettas against Syria and the *Hamas* and *Hezbollah* groups. According to Lebanese commentator Samir Atallah, the Russians seem to have agreed to defer to the Americans over everything of consequence related to the WANA region. Russia has joined the West, "and everything else that is said after the summit will only be a distribution of roles, like in an orchestra", he says. This means "if Iraq is destroyed, Moscow will suffice with a statement issued by its Foreign Ministry's Undersecretary for Middle, Near or Far Eastern affairs", Atallah says.

Zuhair Qusaibati writing for the Saudi pan-Arab daily *Al-Hayat* says the Moscow summit will have "buried the dreams" of anyone who was hoping Russia would recover and re-establish its presence on the world and regional stages. Russia is being "brought into the American orbit" as part of package of strategic and economic understandings under which the Americans have been guaranteed a role in Central Asia and the Southern Caucasus for the post-Afghan period, he writes. The regime in Baghdad is one of the "losers" from the Moscow Summit despite attempts to deny reports that the Russians have agreed to "sell the Iraqi Card" to Washington in exchange for various forms of compensation (including promised US and EV investment in Russia), according to Qusaibati. Baghdad knows that the Russian veto in the UN Security Council lost its efficacy long ago. Now Iraq's outstanding Soviet-era debts to Moscow have also lost their appeal to Russia, which was reportedly promised a share of oil projects and investments in post-Saddam Iraq, he writes. Qusaibati continues by asserting that the Arabs top the "list of losers from the inauguration of the era of full partnership between America and Russia". The Arabs were faulted for failing to rebuild their bonds of friendship with the Russians under Boris Yeltsin, when the Russians had suffered an internal collapse after their loss of an empire of allies, he recalls. But Putin's Russia had to "yield to a knockout blow," the Arabs can henceforth expect to find Moscow faithfully toeing Washington's line on West Asian issues.

Iyad Abu-Shakra writing for *As Sharaq al Awsat* says the Arab world is "currently undergoing an experience comparable to what the Russians went through during the Mikhail Gorbachev era." At the time, their politicians and citizens, like ours today, were either extremely naive about the intentions of their ideological adversaries, or utterly ignorant about the best way to improve their internal condition. As a result, "*perestroika and glasnost* ended with the collapse and disintegration of a Soviet State and the relegation of Russia to a second-rank power". According to Abu-Shakra, this is what the Moscow summit confirmed at a time when the US has been affirming its strategic objectives, and doing so in the kind of threatening tones that accompanied the publication of its list of state sponsors of terrorism. The US has made it clear that its current policy "is to remove hostile regimes from power, one after the other, even if that means dismembering the countries they rule and redrawing their maps just as we saw in the former Soviet Union & EU notably Yugoslavia". The only difference is that the word 'communism' is being replaced with 'terrorism', Abu-Shakra remarks.[15]

The US found many partners in its fight against terrorism. In Indian the NDA government led by A.B.Vajpayee also enthusiastically supported the US on this issue. L.K. Advani, India's Home Minister offered all possible help and cooperation in the fight against terror. But the US needed Pakistani help in this fight and so preferred to utilize help from Parvez Musharraf. Russia was also willing to cooperate with US in order to defeat extremism and terrorism. The Russian massacre of Chechens and the destruction of Grozny and much of the Caucasus province had fuelled insurgency. The Chechens launched a violent struggle against Russian oppression. They were supported by many Arab fighters - veterans from the Afghan War and closely linked with Al Qaeda. They played havoc in Moscow theatre in 2002, hostage taken at a large hospital, downing of two Russian civilian planes, several hostage taking incidents, killing of Kremlin backed president of Chechnya Akhmad Kadyrov in V-day parade in Grozny and in many other daring acts of violence. Vladimir Putin who replaced Boris Yelstin became President of Russia and promised security, an end to Mafia, criminal gangs, solution to the Chechanya issue. Not only he has failed to contain the Chechen fighters, but the escalating violence has left him weak and vulnerable on this issue. Chechanya is one place in Russia where insurgents are active. Unable to reach out to the West with their numerous attacks on Russian troops in the region, now the rebels are taking their struggle beyond Chechanya and deep into Russian cities. An Islamic group called "*the Islambouli Brigades*" claimed responsibility for downing the Russian civilian planes. This only confirms Russia's claim that Chechanya has become a haven for international terrorists. Like in Kashmir, in Chechanya also several foreign militants have been killed in recent years. One newspaper wrote on this issue.

> The Islamist connection in the outrage (Russia's 8/24) adds urgency to Russian demands that the West should renounce double standards in dealing with terrorism by giving shelter to Chechen rebel emissaries, as several Western countries including Britain and the USA, have done recently. 8/24 should serve as a wake up call to the international community to jointly tackle terrorism, one of the worst scourges of the 21st century.[16]

The Americans and the Europeans have been repeatedly urging the Russian President Vladimir Putin to talk to Chechen rebels in order to find a solution to the escalating violence. Some reports suggest that the Chechen militants are being financed and armed by the West, Israel and pro-US Arab States. Putin came down harshly on the West for advising him to do what they themselves are unwilling to do regarding Osama bin Laden. Putin said:

> Europe has rejected the offer of talks from No.1 terrorist Osama bin Laden. The question arises why they turned down his appeal if they addressed similar calls to us. If they do not want to sit down at the negotiating table with Osama bin Laden, they have no right to force us to the negotiating table with his disciples, with those who have undergone training in his camps. Let them (Europeans) try to talk to Osama bin Laden and we will see where it gets them. They are very good at teaching others, but when it comes to themselves they want to be clean, neat and shining.[17]

The Chechens have throughout aspired for an independent state. The Russians have tried to brutally suppress them even before in the Soviet Union. During 1994-95 the Chechens again rebelled and Russian army tried to crush them but due to international pressure they had to stop military action. During 1995-96 Zelimkhan Yandarbiyev became the president of the breakaway Chechen republic. The Russians never recognized him and accused him of being a terrorist. During the later years of Yelstin presidency and subsequently under Putin things deteriorated as a bloody war with Russian forces was unleashed. The Russians feared of a spill over effect on their other Caucasus republics with large Muslim population, if Chechanya secedes from the Russian republic. Since Putin came to power there has been a general revival of Russian power to restore some of the muscle to its global image. The invasion of Chechanya was obviously an attempt to wipe out what was seen as a moment of weakness in 1994-95 on the part of Russia.

The Russian army used very brutal methods to crush the Chechen revolt. Their capital Grozny was razed to the ground and hundreds and thousands of Chechens were killed. Some fled the area. Zelimkhan Yandarbiyev was one of them who fled Chechanya in 1999 and was received as a guest of Qatar, which has a record of giving asylum to dissident Islamic leaders. He was killed in Doha, Qatar on 13 February 2004. Russian security services alleged that Zelimkhan was a member of the Al Qaeda who helped finance the Nord Ost theatre siege in Moscow in October 2002 in which over 120 people lost their lives. [mostly by gas sprayed by Russian police to secure the release of hostages]. He was also accused of heading an international fund raising campaign for Chechen fighters. Tensions escalated between Russia and Qatar when two Russian agents were arrested for the murder of Zelimkhan. During the trial of the two Russians it emerged that the two had confessed for the murder and claimed it was carried out on the orders of Russian Defence Minister Sergei Ivanov with the help of the foreign ministry which facilitated them by smuggling arms through the diplomatic Bag. It later transpired that the two Russians were members of the Russian secret service but Russia's foreign Minister claimed they were only in Qatar for purposes of gathering information about terrorism. The Qatari prosecutor originally asked for the death penalty but Judge Ibrahim al Nasr on 30 June 2004 sentenced the two to life imprisonment for the assassination. The judge went out of his way to declare that the murder order came from Moscow. Russia immediately said the allegation was "so ludicrous that it was not possible to comment on it". Later Russian officials said the confessions were obtained under duress or even torture. They said they will appeal against the verdict on the grounds that diplomatic immunity was violated in the course of the arrest, that the court did not investigate the claims of torture and that there was a general lack of evidence. It was also widely speculated that the two Russian agents will be pardoned by the Qatari Emir or be allowed to serve out their life sentences (25 years in Qatar) in Russia. So far no such thing has taken place. Qatari prosecution named Sergei Ivanov, a former KGB officer and a hardliner tipped to succeed the Russian President Vladimir Putin as having ordered the killing. He said Zelimkhan's jeep had been tracked by a Russian satellite. Russian analysts said the claims were absurd as the country's main intelligence services were not under Mr. Ivanov's direct command and their satellites were not capable of such surveillance.

Anyway the Qatar court decision gave a major blow to Russia's global standing especially in the Arab world and established what a small state like Qatar can do to a former super power [of course] with the backing of the US. It must be recalled Qatar has a security pact with US and has allowed the establishment of US Central Command headquarters in Doha. But relations between Moscow and Doha quickly became strained after the murder and the court order. In March 2004 Russia briefly detained two Qatari sports officials passing through Moscow on their way to a match in Serbia. The first secretary of the Russian embassy in Qatar was expelled in return. The two countries officially maintain that ties are good but the court order led to a storm of protest in Russian parliament and press with calls for release of the two jailed agents by any means.[18]

The killing of Zelimkhan has not halted Chechen attacks in Russia. Infact the Chechen fighters have intensified their attacks on neighboring parts of Russia. Chechen women fighters have carried out daring acts of violence and now Russian officials say that use of Chechen suicide bombers is proof that foreign Islamic extremists - Wahhabites from Saudi Arabia - have infested the separatist movement.[19] However, it must be mentioned that the Saudi leaders as well as heads of OIC states have condemned terrorism and have played a crucial role in counter-terrorist efforts. According to the Russian Ambassador to Saudi Arabia Andrei Baklanov, the response of the Saudi leadership to the tragic events in Moscow was very illustrative (Moscow theatre hostage/storming). The Saudi Cabinet met to adopt a special decision in which it emphasized its firmness in condemning all forms of terror and expressed condolences and complete solidarity with the families that lost their relatives. The media widely covered the document. Apparently similar responses came from Crown Prince Abdullah of Saudi Arabia and the Secretary General of the GCC A.Attiyah during visits to Moscow - the former visiting Moscow in early September [9-12] 2003 and the latter visiting in early November 2002. To conclude this issue, it must be stressed that the Chechen issue bears close resemblance to the Kashmir issue especially in terms of outside support to the militants and in this case Pakistan's support to the Kashmiri militants and allowing its territory to send foreign fighters for Jihad in Kashmir. There are lessons both India and Russia can learn from their mutual experiences as far as militant organisations being financed, armed and supported by outside powers is concerned. In both the cases the USA has been the prime mover behind the Chechen militancy and the Kashmiri separatist movement so as to put pressure on India and Russia to achieve its larger strategic goal of weakening its rivals in power game.[20]

The recent seizure of a packed school in Southern Russia (in early September 2004), in which over 350 people including children died, downing of two Russian airliners in the end of August 2004 in which 90 people died, and the suicide bomb blast in a Moscow street on 31 August 2004 that killed 11 people prompted Russia for the first time [in recent times] to seek a meeting of the UN Security Council to discuss unprecedented wave of terrorist attacks on its territory. Explaining Moscow's appeal to the UNSC, the Russian envoy Andrei Denisov, said Russia sought "firm, unqualified support" for its anti-terrorist struggle. The UNSC in a special meeting on 1st September 2004 demanded "the immediate and unconditional release of all hostages of the terrorist attack" in North Ossetia. The Council's statement urged all nations to cooperate with Russian authorities in efforts to bring to justice "the perpetrators, organisers and sponsors of these terrorist acts". That Moscow got immediate support that too unanimous from UNSC speaks for the success of Russian diplomacy. The UN Security Council called the hostage - taking a "heinous act" and denounced acts of terrorism as "criminal and unjustifiable, regardless of their motivation" and reaffirmed UN determination to combat terrorism that "constitutes one of the most serious threats to international peace and security". The Russian President Vladimir Putin pointed out that the terror strikes were directed not only against individuals, but against Russia as a whole. He added: "We are grateful to the UNSC, to all heads of State and Government, who expressed their solidarity with Russia". Meanwhile the Russian Foreign Minister Mr. Sergei Lavrov said the latest terrorist acts also "have international roots". Interestingly, responsibility for the school seizure has been claimed by a new group calling itself "*Salakhin Riadus Shahidi*", which is led by Chechen warlord Shamil Basayev who is possibly linked to Al-Qaeda. As seen earlier "*The Islambouli Brigades*" claimed responsibility for the blowing of two Russian airliners. So far the Western countries especially the US have been reluctant to recognize Chechen struggle as a terrorist issue. It is true that Russia has been consistent in saying that Chechen freedom movement has close relations with global terrorist groups and that it gets funds from such global groups. It is in this context one should see Russian accusations against Zelimkhan who was killed in Qatar and whom the Russians accused of working for fund raising for Chechen guerillas. When Britain gave asylum to Akhmed Zakayev, a representative of the Chechen leader, Aslan Maskhadov, Russia protested to the Tony Blair government. Russia also accused Zakayev of fund raising to Chechen rebels.[21]

Vladimir Putin's decision to send elite commandos to storm the school in Beslan, Northern Ossettia where militants had held hundreds of hostages, led to bloodshed and over 360 people were killed including children. More than 700 people were hospitalized with wounds, majority of them being children. An estimated 30 militants were involved and security forces killed 20 gunmen including 10 Arabs and the rest fled the scene. The region's federal Security Service chief Valery Andreyev said: "There are 10 people originating from the Arab World among 20 killed terrorists" Interfax reported. The Regional President Alexander Dzasokhov said the militants had demanded that Russian troops leave Chechnya - The first clear indication of their demands and of a direct link between the school attack and the ongoing guerilla war in Chechnya - a neighboring region of North Ossettia. Valery Andreyev's regional security service said Chechen commander Magomet Yevloyev led the hostage takers. They said the operation had been planned by Shamil Basayev, Russia's most wanted Chechen rebel, who has been behind several major attacks our Chechenya. Vladimir Putin described the recent spate of terror strikes in Russia as a "total war" unleashed on the country by international terrorism and called for mobilization of Russia in fighting terrorism. The crisis was a major challenge to Putin -either to accept the demands of the hostage takers - which included withdrawal of Russian troops from Chechnya and grant independence to Chechnya so as to save the lives of school children or storm the school. Although he expressed concern for the safety of the hostages but he also made clear his firm resolve not to give in to the extremists as it would have negative effects in his struggle for combating global terrorism. Since North Ossetia is largely Christian and the neighboring Ingushetia Muslim, the Chechen rebels wanted to provoke a clash between the two like the 1992 clash over a disputed territory.[22]

Russia's response to the crisis and Putin's determination not to capitulate in its fight against terrorism is in line with the Moscow summit of May 2002 between Bush and Putin. Russia has sent a strong and unequivocal signal to terrorists worldwide of its determination to suppress terrorism. The swiftness or speed with which the UNSC met and deplored the hostage taking showed western support to Russia in its hour of crisis. It is obvious India did not get such support from the international community in our efforts to end violence in Kashmir. Despite New Delhi's efforts to establish close ties with US/EU as also NDA governments call on USA as natural ally, did not yield India the kind of support Russia received recently. Here again there are clear lessons to be learnt from each others experience - for India and Russia, in addition to the Arab factor as India has also had the experience of foreign fighters in Kashmir.[23]

Another factor, which has united Russia and the US, is the issue of oil. According to Lebanese commentator Samir Atallah under the new bilateral contract, America will be the prime consumer of Russian crude oil and Russia will become the principal beneficiary of US investment funds. The "natural outcome" of this will be for Russia's 400 million eager consumers to join China's 1 billion eager consumers, making a vast market "hungry for the goods that we Arabs are boycotting these days from Coke to Pepsi and from the Big Mac to Sylvester Stallone Sunglasses". According to Atallah both Russia and US have decided to "stand shoulder to shoulder, contractually, against Arab and Islamic oil, from Indonesia to Gabon and from Oman to Nigeria".[24]

Russia has been steadily increasing its oil production, which now stands at 8.8 million barrels per day making it the second largest oil producer after Saudi Arabia. Russian production earlier from its

Siberian oil fields used to be around 6mbpd. But the biggest problem with Russian oil is the issue of transportation from Siberia to world markets especially in the USA and Asia where Russian oil and gas is needed. The transportation of oil from Saudi Arabia is 1.5 times as cheap than the Russian oil from remote Siberia. At the moment the USA is the largest energy consumer in the world - taking about 25 mbpd. The US imports about 65-70 percent of its oil. Bulk of it comes from OPEC especially Arab oil producers. Now due to political reasons US is interested in the import of oil from Russia. Clearly the US is going to help Russia in this field. According to some observers Russia is more predictable now than the Arab oil producers. Not surprisingly during the last couple of years the Russian Fuel and Energy Complex has got substantial western investments for the development of the petroleum infrastructure and for the further increase in oil output. One can see a threat to OPEC from the US and Russia as both appear to be jointly working to reduce the clout of OPEC. Even though OPEC has increased its oil output, still oil prices are rising leading to speculation that it is artificially contrived to help boost the revenues for Russia.

The basic thrust of Russia's aggressive economic diplomacy has become energy. Luckily, Russia's second biggest oil company, won the rights in January 2004 to develop a potentially huge gas field in Saudi Arabia in a tie-up with Saudi Aramco. The deal strengthened newly emerging links between the world's two biggest oil producers that could give Russia greater leverage in global energy markets. The above deal and Saudi investments in Russian oil industry were discussed during Saudi Crown Prince Abdullah's visit to Moscow in September 2003. The USA by encouraging Russia to increase its oil output to meet the growing import needs of the former as also by manipulating the oil prices, Russia is being used by the US to spoil the game of OPEC. This is definitely a short sighted US policy and Putin's willingnes do the bidding will in the long term undermine its own strategic interests for short term gains.[25]

Since the reelection of Vladimir Putin as Russia's President for a second term in March 2004, he has been telling the nation that Russia was still facing a win or die battle it had fought in the cold war, even if the rules of the game had changed. He said; "There is a tough, competitive battle going on in the world. As different from the past, this battle has moved from the realm of military conflict to economic competition".[26]

Apart from tackling the issue of terrorism and cooperation in the field of oil and gas, which Presidents Bush and Putin agreed to at the Moscow summit in May 2002, the Arab-Israeli peace issue came up in the Joint Declaration on a New US-Russia Relationship issued on 24 May 2002. Jordanian commentator Mahmoud Rimawi said the wording of the declaration was clearly intended to enable both countries to "keep their distance" from the WANA region "and that is worrying development seeing as they remain the official co-sponsors of the peace process". He wrote in Amman (Jordan) daily Al Rai, most worrying was the way the joint statement completely ignored Israel's ongoing aggression in the Palestinian territories, while making the "pseudo-academic" observation that "neither conflict nor peace is inevitable" in the West Asian region. Rimawi said: "The fact of the matter is that peace is distant and not at hand, while the conflict is ongoing and raging and that is thanks to the world's inaction and its inability to address Israel's Prime Minister Ariel Sharon with the word 'Enough'!". Reiterating talk of a Palestinian "state" is no substitute for holding back Sharon, he wrote, because what Israel's prime minister has been doing since he and Bush came to power is to systematically destroy the foundations of that state and society (infrastructure). Bush and Putin had nothing to say about that, other than to express their belief that the conflict must be resolved through negotiations as any press commentator could have done, without assuming any of the responsibility "for translating that belief into practice." The major world powers, writes Rimawi, "keep talking about initiatives, hopes and visions for ending 'the conflict', but the policies they pursue show no connection between their declared principles and their actual behavior'. They seem to have given Israel a "green light" to behave outside international law and join their "nuclear club" of the international heavy weights, "even if that means sacrificing one of the peoples (Palestinians) of the region and threatening the interests of at least 20 of its (Arab) countries". It is ironic how Israel, created by the UN, has succeeded in making the Palestine question off-limits to the international community, Rimawi remarks. First it rendered the UN and its resolutions irrelevant. Now under Bush and Putin "Moscow's interest scarcely extends below the orthodox church's property in Jerusalem" while Washington is obsessed with two enemies: *Hamas and Islamic Jihad* who only emerged as a by product of 35 years of Israel's brutal military occupation of West Bank and Gaza. Unfortunately the May 2002 Joint US-Russian Declaration says nothing new to this sad state of affairs and leaves open the question of what negotiated settlement the two sides aspire to. "Does it mean striving for a long-term interim accord on part of the West Bank and Gaza strip, as is Sharon's avowed objective, and deferring a full settlement until after the occupied Palestinian territories have been flooded with more Jewish settlements than they are today?" Rimawi writes.[27]

Another commentator Samir Atallah says what Bush and Putin did was declare "that the President of the US as master of the universe and the President of Russia as the biggest failed aspirant to that throne", will henceforth unite their energies behind two objective: fighting terror and cooperation on oil issues. As far as WANA is concerned the Russians seem to have agreed to defer to the Americans over everything of consequence related to the Arab-Israeli issues.[28]

Before the summit Russia took initiative to revive the Arab Israeli Peace process. In January 2002 Moscow initiated a meeting of the group of cooperation at the foreign ministers level. Putin addressed it with a program of political statement on the situation in the West Asian region that also touched upon the security aspects as well. It was decided to revive the multilateral talks on Arms Control and regional security as part of the Madrid Conference. Little earlier a dialogue between Russia and the Arab World took place in Cairo in 1999 and regional security issues and the West Asian strategic issues were discussed. Suggestions were made to set up arms control measure so as to preserve regional security.[29]

Yemen's President Ali Abdullah Saleh visited Moscow on 6 April 2004 and met Russian President Vladimir Putin and held talks on Iraq, Arab Israeli peace and arms purchases. He had visited Russia in December 2002 and had announced plans to buy six Russian MIG-29 fighter planes, adding to the 176 ordered in a $300 million 2001 deal. Putin in talks with Saleh told him "the region is very difficult and we are attentively following the situation. Russia is ready to do everything to assist the stable development in Yemen and in the region". But he added: "we must note that unfortunately our trade exchange still hasn't reached the desired turnover but for this there are good prospects." President Saleh congratulated Putin on his reelection last month. He said: "Relations between Russia and Yemen have a historic character. We are fully pleased with the success our cooperation has achieved". The struggle against terrorism and developments in Iraq and the Palestinian territories were the center of discussions. The Yemeni President said: "Russia has (a)... vital role to play in the West Asian peace process". Saleh had brought new proposals related to efforts to boost the UN role in stabilizing Iraq. Later a Kremlin official said Yemen and Russia favor widening UN influence.[30]

From the above survey it is clear that due to Russia's economic problems, reduced military capabilities, growing partnership with US/EU and the threat of terrorism, Moscow's circle of friends in the Arab world especially after what happened to Iraq, has dwindled. That only Yemeni President makes a ritualistic annual visit clearly show the limits to Russian power and influence in the Arab world.

Since India established diplomatic ties with Israel in 1992 Indo-Israeli ties had become close especially during the NDA government. Part of the reason is the sustained US interest in strengthening these ties, which were due to growing Indo-US ties especially in the context of Ariel Sharon's brutal suppression of the Palestinians and other aggressive Israeli actions which led to a decline in Indo-Arab ties. The Arab states especially Egypt noted the implications of close Indo-Israeli ties on the Arab World. Not only the US is systematically appropriating India's geopolitical space in the Gulf and West Asian region but is working hard to make Israel the only power in the oil rich and strategically crucial area very close to India. Since India imports 70 percent of its energy from the Gulf region, Pax Americana will lead to eventual pressure on India in addition to the existing pressure from Pakistan exercised by the US for long. This calls for balanced policy towards the region and coordination with Russia whereby both working for the settlement of Israeli-Palestine conflict and urging Israel to withdraw from Syrian occupied lands will be crucial for peace, security and stability in the WANA region. The Iraq war has alerted the Russians (especially due to continued Iraqi resistance) that instability could rapidly spread through

Southern Russia to deep inside the country. Russian predicament [mainly due to Chechnya] was obvious when Putin traveled to Malaysia in October 2003 to attend the OIC summit where Russia was admitted as an associate member of the Islamic grouping. [Saudi Arabia played a crucial in Russia getting membership]. Putin is also working to appoint a special adviser on Islamic affairs. Like in the 1950's to 1970's both India and Russia can work together in the WANA region with the Arab countries to ensure peace, security and stability so very essential for the welfare of both India and Russia. US attempts to unilaterally intervene in Iraq and continued threats to Iran and Syria—with whom India and Russia have close ties and lack of US interest in restraining Israel in its aggressive policies towards the hapless Palestinians and in the name of tackling terrorism spreading instability in the oil rich and strategically crucial area can and should prompt India and Russia to work together. Not only India and Russia are being displaced from the WANA region gradually by the US in order to dominate the oil rich states but religious and extremists groups are getting support and strengthened in the process with serious security implications for both India and Russia. Unlike the US, India and Russia are nearer to the Gulf region [hence to the fire] and what happens there will reach them sooner and faster, hence the significance of Indo-Russian strategic partnership in the Arab world. The potential implications for the US have become very clear, hence the concern.

References

1. A.K. Pasha, *Egypt's Relations with Soviet Union: The Nasser and Sadat Period* (Aligarh: Center of West Asian Studies, 1986) p. 17
2. Ibid, p. 13-14; see also Mohammed Heikal, *Nasser–The Cairo Document* (London: 1972) p. 58; *Karen Dawish, Soviet Foreign Policy Towards Egypt* (London: 1972) p. 11; *The Policy of Soviet Union in the Arab World: A Short Collection f Foreign Policy Documents: The USSR and Arab World* (Moscow: 1975) p. 48.
3. See A.K. Pasha, *Egypt's Quest for Prace: Determinants and Impllications* (New Delhi: 1994) pp. 206-219.
4. M.H. Nuri, "India and the Gulf Crisis", *BIISS Journal* vol. 13, no. 1, 1992, p. 1-50; A.K. Pasha, "India's West Asia Policy", *Strategic Analysis*, vol. xvi, No. 6, September 1993, p. 783-804

5. A.K. Pasha , ed., *The Gulf in Turmoil: A Global Response* (New Delhi: Lancers Books, 1992), pp. 70-126
6. Ibid, pp. 194-201
7. Ibid, p. 89-91
8. A.K. Pasha, *India and West Asia: Continuity and Change* (New Delhi: Lancers Books, 1992), pp. 70-126.
9. A.K. Pasha, ed; *Contemporary Gulf: State, Society, Economy and Foreign Policy* (New Delhi: Detente Publications, 1999) p. 20-28 and p. 318-330; A.K. Pasha, Iraq: Sanctions and Wars (New Delhi: Sterling, 2003) p. 114-115.
10. Ibid, p. 285-298; see also A.K. Pasha, "The Recent Gulf Crisis: India's Options", *Strategic Analysis*, January 1995. vol. xvii, NMo. 10, p. 1271-1286.
11. Stephen Grummon, "Russia's Ambitions in the Persian Gulf", *Middle East Quarterly,* vol. 11, March 1995.
12. Ibid; See also Andrei Baklanov, "Russia and the Arab World shoudld resume Dialog", *International Affairs* (Moscow) 2003, p. 35-40
13. Ibid.
14. A.K. Pasha, "The Iraq Crisis: An Overview", World Focus, vol. 25, No. 1, January 2004, no. 289, p. 3-6
15. "Moscow summit seen as bad news for Arabs and Muslims," Lebanonnews.com, 27 May 2002, Arab Press Review p. 1-3 [The Daily Star {Beirut}].
16. *The Hindu*, 28 August 2004.
17. *The Hindu*, 22 April 2004.
18. *Middle East International,* No. 729, 9 July 2004, p. 12; The Hindu, 14 April 2004, p. 15; see also MEI, no. 721, *The Daily Star (Beirut) 7 April 2004,* p. 7
19. The Hindu, 2 September 2004
20. Andrei Baklanov, *Internation Affairs* (Moscow) 2003, p. 35-40; see also Nirmala Joshi, "India and Russia: Enduring Partnership", India Quarterly, vol. VIII, No. 3 & 4, July-December 2002, pp. 113-28.
21. Vladimir Radyuhin, "Russia Gains Global Support", The Hindu, 3 September, 2004, p. 14.
22. ____, "Putin had to choose between two evils", The Hindu, 4 September, 2004, p. 14
23. Joshi, no. 20, p. 118

24. Lebanonwire.com n. 14, p. 1
25. http://english.pravada.ru/economics/2002/09/18/26864.html [More predictable Russia will make Arabs step into the background]
26. Vladimir Rudyuhin, "Russia's economic displomacy", The Hindu, 27 April 2004, p. 10.
27. Ibid
28. Lebanonwire.com, p. 1-3
29. Baklanov, n. 20.
30. The Daily Star [Beirut] 7 April and 8 April 2004.

12

Russian Foreign Policy—The Emerging Contours

Dr. Jagdish P. Sharma

Every historical period is marked to some extent by change, but today the pace of change appears more rapid, surprising and the consequences more profound, dangerous and radical than ever before. Indeed, the cascade of recent events suggests that a revolutionary restructuring of world politics, society and economy has occurred. The restructuring of economy, foreign policy, politics is noticed by many experts and is reflected in the later trends. The nations of the world are drawing more closely together in transportation, communications, ideas, trade, commerce, and even peace and security. Similarly, restructuring of society is also suggested by many disintegrating trends that may presage disorder, caused by such phenomena as social and ethnic unrest, resurgence of religious and secular nationalism, environmental degradation, weapons testing, proliferation and control, and the domination of a Superpower. Together, the countervailing forces of integration and disruption point toward a transformation in world politics that matches in its extensive nature and importance the system disrupting convulsions that swept the world following World War I and World War II. The present period is comparable to the late 1940s or early 1950s, when a new era coloured by cold war commenced.

At that time, states sought to find new policies and institutions to deal with new conditions. The search for peace, security and redefined national interest is still changing. The post cold war world is now much in evidence. To most observers it appears that world politics is entering a new phase. Throughout history, important turning points have been perceived at the end of major wars, which disrupted pre-existing international arrangements. World Wars I and II symbolised fundamental breaks with the past because each set in motion major transformations in world politics. The end of the cold war is a historical breakpoint of no less epic significance. The conclusion of the ideological conflict between communism and capitalism at the root of the East-West dispute give " the luxury of some genuine choices for the first time since 1945" (Hyland, 1990).

It appears we are now at the threshold of a new era in world politics, having just experienced, as US President George Bush in 1992 put it, changes "of biblical proportions". The year 1989 marked the beginning of the end of a long period of uncertainty in world politics. The geo-political and ideological contours of the cold war period impacted on almost every aspect of world politics for around forty-five years. With the collapse of polarization between the two Superpowers and the threat of all-out nuclear warfare in rapid retreat, other significant concerns for world politics gained prominence. An early version of the new agenda that was put forward in 1991 identified a number of global policy concerns including the environment, drug trafficking, terrorism, cross-border infiltration, religious fundamentalism, migration and human rights.

Perhaps, the most difficult task in the development of international relations in the 1990s was to determine the general nature of goals that States including Russia set for themselves. The management of inter-state relations constitutes the goals of foreign policy, which one could describe in general as the art of adjusting the varying and often clashing interests of states to the advantage of the state concerned. In managing its foreign policy, the State of Russia engaged in seeking common ground among its national interests, in narrowing areas of disagreement with major powers and in finding formulae that permit them to co-adjust with the changing situation.

During the last 15 years Russia has undergone an extraordinary transformation. It has changed from a communist dictatorship to a multi-party democracy in which officials are chosen in regular elections. Its centrally planned economy has been reshaped into a capitalist order based on markets and private property. Its army has withdrawn peacefully from both Eastern Europe and other former Soviet republics, allowing the latter to become independent countries. Twenty years ago only the most naive idealist could have imagined such a metamorphosis. Russia has come to be viewed as a disastrous failure and the 1990s as a decade of catastrophe for its people. Western academics have described Russia not as a middle-income country struggling to overcome its Communist past and find its place in the world, but as a collapsed state inhabited by criminals and threatening other countries with multiple contagions.

Although Russia's transition has been painful in many ways, the country has made remarkable economic and social progress since the end of communism. It began the 1990s as a highly distorted and disintegrating centrally planned economy, with severe shortages of consumer goods and a massive military establishment. It ended the decade as a middle income capitalist economy. Although economic output fell initially after the Soviet Union collapsed, credible analysts suggest that the decline had been reversed by 2003. The 1990s were a decade of extreme macroeconomic turbulence in Russia. Between December 1991 and December 2001, the Russian rouble's value dropped by more than 99 per cent against the US dollar. The manner in which economic reforms were carried out in Russia is said to have exacerbated economic inequality. Today the country's political order has changed beyond recognition. The dictatorship of the party has given way lo electoral democracy. Russia's once-powerful Communists no longer control all aspects of social life or send dissidents to labour camps.

Instead, they campaign for seats in parliament. Some see the sudden spurt of growth over the last four years as an indicator of more improvements to come, and they expect Russia soon to join the ranks of important middle-income countries. They emphasize the country's human capital, its reformed tax system, and its mostly open economy.[1]

The foreign policy of Russia like that of any other country is fashioned by the needs of development and progress. It aims at the enhancement of peace, prosperity, security and stability of the state. To a great extent the policy is determined by the country's strategic location, geography, climate, economic and regional interest, historic traditions, ideology as well as the relative strength of the other centres of power. At the initial stages the Russian foreign policy was also influenced by suspicion towards Western Europe. This attitude stemmed from the continued attempt to crush the Russian state during the early decades, as well as their refusal to give recognition to the communist government of Russia. Yet two years later the NATO-Russia council was unveiled as a new "bridge of security across Europe". 47 per cent of Russians, however, still consider the North Atlantic alliance a threat to their national security.

The "Great Game" geopolitical rivalry between Russia and the West for influence across the Eurasian steppe is over. Russia failed in its attempt to monopolise the region's transportation links, but the construction of the Baku-Ceyhan pipeline is one signal victory for it. Central Asia's gas reserves are controlled by Gazprom and, as in Soviet times, will continue to pass through Russia's- controlled routes. Europe has realized that there is nothing further to be gained by continuing to compete with Russia. This is the reality: Moscow has sufficient economic and strategic leverages to frustrate further western plans for the region if Russian interests are not taken into consideration. Russia will continue to play a critical role in the Caucasus and Central Asia irrespective of American intent. Cooperation with Russia is the only way forward. Russia continues to have the most effective network of contacts in Euroasia. The American ambassador to Russia, Alexender Vershbow, has declared that, "NATO sees Russia as a partner". If that is the case then it is time to institutionalise cooperation between Russia and the west to deal with common threats.[2]

The aims and objectives of Russian Foreign Policy are stated in the following terms (a) peaceful co-existence of states with different political and social systems; (b) equality and independence of nations; and (c) non-interference in internal affairs of other countries. Russia will continue to be a nuclear power even if the chances of a nuclear world war breaking out do not seem a possibility. At the same time the country will take an interest in Disarmament.

In the Arab and Afro-Asian and Latin American regions the current policy is to provide support to the national liberation movements like Palestine Liberation Organisation, fighting for the cause of Independent Iraq and its people, upholding Third World causes including the struggle for independence of Western Sahara.

It is not necessary to insist that such states become close to Russia in order to merit Russian support and assistance. As far as relations with the remaining Socialist or Communist states are concerned, the present Russian position is that all members of the Socialist Camp are equal and all governing democratic and socialist parties are autonomous. The above policy framework constitute the principal guidelines of present Russian policies. Clearly, they are specifically distinct from the hardline followed during pre 1990s era. Some of the basic shifts in foreign policy orientation actually took place during the last years of President Mikhail Gorbachev's period.

Russia and Afro-Arab and Asian World

Russia has played an important role in the past in helping the Arab and Afro-Asian countries. Egypt and other Arab-African states were supported in the fight against Israel. A large number of Russian army officers were stationed in Egypt during 1960s and 1970s.

The Afro-Arab countries expelled the Russians in early 1970s because they failed to get the expected military help from Russia. This made the Russian position somewhat awkward. Still Russia was prepared to help Afro-Arab and Asian countries against Israel. Russia attached great importance to Arab-African and Arab-Asian world, because it had been a great source of oil and other strategic and economic resources. Recently when opening his formal talks with Egyptian leader, Hosni Mubarak, Russian President Vladimir Putin said,

"we see Egypt as our privileged partner, especially in the Middle East, African affairs".

Egypt is a country that has long and close relations with Russia" Putin said: In his words, Moscow treats Mubarak as a close friend who has special relations with Russia, and "who has spent many years studying in our country". Egyptian President Hosni Mubarak reiterated his interest in maintaining and developing cooperation with Russia. He said, "I am always interested in stable relations with Russia in making cooperation as strong as possible, and also in developing cooperation with the Russian Federation."

Mubarak recalled that the bilateral relations have a long history. " They began in the 1950s, during the revolution, under President Nasser". He stressed that his country highly assessed Russian-

Egyptian relations that are on the rise today. According to the Egyptian leader, Russia has always helped Egypt a lot at various stages of the country's history. " Russia has provided aid in weapons, in economic tasks and industrial development. Many facilities built with Russia's help have become symbols of our cooperation", the Egyptian leader said citing a metal working plant as an example.[3]

On Iraq, the Russian government consistently condemned intermittent US missile attacks against the country during the 1990s and in the recent years. In 1996, in contravention of a UN embargo, Russia concluded an agreement with Iraq on the development of petroleum fields in that country. In late 1997, following Iraq's refusal to permit weapons inspectors of the UN Special Commission (UNSCOM) access to contentious sites, the Russian Government intervened in an attempt to avert a renewal of hostilities. The conclusion of an agreement between the UN and Iraq in late February 1998 was regarded by Russia as a significant diplomatic success. In response to US and British air attacks on Iraq in Mid-December 1998, Russia temporarily recalled its ambassadors from the USA and United Kingdom. Russia resumed scheduled flights to Iraq in late 2000, in contravention of UN sanctions. In mid 2001 Russia, which supported Iraq in its demands that the sanctions regime in force since 1990 should be revoked, effectively blocked a British-drafted proposal before the Security Council for the introduction of a new, US-initiated, programme of 'Smart' sanctions. Russia under President Putin urged the United States to avoid the use of unilateral force, and encouraged Iraq's compliance with UN demands regarding weapons inspections, so as to facilitate the lifting of sanctions. Although Russia voted to support UN Security Council Resolution 1441, approved in November 2002, which provided for expeditious return of weapons Inspectors to Iraq under the auspices of the UN Monitoring. Verification and Inspection Commission (UNMOVIC), it was a leading opponent, with France and Germany, of attempts, led by the US and UK in February-March 2003, to approve military action in Iraq.[4]

The alarming situation in Iraq was one of the main subjects discussed during the talks and meetings of Russian Foreign Minister Igor Ivanov in Tehran on March 11, 2003. Ivanov confirmed Russia's invariable position on Iraq: the situation must be solved by political means. According to Ivanov, a military action taken against Iraq would be at variance with the UN Charter and the norms of international law. It would seriously destabilise the situation in the region and bring suffering to the Iraqi people. Moreover, it would lead to the renewed activity of terrorist and extremist groups.[5]

Indo-Russian Relations

The friendship of the Soviet era is fully reflected in the current Russian policy towards India. The Russian Federation also continues to have a special place in India's foreign policy. Russian President Putin congratulated Dr. Manmohan Singh on taking office as Prime Minister of the Republic of India. According to the Presidential press service, the congratulatory message said:

"Russia knows that you have inspired important economic reforms that helped to make India a leading world power. We also remember your personal contribution to comprehensive development of relations with Russia.

"I would like to emphasise that, in spite of great structural changes that our countries have undergone in last decades, Russian-Indian cooperation has consistently been based on shared or close basic interests, mutual respect and good attitude of our brotherly peoples.

I am sure that sustained orientation to strengthing our strategic partnership will remain a solid basis for the development of comprehensive cooperation between India and Russia on bilateral, regional, and global issues. We are sure of your personal support in this."[6]

India and Russia expressed satisfaction with the progress in bilateral cooperation in all fields during the recent talks in Moscow between the visiting National Security Adviser, J.N.Dixit, and the Russian Security Council Chief, Igor Ivanov. The talks focused on global security and stability, besides exchange of views on Afghanistan, Iraq and West Asia. Mr Dixit's visit came a week after the Foreign Secretary Shasank's visit to Moscow for a meeting of the Indo-Russian joint Group on Global Challenges.[7]

Russia like India, has been a victim of terrorism with global links for well over a decade now. The Russian Federation deals with terrorism in a rather robust manner. This was evident when Russian special forces stormed a theatre taken over by terrorists in the heart of Moscow or when Russian Security Agencies relentlessly pursued terrorist leader Shamil Basaev across the world.[8]

India established diplomatic relations with the then Soviet Union on April 13,1947. Even before independence there was a substantial area of agreement between the Indian National Movement and the leadership in USSR. In the earlier years after independence, India and USSR could not come closer to each other. India's independent foreign policy and non-alignment were looked upon by the Soviet bloc as 'only a mask to cover collaboration with Anglo-American imperialism'. However, the first five years of India's independence convinced the Soviet Union and her allies that India was keen to preserve her independence in international affairs. By 1953, the Soviet Union had realized that India's non-alignment was a useful factor, working not only in favour of peace, but also helping in the elimination of foreign domination in Asia. Late Prime Minister Jawahar Lal Nehru's visit to the USSR in 1955 and the visit of Soviet leaders to India in 1956 marked a turning point in bilateral relations.

The Soviet Union also displayed understanding of the peculiarities of the sub-continental politics which were largely a legacy of the past colonial rule, complicated by continuing intrigues and interferences by outside powers. In particular the Soviet Union fully endorsed India's stand on the issue of Kashmir. The Soviets even vetoed some of the anti-India resolutions in the UN. Both Soviet Union and India had found several areas of common interest in the pursuit of their respective foreign policies and had cooperated in many areas. The fruitful and mutually beneficial cooperation between the two countries culminated eventually in the formal signing of a treaty of Peace, Friendship and Cooperation on 9 August 1971. This treaty significantly acknowledged India's policy of non-alignment and endorsed the principles of peaceful co-existence. Now, even after the dismemberment of USSR and the emergence of CIS along with Russia, with new priorities, the cordial relations have remained intact. During Prime Minister Rajiv Gandhi's six day visit to the USSR in May 1985, he reassured the then Soviet leader, Mikhail Gorbachev that there would be no change whatever in long standing friendship and cooperation with the Soviet Union. Rajiv Gandhi made it clear to the Soviet leadership that India's quest for new advanced western technology would not come into the way of commitment towards the promotion of Indo-Soviet friendship and cooperation.[9]

The current emphasis of Russia in foreign policy is on a relationship based on new reality, taking into account the new political and economic interests of the country.[10] President Boris Yeltstin's visit to India in January 1993 paved the way for further development of trade and economic relations.[11] Prime Minister P.V.Narsimha Rao's visit to Moscow in July 1994 and various agreements signed by the two countries further consolidated the friendly ties between the two countries. President Putin visited India from 3-5 December 2002. The visit reinforced the traditional ties of warmth and friendship between the two countries and enabled them to exchange views on important issues of bilateral and international concern. During the visit, Russia reaffirmed its support to India as a strong and appropriate candidate for permanent membership in an expanded United Nations Security Council. The Joint Declaration on Strengthening and Enhancing Economic, Scientific and Technological Cooperation set out the ideas of the two countries towards deepening and expansion of bilateral cooperation in economic, science, defence and technology fields. The then Minister of External Affairs Mr. Yashwant Sinha visited Russia on 19-20 February 2003. Here it was stressed that bilateral relations between India and Russia are excellent, and have been marked by frequent high-level contacts.[12] This is possible because of congruence of Indo-Russian strategic interests".

President Putin recently summed up the salient features of Russian policy in these words,

> "We need to make our foreign policy adequate to the goals and capabilities of the new stage of development. In other words, we need to use the tools of foreign policy for a more appreciable practical return in the economy, and in the realization of important national tasks. ———We are interested in further integration of the Russian economy into the international economy, including joining the WTO on conditions that are beneficial for us.—The expansion of European Union should not just bring us closer geographically, but also economically and spiritually.————
>
> We will continue to develop political and economic dialogue with the USA and with such major partners as China, India and

Japan, and we will work with other countries."[13]

Observers are convinced that as Russia develops as a stronger economic power, its influence in international politics will be all the more great.

References

1. Andrei Shleilfer and Daniel Treisman, "Rethinking Russia", *Foreign Affairs* (New York) Vol 83, no.2. March/April 2004, pp. 20-37. For details also see Isaiah Bertin, *The Soviet Mind: Russian* Culture under Communism edited by Henry Hardy, US: Brookings Institution Press, 2004.
2. Ian Bremmer and Nikolas Gvosdev, " NATO looks east : Why not really make Russia a Partner?" *International Herald Tribune* June 22, 2004.
3. Quoted in *News from* Russia (Embassy of the Russian Federation in India) Vol. VII, No.6, June 1, 2004, p. 13.
4. For details see *Europa year Book* London; Europa Publications, 2003, p. 3478.
5. Quoted in *Daily Review* (Moscow) March 12, 2003.
6. Quoted in *News from Russia* ,Vol. VIII, No.6, June 1, 2004. p. 17.
7. The Hindu (New Delhi) July 2, 2004.
8. G.Parthasarathy, "Russia and global terrorism" in *Pioneer (New Delhi) July* 1, 2004.
9. N. Jayapalan, *Foreign Policy of India* Delhi; Atlantic Publishers, 2001, pp. 187-188.
10. *The Hindustan Times* (New Delhi) July 2, 1994.
11. *The Patriot* (New Delhi) May 9, 1994.
12. *India 2004* Government of India publication, pp.416-417.
13. Quoted in *News From Russia* May 26, 2004.

13

Russia Emerging as a World Economic Power and Indo-Russian Economic Cooperation

V.D. Chopra

Russian Economy

Russia has emerged as a world power after the disintegration of the Soviet Union, if economic statistics and its foreign policy contours are any indications.

After a disastrous decade under the former President, Boris Yeltsin, Russia is on the way to economic revival. In the past four years, it has registered the highest growth rates in half a century.

The economic stagnation, which it suffered in the 1990s was even worse than during World War II. During 1940-1946, Soviet industrial production fell by 4 per cent. In 1990-1999 the fall was almost 60 per cent, while the GDP fell 54 per cent. Russia's economy witnessed a 20 per cent growth in the recent past and surged 7.2 per cent in the first six months of the 2003, placing Russia among the world's fastest growing economies. The country's foreign exchange reserves increased from $11 billion three years ago to $64 billion in 2003. Instead of increasing foreign debts, it has managed to decrease them by one fourth over three years. Significantly, it is discharging its foreign debt. It has repaid $17.3 billion in 2003, reducing its debt-to-GDP ratio to 35 per cent, lower than that of Germany, France or Italy.

In the first six months of 2003 foreign investments in Russia were $12.66 billion. Russia's oil and gas industry has been the driving force that pulled the economy from the mire of the preceding decade. In the past three years oil and gas exports have increased by 18 per cent.

This shows how grave mistakes in social and economic reforms during Boris Yeltsin regime had led to extremely serious consequences, pushing one third of Russia's population below the poverty line. People lost all their savings and suffered from long wage delays.

As against this, now the GDP has grown by almost 30 per cent, inflation has dropped by 200 per cent, hard currency reserves have risen to an all-time high of $84 billion, real per capita incomes have increased by 50 per cent, and the number of poor has been reduced by one third, Russian President Vladimir Putin claimed recently. This indeed is a remarkable achievement and it has put Russia on the economic map of the world. There is something more to it, if recent statistics are taken into account.

Russia's GDP grew 8 per cent in January-April 2004 compared to the same period last year. In April, the GDP growth was 7.8 per cent, according to the Economy Ministry's social and economic survey. The GDP is expected to grow 6.5 per cent in 2004 (down from 7.3 per cent in 2003), and industrial production is expected to increase 6.1 per cent (down from 7 per cent last year). Lower expectations for economic growth in the second half of 2004 are due to the fact that the Russian economy grew more rapidly in the second half of 2003.

According to the Economic Ministry, inflation was 0.5 per cent in Russia in May 2004, and 5.1 per cent in January-May 2004. In the estimate of the Statistics Service, inflation was 4.6 per cent in January-April. The inflation slowdown was due to a restricted rise in natural monopoly prices and tariffs, and the strengthening of the rouble.

In the estimate of the Economic Ministry, fixed investment increased to RUR 574.6 billion (about $19.8 billion) in January-April 2004, 12.9 per cent more than in the same period last year. A rise in investment is due to high oil and gas prices, which boosted investment in the fuel and energy sector; lower yields on rouble instruments, stimulating investors to invest in the real sector of the economy; the improving financial position of Russian companies, and overall economic stability in the country. The trade surplus was $24.3 billion in January-April 2004, which is 25 per cent more than in the corresponding period last year ($19.3 billion).

The Economic Ministry of the Russian Federation has revised its 2004 GDP forecast from 6.4 per cent to 6.6 per cent, said Andrey Klepach, Chairman of the Economic Ministry's Department for Macroeconomic Forecasting. Under an optimistic scenario, he said, the GDP would grow 5.9 per cent in 2005, 6 per cent in 2006 and 6.1 per cent in 2007. Under a more conservative scenario, based on the oil price of $20 per barrel, the Russian economy would grow 5 per cent in 2005, 4.8 per cent in 2006, and 4.8 per cent in 2007. According to Mr. Klepach, the effectiveness of the economy will increase. He said investment in Russia was expected to rise 10.4 per cent in 2004, retail trade–8.9 per cent, and paid consumer services–5.6 per cent. Under a more conservative scenario, manufacturing growth in 2004 is projected to be 6.3 per cent, 5.8 per cent in 2006 and 5.7 per cent in 2007. A slowdown in manufacturing growth will be largely due to lower oil production and growing competition. Retail trade is expected to rise by 8 per cent in 2005.

Mr. Klepach stressed that an annual growth of 6 per cent was not enough to double the GDP by 2010. In his opinion, under the circumstances, Russia is unlikely to achieve this goal. "We do not have a planned economy. Potentially, we can grow faster, but we need not only directions from above: much depends on the performance of Russian companies," the official said. "We need time and serious decisions, as well as an appropriate strategy for oil industries," he added.

In Mr. Klepach's opinion, if business and the government offer a new strategy, these plans will be more realistic. According to him a 10 per cent annual inflation is a high rate for Russia. In January-April 2003, inflation was 4.6 per cent, against 6.2 per cent in the same period last year. In May 2003, inflation was 0.8 per cent.

Mr. Klepach said the rouble had strengthened against the dollar by 5.3 per cent 6 in real terms in January-April 2004, and the rouble's real exchange rate against the euro was up 8.3 per cent. The rouble strengthened by 5.6 per cent against the basket of currencies of Russia's main trade partners. The rouble is expected to strengthen 6 per cent against the basket of currencies in January-May 2004.

The rouble's real exchange rate against the dollar rose 5.2 per cent in the first quarter of 2004, and the rouble strengthened against the dollar by 6 per cent in real terms. The rouble's real effective exchange rate was up 4.7 per cent.

According to Mr. Klepach, Russia's trade surplus was $24 billion in January-April 2004, and exports amounted to $51 billion, up 23 per cent compared with January-April 2003, while imports increased 21 per cent to $27 billion. He further said the Macroeconomic Forecasting Department was going to revise its industrial production forecast for 2004 from 5.9 per cent to 6.1 per cent. According to him, industrial production was up 7.4 per cent in January-April 2004 compared to the same period a year earlier. In April, manufacturing growth was 6.7 per cent.

However, In March, Russia's industrial growth was 0 per cent compared with February, while the GDP continued to grow, Russian Economy Minister German Gref said at a meeting of Russian President Vladimir Putin.

The World Bank will invest $1 billion to 1.5 billion in Russia over the next three years, World Bank President, James Wolfensohn told reporters recently. According to him, Russia-World Bank relations have become more mature. Mr. Wolfensohn said Russia had significant resources at the moment, and it did not need aid from international financial organisations, but the World Bank continued cooperating with Russia, acting as a "knowledge bank".

It is relevant to mention here that Russia raised the volume of oil exports from 15.7 per cent to 55.08 metric tons in January-March 2004, compared to that in the corresponding period of 2003, the Federal Customs Service reported. The amount of oil export revenues reached $10.28 billion during the first three months of 2004, exceeding the corresponding figure for January-March of last year by 17.2 per cent. The volume of oil exports to non-CIS countries reached 49.19 metric tons, totaling $9.37 billion, and the volume of exports to CIS countries amounted to 5.89 metric tons, totaling $912.8 m.

The export of oil products reached 18.41 metric tons in January-March 2004 (a decrease by 11.7 per cent). The volume of gasoline export amounted to 1.19 metric tons, totaling $307.5 m, and the export of diesel fuel reached 7.03 metric tons, totaling $1.73 m.

48.7 billion cubic m of gas, totaling $5.4 billion, were exported during January-March 2004, of which 39.5 billion cubic m were supplied to non-CIS countries. The export of electrical power reached 4.96 billion kilowatt-hours, totaling $116.7 m.

The proportion of fuel and energy products in the total volume of exports to non-CIS countries reached 59.3 per cent in January-March 2004 (compared to 64.3 per cent in January-March of last year).

For the whole of 2004 the ministry forecasts a growth in oil production of 6.9 per cent to 450 million tons, in gas production by 1.1 per cent to 627 billion cubic metres.

In the first quarter of 2004, the volume of exports from Russia exceeded imports almost by 100 per cent. The Russian Federal State Statistics Service's report says that exports totalled $37,289 million (a 20 per cent growth against the same period in 2003), and imports, $19,195 million (21.3 per cent).

In the first quarter of 2004, the foreign trade turnover of the Russian Federation on the methodology of the balance of payment in the established prices totalled $56,684 million exceeding the indices of the first quarter of 2003 by 20.4 per cent.

Russia's foreign trade turnover in March 2004 totalled $21,128 million, which exceeds the figures of the same period last year by 20.3 per cent. In March 2004, the volume of exports from the Russian Federation totalled $13,552 million (16.9 per cent), imports $7,576 million (26.7 per cent).

The volume of export operations with countries outside of the CIS totalled in the first quarter $31,370 million, which exceeds last year's figures by 18.4 per cent; in March the export volume totalled $11,244 million (13.7 per cent). For imports, these data were correspondingly for the first quarter and for March $15,251 million and $6,033 million (growth by 19.7 per cent and 24.4 per cent).

The volumes of trade operations with the CIS countries for the accounting period also grew. Thus, the exports totalled in the first quarter $5,919 million, which exceeds last year's figures by 29.2 per cent; in March, the volume of exports was $2,308 million (35.4 per cent). For imports, these data were correspondingly for the first quarter and March $3,944 million and $1,543 million (growth by 27.8 per cent and 36.8 per cent).

The balance of payment is formed by the Bank of Russia in line with the Federal Law on the Central Bank of Russia. It is a statistical report that reflects all foreign economic operations of the Russian Federation with other countries. Foreign trade is the component part of the account of current operations of the balance of payment. Foreign trade includes data of the customs statistics of the foreign trade, data on the volumes of exports (imports) of goods, as well as additional calculations of the Bank of Russia to the statistical data on foreign trade.

It is in this background that an objective estimate should be made on the potentialities of Indo-Russian economic cooperation.

Indo-Russian Economic Cooperation

India is a large and long-term market for Russia's defence exports and exports of oil and hydrocarbons. Russia has security and trading interests in the northern reaches of the Indian Ocean. A friendly India straddling the Indian Ocean rim is and will be—a strategic asset to the Russian leadership. Russia, like India, has a plural civil society. It is, therefore, concerned about preserving its multi-dimensional national identity, an interest, which India shares in terms of its national consolidation. While Russia has adjusted to its diminished international stature, it believes in the creation of a multi-polar world order.

Russia has proved to be a reliable partner in the transfer of sophisticated technologies of use to India—despite the expanding restrictive regimes sought to be imposed on transfer of such technologies. Russia is not only a large expanding market for Indian exports across the board—from raw materials to finished products—but is also a market for Indian investment and joint collaboration projects.

There is also a progressive concretisation of these interests in bilateral relations. Russia and India have managed the transition from economic and technological interaction conducted under governmental arrangements to the conduct of these relations by private sectors. A wide range of inter-State and inter-departmental agreements have been put in place over the last four years in a number of specialised spheres. These are implemented and monitored by a Russia India inter-governmental commission on trade, economics, scientific and technological cooperation.

Russian companies are now participating in the construction of nuclear and hydel-power plants, highways, modernisation and construction of steel plants, mining, oil and gas exploration in the Arabian Sea and the Bay of Bengal, as well as in the Northeastern States. Russian companies are also involved in aluminium production, modernisation of railways, construction of water desalination plants and subways in India. The largest foreign investment of an Indian company has been made in Russia: ONGC-Videsh Limited has invested $1.7 billion for the development of oil and gas supplies at the Sakhalin-I Project in the Russian far east as pointed out by Mr. J.N. Dixit former Foreign Secretary in one of his articles.

Indo-Russian Trade Growing

Indo-Russian commerce, which had declined in the decade following the dissolution of the former Soviet Union, shows signs of renewal. There are commissions in place to oversee the economic revival, in which the Russian and Indian leaderships have invested considerable political will.

With their economy moving into a higher, more profitable gear, Russian businesses are viewing the Indian market with renewed interest, as are their Indian counterparts, whose presence in Russia becomes more visible by the day.

Russia has significant technology to offer, at prices that are better suited to Indian pockets than those on offer from the West. Russian science and technology are world class, as Indian buyers are discovering.

Both sides are also ripe for collaborative ventures in many fields. Recent statistics reveal a quantum leap in Indo-Russian trade, from an annual $1.5 billion to $3.3 billion over the past two years. The pointers encourage further optimism. For instance, the Russian company Techno-prom-export has won a tender to modernise the Obra thermal power plant, the Leningrad Metal Works is in the running for the contract to build the Naria Mangalam HEP plant, while Gazprom is negotiating a tender to develop Indian oil and gas fields. For its part, India's ONGC has invested $1.7 billion in Russia's Sakhalin oil exploration, and Russia, in turn, is helping construct a 2,000 mw nuclear power plant - a technological marvel, say experts - on India's Tamil Nadu coast.

An attempt was made to revive the mechanism of 'ordered' trade in a modified form under the Indo-Russian Trade and Economic Agreement signed in May 1992. However, during President Yeltsin's visit to India in January 1993, it was decided that instead of being governed by inter governmental protocols, Indo-Russian trade should be conducted as per normal international practice.

In January 1993, a debt repayment agreement was also reached which provided for an annual repayment of about US $ 1 billion equivalent in rupees to Russia over a period of 12 years with smaller amounts thereafter for a further period of 33 years. The rupee debt funds were to be used by the Russian side for import of goods and trade-related services from India. Approximately 80 per cent of Indian exports to Russia are routed through the rupee debt funds. In the EXIM policy announced for financial year 1999-2000, the value addition norms under the rupee trade regime were recognised at par with dollar exports (i.e., 33.5 per cent uniformly for all goods). Russian exports to India are against freely convertible currencies.

The rupee debt funds are maintained in a central account with RBI. Under a 3 year perspective plan, which came to an end in 1997 for purchase of certain commodities / goods, a part of the rupee debt funds was allocated for import of tea, tobacco, soya meal and pharmaceuticals by designated Russian agencies. The balance was allocated to various states or importing organisations in Russia on the basis of rouble coverage or was auctioned.

In January 1998, this mechanism was replaced with a weekly auction of rupee debt funds conducted by the Vnesheconom Bank (Bank for Foreign Economic Affairs). At the 5th session of the Indo-Russian Inter Governmental Commission (IGC) held in November 1998, the Russian side informed that rupee debt funds would be utilised both through auctions and allocations. During 1999, allocations made for import of pharmaceuticals and medical equipment from India were utilised by several Ministries of the Russian Federation. Since 2000, the utilisation of rupee funds has continued through the auctions.

In 1998-1999 India's exports to Russia totalled Rs. 3,038 crore as against Rs.3,306 crore in the preceding year. Russia's exports to India were Rs. 2,526 crore and Rs. 2,221 crore in 1997-1998 and 1998-1999, respectively. In 1999-2000 Indian exports picked up to reach a level of Rs. 4,107 crore (US $950 million). In rupee terms exports recorded an increase of 40.8 per cent (in dollar terms 36.6 per cent) over the corresponding period of 1998-1999. Russian exports to India also increased to Rs. 2,700 crore (US $ 620 million). In 2000-2001 India's exports to Russia totalled Rs. 4,054.65 crore as against Rs.4,107.23 crore in the preceding year. Russia's exports to India were Rs. 2,344.46 crore and Rs. 2,700.43 crore in 2000-2001 and 1999-2000, respectively. In 1999-2000 Indian exports picked up and recorded an increase of almost 40 per cent (in dollar terms 36.6 per cent) over the corresponding period of 1998-99. However, it declined marginally by 1.28 per cent (in rupee terms) and 6.36 per cent (in dollar terms) in 2000-01.

Statistics on Indo-Russian bilateral trade turnover are as follows:

Rs. In billion *(in brackets in US$ billion*)

Year	*Indian Exports*	*Indian Imports*	*Turnover*	*% Change*
1993-1994	20.05 (0.67)	8.10 (0.27)	28.15 (0.94)	N.A.
1994-1995	25.41 (0.85)	15.72 (0.52)	41.13 (1.37)	44
1995-1996	35.03 (1.16)	28.53 (0.94)	63.56 (2.1)	54
1996-1997	27.66 (0.92)	22.30 (0.74)	49.96 (1.66)	(-)21.4
1997-1998	33.06 (1.07)	25.26 (0.81)	58.31 (1.88)	14.1
1998-1999	30.38 (0.72)	22.21 (0.53)	52.59 (1.25)	(-) 23.3
1999-2000	41.22 (0.95)	26.75 (0.65)	67.97 (1.57)	31.27
2000-2001	39.68 (0.869)	23.59 (0.516)	63.27 (1.385)	(-) 6.91
2001-2002	38.07 (0.798)	25.54 (0.536)	63.61 (1.334)	0.53
2002-2003	33.76 (0.698)	28.53 (0.589)	62.29 (1.287)	(-) 2.05

Source: DGCI & S.

Main items of export from India are tea (share in total export to Russia in 2000-2001 constitutes 13.38 per cent), readymade cotton garment (23.42 per cent), drugs and pharmaceuticals (12.25 per cent), cotton yarn and fabrics (7.53 per cent), coffee (7.06 per cent), readymade woollen garments (4.06 per cent) unmanufactured tobacco (3.09 per cent), readymade synthetic fibre garments (2.60 per cent) etc. Major imports from Russia were manufactured fertilisers (16.78 per cent), nonferrous metals (11.51 per cent), newsprint (12.39 per cent), iron and steel (19.69 per cent), etc.

According to a market research on "Indian Goods on the Russian Market" conducted by the COMCON Research International in August-September, 2000 for the India Trade Promotion Organisation (ITPO), Moscow, although the basic image of Indian goods is favourable, India is still perceived as an agrarian country.

The stereotype of India as a low-tech country makes Russian consumers suspicious of such Indian products as software, machinery and auto-spares. In recent years Indian products have virtually disappeared from the Russian market, and the images of India and Indian goods have somewhat faded. A study notes that the trade between Russia and India within the framework of debt repayment scheme has generally been detrimental to market mechanisms and that the system of rebates granted to some Russian traders has been more corruptive than helpful leading to illegal re-export of Indian goods to third countries.

Main items of export from India are readymade cotton garments (share in total export to Russia in 2002-2003 constitutes 30.08 per cent), drugs and pharmaceuticals (14.73 per cent), tea (8.13 per cent), coffee (6.27 per cent), processed minerals (5.46 per cent), unmanufactured tobacco (3.45 per cent), etc. Major imports from Russia were iron and steel (17.50 per cent), manufactured fertilisers (14.54 per cent), nonferrous metals (11.55 per cent), newsprint (10.30 per cent), etc.

Initiatives have been taken to bridge the information gap between the business sectors by trying to bring them together on common platforms and through increased exposure to each other's market. Rapid expansion in both economies has led to emergence of new capabilities and requirements. The Joint Business Council (FICCI & RFCCI) was revived in February 2003. A large Indian trade exhibition was held in Moscow in the same month. The number of visiting trade delegations is increasing. Russian companies are also bidding for projects in India. Several new sectors have started getting attention including automobiles and components, engineering goods, plastics, food processing, tourism, IT and telecom.

Contacts between commercial banks and financial institutions have expanded. A commercial bank promoted by State Bank of India and Canara Bank is due to commence operation in Moscow in 2004. More Russian Banks are opening their representative offices in India. EXIM Bank has extended two separate lines of credit worth US $10 million and 25 million to two Russian Banks. An additional Line of Credit to a third bank is being negotiated. The ECGC has signed a Cooperative Agreement with Vneshtorg Bank.

The Indo-Russian Inter-Governmental Cornmission (IRIGC) was set up through an agreement signed on May 4, 1992, during the visit to India of Russian State Secretary, H. E. Mr. Gennady Burbulis. Twelve Working Groups are constituted under the IGC. According to the agreement, the IRIGC is to meet at least once a year. The IRIGC has held nine sessions till date, the first in Moscow (September 1994); the second in New Delhi (October 1995), the third in Moscow (February 1997); the fourth in New Delhi (December, 1997); the fifth in Moscow (November 1998); the sixth in New Delhi (January 2000); the seventh in Moscow (January 2001) and, the eighth in New Delhi on 7 February 2002. In addition, the Co-Chairmen of the IRIGC meet for an inter-sessional review. The last meeting of the IRIGC was held in Moscow in May 2003.

Conclusion

This study shows after the disintegration of the Soviet Union, Indo-Russian relations have been elevated once again to new heights. The moral of this trend is that Indo-Russian strategic partnership has begun to assume a new economic content and if this trend develops,Indo-Russian relations will become a major stimulus in building a multipolar world. In this connection one important factor should be kept in the forefront. Russia is one of the biggest oil producing countries in the world and it has begun to wield this instrument to carve out a significant role in the political economy of the world.

"Russia has embarked on a new geopolitical game, playing its energy card to reclaim global clout. Its vast energy reserves and control over the markets in the former Soviet Union are to be leveraged to turn Russia into a superpower. As global energy demand soars, the Russian President, Vladimir Putin, wants to position Russia as a key broker in the international market and use oil and gas exports as instruments to speed up the country's economic revival and enhance its geopolitical weight."

"After dropping nearly 50 per cent from the Soviet era peak, Russia's oil output has soared again to exceed 450 million tonnes together with gas condensates by the end of the current year making it the world's second largest producer behind only Saudi Arabia. Total oil reserves are a State secret in Russia, but the former Energy

Minister, Yuri Shafranik estimates that Russia may have 44 billion tonnes of oil more than Saudi Arabia does. Russia currently exports over 6.5 million barrels a day, taking crude oil and product together and plans to boost exports to about 9 million barrels a day by the end of the decade - roughly equal to Saudi Arabia's current exports", according to a columnist, Vladimir Radyuhin.

It is relevant to mention here that Russian President Vladimir Putin has sent a message to Indian Prime Minister, Dr. Manmohan Singh. He has underlined in this message "I am confident that the policy of strengthening strategic partnership will continue to provide a solid basis for multifaceted Russian-Indian cooperation in bilateral, regional and global affairs. I firmly count on your personal support for this endeavour". He did not leave at that. He said, Dr. Manmohan Singh "is the man who had launched major economic reforms that helped transform India into a leading global power". President Putin has visited India for an annual bilateral summit in December 2004. High-level meetings between the leaders of the two countries have given a new momentum to the bilateral and multilateral relations.

14
Economic Cooperation between India and Russia

R K Wadhwa

Foreign trade occupies an important place in the process of economic development of a country. Mercantilists advocated all measures to increase international trade. The protagonists of free trade doctrine have argued for long that it benefits all the participant countries. David Ricardo formulated the comparative cost theory to prove this proposition. J S Mill modified it and others also intended to put forth the gains from trade. However, the pattern of international trade, more specially between developed and underdeveloped countries, tells the story of pauperization and exploitation of the later by the former. Gunnar Myrdal has noted that the developed countries had an obvious interest in using the dependent countries as markets for the products of their manufacturing industries and forced a pattern of trade on dependent countries that was decisively oriented towards export of primary goods at cheap prices from the latter to their home countries. The trade relations between England and India during the pre-Independence period are a glaring example of this exploitation.

Historical Perspective

During the two hundred years of the alien rule the development of Indian economy was distorted to suit the British imperialists. Consequently on the eve of Independence, Indian economy was colonial in character. It was by no means independent. Another feature of Indian economy on the eve of independence was the domination by British capital. It held strategic positions in the industrial sector. The dominance of foreign capital was, to a great extent, responsible for the lopsided development of Indian economy. Foreign capital and the British government were positively against the development of an independent Indian economy. They did not like India developing those industries which would drive their own products from the Indian market. The high profitability of marketing here of capital goods produced in Britain discouraged them from organising their production in India.

When India got independence it was looking for building up a strong independent industrialized economy. The so-called growth economists and development specialists from the Western world suggested that out of the three important factors of production, i.e., land (natural resources), labour, and capital, the country had the first two but lacked the third one, i.e., capital. They suggested that there could be two sources of capital (i) internal and (ii) external. Since the national income of India was very low, the amount of domestic capital formation was not of much significance. The other alternative was to approach Western countries and international institutions like World Bank which were dominated by them. As the stock of foreign exchange at the disposal of the country was limited, the only option left before India was the 'aid' from the western countries, but that could be secured only when India fashioned its policies and strategy of development according to the dictates of the 'aid-givers' - which in other words meant no escape from neo-colonialisam or hope of building up an independent economy for India. Besides, the Western countries and the World Bank opposed India's move to build a public sector and establish basic and heavy industries.

The only country which correctly understood the significance of India's strategy of economic development was the Soviet Union. If one looks deeper in the happenings since 1950, one will find that Indo-Soviet economic cooperation has contributed a great deal to enable India to preserve its political independence, sovereignty and territorial integrity. Not only this, it has made them more secure by helping India build an independent national economy. The significance of this statement will be clear if we look back at the path traversed by the Indian economy since Independence.

The construction of an iron and steel plant in Bhilai was one of the first industrial projects to come up in public sector. Soviet assistance to India had a purposeful character from the outset. It is true that it looked like credit coming from any other source, but who else in the world in the 1950s offered India even commercial credit for the construction of steel plants and heavy engineering works? The importance of Bhilai is determined first of all by the fact that it opened a highly important chapter in the history of the Third World. For the first time assistance rendered to a Third World country was channeled into accelerating the development of an independent economy.

Indo-Soviet Cooperation

The greatest significance of India's trade and economic cooperation with the Soviet Union lies in the fact that it gave India an opportunity to overcome its colonial legacy at a crucial period in its history, when the country was asserting its policy of non-alignment and economic independence.

The Soviet Union's assistance to India in building about 70 large industrial enterprises and other projects in the public sector formed the nucleus of the national economy, the basis for stepping up the rate of extended reproduction. The building of large enterprises in key industries immediately affected several branches of the national economy, leading, in the final analysis, to a comprehensive and balanced economic development. The enterprises built in cooperation with the Soviet Union contributed 80 per cent of India's production of metallurgical equipment, and hydraulic turbines for power stations, over 50 per cent of its oil production, 30 per cent of oil processing, 30 per cent of the country's steel output and a substantial part of its power generation.

A remarkable feature of Soviet assistance to India has been that enterprises built with Soviet assistance belong wholly to India. The Soviet Union does not own a single shop at the state-owned enterprises and does not participate in the distribution of their profit.

A significant trend in the development of Soviet-India economic and technical cooperation was the help given to India in building projects which were economically inter-connected. For instance, the Soviet Union had rendered assistance in the construction of a mining complex for the extraction of iron ore, coal and limestone as raw materials to be used by steel plants and heavy machine-building enterprises. For this purpose it had provided the necessary personnel, training programmes and the services of design organisations. Another project dealt with the prospecting, extraction and processing of oil and gas and the training of personnel.

India's cooperation with the Soviet Union accelerated the pace of the country's industrialization. The importance of Indo-Soviet economic and technical cooperation was universally recognized by statesmen, politicians and the general public in India.

"The Soviet Union has given us many precious gifts; the most precious gifts of these is friendship." —*Jawaharlal Nehru*

"Today, we have the best of relations with the Soviet Union, and we are the best of friends." —*Lal Bahadur Shastri*

"I should like to express our deep appreciation of the invaluable help that Indo-Soviet cooperation has brought to us in our advance towards a self reliant, modern industrial economy. A special feature of this help is that it flows into our state sector, to which we have assigned a vital role in our planning, and more particularly into key branches of industry, such as metallurgy, machine-building, oil and power generation, on which the future growth of the economy so largely depends."—*Indira Gandhi*

The emergence of Soviet power was welcomed by Indian patriotic opinion as a positive factor contributing to the final liberation of the oppressed people. This is what India's two greatest sons wrote about the Great October Socialist Revolution of 1917:

"There is no questioning the fact that the Bolshevik ideal has behind it the purest sacrifices of countless men and women who have given up their all for its sake; and the ideal that is sanctified by sacrifices of such master spirits as Lenin cannot go in vain; the noble example of their renunciation will be emblazoned for ever and quicken and purify the ideal as time passes." (Mahatma Gandhi, *Young India,* 1928).

"I have no doubt that the Soviet Revolution had advanced human society by a great leap and had lit a bright flame which could not be smothered, and that it had laid the foundations for that new civilization towards which the world could advance." *(Jawaharlal Nehru, Discovery of India).*

Indo-Soviet Trade

Economic and trading relations between India and the Soviet Union date back to the fifth century when Armenian merchants had established trade relations with the Indian people. In the 17th century, a group of Armenians settled in Kolkata played an important role in the economic life of the country. Indian traders were also active at Astrakhan and in the Volga delta region during the same period. Indian black pepper, ginger, sandalwood, handlooms and other commodities were, thus, well-known in ancient and medieval Russia. After the victory of the Great October Socialist Revolution in Russia, the first Soviet products to enter the Indian market, in 1925, were crude oil, petrol, kerosene and sugar. But trade contacts between the two countries were reduced to nil by the British colonialists. However, the first Soviet trade agency was established in Kolkata in 1943 and her trade ties with India, though very much restricted, revealed the wide potential of expansion once India gained Independence.

Since 1950s a sea change has come about in both the direction and the composition of India's foreign trade. For this the Indo-Soviet economic cooperation has been, to a large extent, responsible. Moreover, the Indo-Soviet cooperation has been the initiator of a number of novelties in bilateral trade relations.*

Trade Growth in the Pre-Disintegration Period

The trading relation between the two countries is not altogether new. But its total amount was almost negligible during the British rule. On the eve of planning in 1950-51, total trade turnover between the two countries stood at Rs 1.56 crore. For the three years before the signing of the first five-year trade agreement, the average annual

* Taliking of the trade relations and economic cooperation an official document of the UNCTAD (UNCTAD IV: Trade Relations Among Countries Having Different Economic and Social Systems, Nairobi, May 1976, page 7) has said: "Economic relations have been extended on a larger basis to cover some new field of activities, such as cooperation and sepecialisation in production. A valuable contribution to the development of their mutual trde has been made through various new approaches and institutional innovations, such as the conclusion of a considerable number of inter-governmental agreements on technical and scientific cooperation in addition to traditional trade and economic cooperation agreements, setting up of permanent mixed intergovernmental commissions and establishments in some cases of working groups on cooperation in planning, etc."

trade turnover was Rs 3.65 crore. After that trade relations between the two countries have been governed by the five year bilateral trade agreements. Indo-Russia trade relations occupy an important place in a comprehensive and diverse complex of politico-economic relations between the two countries. Starting with a modest trade turnover of Rs 1.56 crore in 1950-51, the Indo-Soviet trade registered a phenomenal and impressive growth at Rs 7803 crore in 1990-91. As a result, total trade turnover between the two countries increased from 0.12 per cent of India's total trade in 1950-51 to a peak of 11.63 per cent in 1980-81, and marginally dropped to 11.45 per cent in 1990-91. While India's exports to USSR grew from 0.22 per cent in 1950-51 to a peak of 21.28 per cent during 1981-82, India's imports from USSR rose from 0.034 per cent to 8.36 per cent during the period. The decade of 80s experienced wide fluctuations both in India's exports and imports. By the year 1990-91 while the exports dipped to 16.14 per cent, imports declined to 6.05 per cent. The sluggishness in the trade could be attributed to collapsing prices of oil and oil products that created difficulties in Indo-Soviet trade and settlement.

The following graph shows the trend in Indo-Russian Bilateral Trade in the Pre-Disintegration period, i.e., 1950-51 to 1990-91 (Data in Table 1)

Fig. 1.

Trend in Indo-Russian Bilteral Trade in the Pre-Disintegration Period

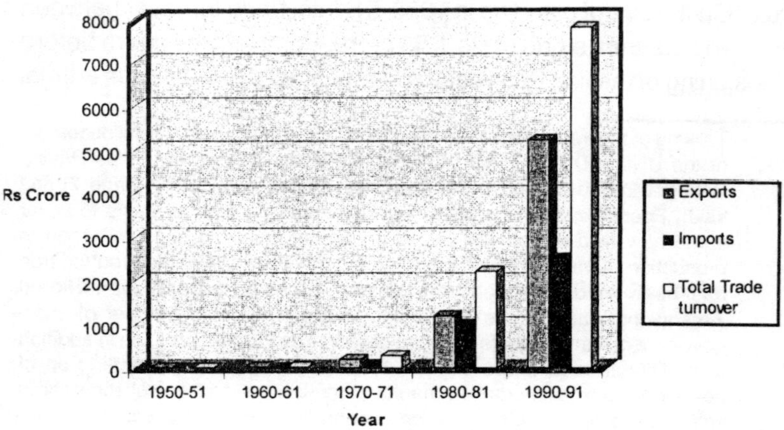

The important features of Indo-Soviet Trade Relations include:

1. Indo-Soviet trade relations have been based on the principle of equality and mutual benefit
2. Indian currency rupee has been accepted for the purpose of calculating the total trade turn over, and thus imposed no foreign exchange burden on India
3. They offer maximum opportunity to the two countries to develop their trade
4. The novel scheme of production cooperation between the two countries in the fourth trade agreement seemed to be primarily intended to help India tide over her difficulties arising out of the limited availability of foreign exchange and to overcome the teething troubles of nascent industries. Thus, through trade, the Soviet Union tried to render economic assistance to India.
5. The trade agreements provided stability in Indo-Soviet trading relations. This has been one of the most important features of Indo-Soviet trade. They ensured India about the quantity of goods to be exported to the Soviet Union in advance and enabled her to buy capital goods and equipments as well as other items required by her plans of economic development. This worked both as a preventive against import of non-essential items as well as an element of certainty in her exports.
6. The Soviet economic system has been free from uneven and cyclical changes faced by the capitalist countries, India is assured of firm demand and stable prices of her products. In this way, it made possible for India to enlist foreign trade as a mechanism of economic development in her national plan.
7. The Soviet Union neither seeks any indirect trade privileges nor any advantages other than agreed upon in trade agreements. And it does not oppose measures India wishes to take in order to protect her economy from foreign competition.
8. The shipping arrangements also save a lot of foreign exchange for India
9. They also intend to jointly cultivate markets in third countries which goes to expand the base of India's foreign trade in those countries
10. Trade and economic relations with Soviet Union have influenced western countries to make certain concessions to India in their trade and economic relations. Based on direct government to

government contracts, the entire earnings from export and import operation of Indo-Soviet trade accrue to the Indian Government.

Gains for India

The three decades of Indo-Soviet Trade relations have shown that India enjoyed certain distinct advantages in her trade relations with the USSR. This enabled India to solve many of her problems faced in the course of trading relations with the rest of the world.

- India does not have BOP problem with the USSR. Trade agreements based on non-convertible rupee payments facility have successfully avoided them, while on the contrary India had to face the problem of huge deficits in her trade with the rest of the world.
- India had accumulated trade surpluses in her trade with the USSR which obliged the latter to supply more sophisticated and necessary items so badly needed by India to pursue her developmental programmes.
- In their trade relations, both the countries provide most favoured nations treatment to each other in custom duties and other taxes that helped India to increase her exports to Soviet Union.
- Indo-Soviet growing trade relations also helped India to diversify her trade with other East European countries also, who after being influenced by the successful implementation of the non-convertible rupee payment trade relationship with the Soviet Union concluded such agreements with India.
- Phenomenal growth and consequent diversification of India's trade with the Soviet Union and her East European COMECON allies strengthened India's bargaining position with the rest of the world. It ended India's full dependence on western markets for her import needs and opened up new vistas for her exports - traditional as well as manufactured non-traditional exports. This trade relationship enabled India to stand in good stead and now India finds herself in a better position to claim for better terms of trade in the Sterling and Dollar areas.

Indo-Russia Trade in the Post-Disintegration Period

Following the break-up of Soviet Union, while Russia's international trade has been growing, India's share has been falling.

Indo-Russian trade turnover has drastically slumped from US $ 5.5 billion in 1991 to US $ 1.2 billion in 2001 registering a decline of 78 per cent. The trade turnover in the year 2002, however, picked up by 73 per cent over the previous year. In rupee terms it has declined from Rs 7803 crore in 1990-91 to Rs. 6909 crore in 2002-2003 –a fall of 11 per cent. A sharp decline in the total trade was witnessed in the year 1992-93 immediately after the disintegration-a fall of 67 per cent in exports and 71 per cent in imports. Though in absolute terms the trade has experienced a rising trend with intermittent fluctuations in subsequent years, in per centage terms the share has continued to decline - witnessing a steep fall from 11.45 per cent in 1990-91 to a low of 1.26 per cent in 2002-03. The following graph shows the trend in Indo-Russia Bilateral Trade in the Post-Disintegration period (1991-92 to 2002-03) (Date in Table 2).

Fig. 2.

Trend in Indo-Russian Bilateral Trade in the Post-Disintegration Period (Rs Crore)

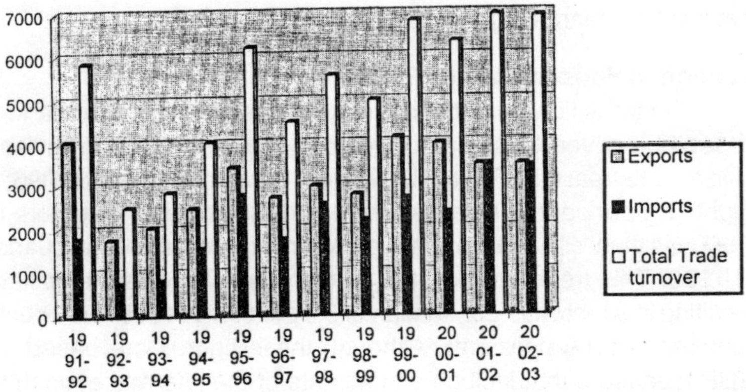

One of the reasons for the decline in Indo-Russia–trade could be that the bulk of the trade was being conducted with other republics of the USSR. Secondly, during the days of Soviet Union, public sector was playing an important role in setting up industrial units and it found economic cooperation with the Soviet Union more beneficial. The imports were paid for either in rupee or by exporting a part of the output of units set up with Soviet collaboration. Liberalisation, privatization, and globalization are the other important developments, which have been instrumental for both the countries to look towards West and European Union.

Though India continues to enjoy a favourable balance of trade with Russia even after the disintegration of USSR, the gap in the trade balance has come to zero in 2001-02. However, in 2002-03 India witnessed a marginal trade surplus of Rs 49 crore with Russia. It is also reported that the favourable balance of trade in the previous years was somewhat misleading as the trade figures did not include the purchase of Russian defence equipment by India, payments for which were made through Indian exports.

It is worthwhile mentioning here that apart from the official trade between the two countries, substantial amount of Indian goods enter Russia either by way of shuttle trade (brought by Russians visiting India in large numbers) or through export of Indian-origin goods to Russia from Singapore, Hong Kong, Thailand, Malaysia and Middle East. Similarly, India purchases industrial raw materials of Russian origin (e.g., metals scraps, fertilisers, paper and paper products) from Canada, USA and Israel due to absence of established Russian international marketing mechanisms.

Economic Performance of Russia

The transition from the centrally planned system to a market-based one severely disrupted the economy. According to revised official data, real GDP fell by 37 per cent between 1991 and 1996; a slight (1.4 per cent, previously estimated at 0.9 per cent) upturn in 1997 was then followed by renewed construction in the second quarter of 1998. This trend accelerated as the financial crisis intensified, resulting in a real GDP contraction of 5.3 per cent in 1998 (previously estimated at 4.9 per cent). Although these figures are based on GDP measures that include an estimate of the informal economy, they probably overstate the depth of the post-Soviet depression, owing to the exaggeration of Soviet-era output and the possibility that estimates of the growth in unrecorded activity are still too low, despite frequent revisions.

Nonetheless, the most important reasons for the length and depth of the post-Soviet depression, which exceeded post-communist output contractions in most of central Europe, include the following:

- the much longer period of communism and central planning;
- the unraveling of economic ties attendant on the collapse of the Soviet Union, and the subsequent replacement of the rouble zone by a number of non convertible currencies;
- sharp falls in the production of a range of goods for which demand collapsed as a result of the shift from planners' to consumers' preferences, and the resulting shrinkage of the state sector;
- the length of time to achieve macroeconomic stabilization and impose hard budget constrains on entries; and
- high levels of political uncertainty, which fuelled doubts about the durability of reforms.

Although it preceded the financial collapse, the resumption of Russia's output decline was caused by many of the factors that eventually destroyed the government's stabilization strategy: falling prices for Russia's principal export commodities, investor nervousness and the monetary tightening that took place as the RCB attempted to defend the beleaguered rouble.

The sharp devaluation of the rouble in August 1998 (the real effective exchange rate collapsed by some 45 per cent in 1998-99) delivered a stronger than expected boost to the Russian economy. Gross industrial output, which had fallen continuously since 1990, jumped by 9.4 per cent in 1999 (on a value-added basis; previously estimated at 7.5 per cent), as Russian enterprises took advantage of the gains in competitiveness brought about by the devaluation. Record high international oil prices helped to sustain the recovery in 2000, when industrial output rose by another 12.4 per cent (previously 10.6 per cent), and this underpinned real GDP growth of 10 per cent (previously 9 per cent)–the best economic performance in 30 years. Growth slowed in 2001 and 2002, to 5 per cent and 4.3 per cent respectively, and the engine of growth shifted from net exports to domestic demand. Investment spending held up well in 2001 but slumped in 2002, and it remains heavily concentrated in oil and gas, as well as the public sector. An investment recovery in early 2003 appeared to support the claim that the 2002 investment collapse was mainly a statistical artifact induced by the tax changes introduced at the start of the year.

Retail trade and services, which have undergone a dramatic transformation since 1991, accounted for 54 per cent of GDP in 2002, compared with less than 36 per cent in 1990. The share of agriculture in total output has fallen from 14 per cent in 1991 to 5 per cent in 2002. However, this collapse led to underemployment among rural labourers, and therefore agriculture still accounted for more than 13 per cent of official employment in 2000. Industry, which accounted for almost half of total GDP in 1990, saw its share fall to 30.5 per cent in 2002.

As a result of central planning and resource endowments, the industrial sector is heavily skewed towards heavy industries. Fuels and energy account for almost 20 per cent of industrial output, and metallurgy for around 17 per cent. Once electricity (10 per cent) and food (14-15 per cent) are added, it becomes clear that manufacturing of high technology and consumer goods makes up a very small part of the Russian economy. Machine-building and metalworking remains the largest processing industry, accounting for just under 20 per cent of industrial production in 2001, followed by chemicals. The fastest growth since the rouble-devaluation in 1998 has been seen in the sectors that suffered most during 1992-98, including light industry; however, light industry accounts for less than 2 per cent of industrial output.

Pattern of Russia's International Trade

The disintegration of the Soviet Union in 1991 into 15 independent Republics has had positive effects on the trade fronts. Russia's total foreign trade turnover grew rapidly in 1992-97 witnessing an increase of 83.5 per cent from US $ 75 billion to US $ 137 billion. The years 1998 and 1999, however, experienced a fall in the foreign trade by 16.8 per cent and 25.5 per cent respectively mainly due to the weak domestic demand and the rouble crisis. The recovery in the foreign trade of Russia started in the year 2000 by attaining the 1997 level of US $ 137 billion and further increased to US $ 153 billion in 2002–an increase of 11.6 per cent. The following graph shows the trend in International Trade of Russia during 1992-2002 (Data in Table 3)

Fig. 3.

Trend in International Trade of Russia (US $ Mn)

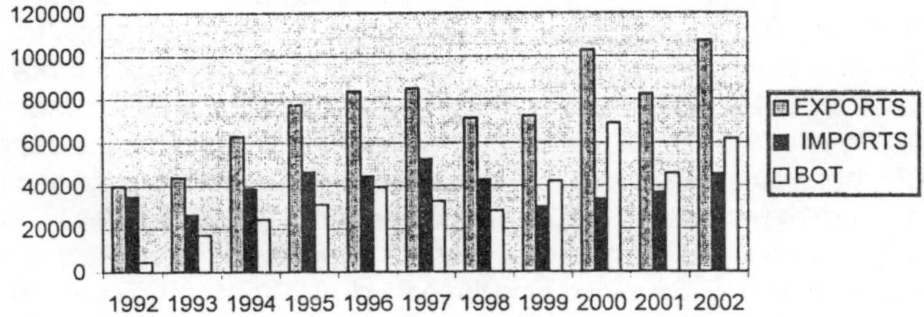

The disruption of payment arrangements with other former Soviet Republics (alongwith their ability to pay) and the evident constraints of the autarky attempted under communism made integration with the world economy a priority for reformers. The economy which till 1989 was experiencing a trade deficit to the tune of US $ 17 billion recorded a trade surplus of US $ 5 billion for the first time in 1992. Although collapsing domestic demand led to a sharp fall in imports in 1993, exports grew strongly, leading to large trade surpluses. The main spurs for this export growth were weak domestic demand for raw materials and semi-finished goods, an undervalued rouble exchange rate, and the profit to be gained from diverting previously subsidized intra-Soviet exports to hard-currency markets where world prices could be charged. Imports subsequently picked up as well. The collapse of rouble in 1998 had an adverse impact on exports which for the first time declined by 16 per cent. The imports too recorded a negative growth of 18 per cent in 1998 and further declined by 29 per cent in 1999. The continued reform process, however, gave a boost to growth in foreign trade that witnessed a rise of 33.2 per cent in 2000 over the previous year.

Since 1992 the trade surplus has been on the rise and grown more than 12 times at US $ 62 billion in 2002 with a peak level of US $ 69 billion achieved in 2000. While exports grew by 168 per cent in 2002 at US $ 107 billion from US $ 40 billion in 1992, imports witnessed an increase of 30 per cent during the period.

Direction of Trade

Following collapse of the Soviet Union, there has been a dramatic shift in the direction of Russia's foreign trade. Its closer move to the West in general and European Union in particular is considered to be the major contributing factor for the big shift. Not only share of developing countries like India but of CIS countries (formerly Soviet Republics) has declined. As could be seen from Table 2, the Indo-Russian trade got a setback from Rs 7803 crore in 1990-91 to Rs 6909 crore in 2002-03—a drop in the share of India's total trade from 11.45 per cent to 1.26 per cent. Similarly, the share of other Soviet Republics in Russia's exports drastically declined to around 14 per cent in 2002 from 70 per cent in 1990. However, the share of non-CIS countries in Russia's imports has increased to 70 per cent from 47 per cent during the period. In 2002 non-CIS countries accounted for 83 per cent of Russia's foreign trade turnover, with the EU alone, accounting for more than one-third. Germany is the major trading partner in the EU and accounted for 14 per cent of total trade in 2002. CIS markets, however, remain important for exporters in such sectors as machine building, where products are not competitive in the West. Trade with former Comecon states, which fell sharply in 1992-94, has also begun to cover.

Outside the Soviet Union, most of Russia's communist-era trade was with client states within Comecon. Trade with the West was limited and sometimes involved the barter of raw materials for manufactured products. Problems with inter-enterprise payments and the break-up of the rouble zone into more than a dozen non-convertible currencies disrupted trade with the CIS. In addition, collapsing domestic demand led to rising exports of energy, minerals and semi-finished goods to non-CIS states. Russian imports from non-CIS countries also grew rapidly, prompted by the new demand for consumer and capital goods not available there and assisted by the rouble's real appreciation against the main currencies of the West during 1992-97.

Composition of Russia's Trade

Russia's exports are now dominated by fuels and metals as against engineering and metal products which were the main export categories at the time of the Soviet Union's disintegration. The end of Communist rule has not only paved the way for substantial realignment of prices turning fuels into the largest visible export but ended the economy's dependence on primary commodity exports that was concealed by their artificially low prices to countries belonging to the Council for Mutual Economic Assistance (CMEA or Comecon). Mineral fuels accounting for 55 per cent of total exports indicated a growth of 89.2 per cent at US $ 58 billion in 2002 from US $ 31 billion in 1998. Though metals are the second most important export product its share has declined from 21.6 per cent in 2000 to 14 per cent in 2002. Russia's modest success in selling steel and other metals abroad has made it a prime target of anti-dumping actions and other trade restrictions in developed market economies. Share of higher value-added exports like machinery and equipment, chemicals, pulp, paper, and other manufactures account for less than 20 per cent of total exports.

The import bill is mainly dominated by the import of machinery and transport equipment, and food and agricultural products which together constitute nearly 59 per cent of total imports into the country. Machinery and equipment (including cars) accounted for around 36 per cent of imports outside CIS states in 2002. The rise in import of food and agricultural products reflects the depleted state of Russian agriculture and its inability to cater for new consumer tastes. In absolute terms import of food and agricultural products has increased from US $ 8.1 billion in 1999 to US $ 10.3 billion in 2002 - an increase of 27 per cent. Imports of chemicals and metals have risen by 59 per cent and 32 per cent in 2002 over 1999.

Composition of Indo-Russia Trade

There has been a major shift in the composition of India's exports to Russia. As supplier of traditional and low value items like black pepper, tea, ginger, jute, sandalwood, handloom, etc. to the ancient and medieval Russia, India has now emerged as supplier of non-traditional and valued added items to Russia. During the year 2002-03 readymade garments as a group accounting for 37 per cent of India's exports to Russia has trebled from US $ 81 million in 1996-97 to US $ 256 million in 2002-03 in a span of six years which reflects that the Indian garments have wide acceptance among Russian consumers and is continuously growing. Among this group RMG of cotton include accessories alone accounted for 30 per cent of total exports in 2002-03 and witnessed a seven fold increase from US $ 30 million in 1996-97 to US $ 210 million in 2002-03. As against this export of cotton yarn, fabrics and made ups having witnessed a steady growth till 2000-01 suddenly dropped by 60 per cent in 2001-02 and further by 43.73 per cent in 2002-03. Tea, which was occupying the top position in the export basket till 1999-00, registered a fall of 45.84 per cent in 2002-2003. The drastic fall in exports of tea could be attributed to stiff competition from other global suppliers like Sri Lanka and Kenya. Transport equipment registering a nearly three-fold increase in 2002-03 over the previous year has emerged as the potential item of export. Export of drugs and pharmaceuticals has shown an upward trend over the last few years. Other potential items emerging in the India's export basket to Russia include coffee, processed fruits and juices, tobacco unmanufactured, processed minerals and other ores and minerals, iron ore, dyes, intermediates etc, handicrafts exclude handmade carpets, glass and glassware products, etc.

As regards imports, iron and steel accounting for 17 per cent of total imports has placed fertilizers with 15 per cent at the second position in 2002-03. The import demand of these commodities has been very erratic during 1996-97 and 2002-03. Import of non-ferrous metals has witnessed a steady decline and nearly halved in 2002-03 over 1996-97 level. As against this demand for synthetic and reclaimed rubber rose by nearly eight times during 1996-97 to 2002-03. Potential items of import interest to India which have shown a steady growth over the period include printed books, newspapers, etc, electronic goods, other crude minerals, pulses, manufactures of metals etc. Other principal items of import from Russia include non-electrical machinery, and coal & coke briquettes.

Indo-Russia-China Strategic Partnership

Russia as a Eurasian power is naturally interested in seeing Asia as a peaceful, sustainable, economically growing and integrated continent, free from geo-political rivalry or claims for dominance, whatever their source. Similar viewpoint has been expressed by the experts of India and China, the two major powers in Asia. In the recent years in the wake of globalisation the nations of the world have realized that if the economies want to achieve sustainable economic growth and development for the upliftment of the people, the nations have to be free from geo-political rivalry. To achieve this goal, the only option left before the nations is to foster trade and economic cooperation among themselves. Several initiatives in this direction have been under way between India-Russia-China like opening up the famous Silk Route, construction of Indo-Russia-Iran transport corridor which shall reduce one-third of transportation cost. Since India-Russia-China are industrially strong in the region these countries can think of strategic partnership in areas of mutual interest. Considering their strengths and weaknesses the three countries can join hands to increase productivity and avoid inter-se competition in various sectors like electronic components, laser technology, radar equipment, aircraft/spacecraft parts and spares, satellite navigation, household electric devices, education, banking and financial sector. Thus through mutual cooperation the countries can benefit from each other and export to the rest of the world.

Prospects of Trade and Economic Cooperation

India and Russia continue to sustain the close and cordial political relations in the post-Soviet era. In recent years both the countries have been pursuing the course for establishing a strategic partnership that is regarded as the ultimate form of relationship between the two independent states. This goal indeed demands that the present relationship be enhanced to a qualitatively new level, particularly in the trade and economic spheres. This is reflected in the exchange of visits between the two countries at the levels of heads of state and prime ministers, besides other political levels, exchange of trade delegations, etc. Several agreements and Memoranda of Understanding have been signed during these exchanges to further strengthen the economic relations. These agreements covering bilateral cooperation have been in the areas of telecommunications, air services, business, cultural, tourism, industrial, banking, financial, and scientific fields.

Several initiatives have also been taken by the Government of India to get Russian regions interested in India. In order to promote cooperation with the regions a Working Group has been set up under the Inter-governmental Joint Commission, the apex decision body for shaping bilateral ties. To encourage bilateral ties in the education field, the Government of India announced a grant of ten million roubles for opening a Centre for Indian Studies in the local universities of Russia. E-learning is another sector where India can help the young graduates of Russia to improve their skills.

Another area where both the countries can strengthen the bilateral ties is the rough diamonds, gems and jewellery sector. Russia being one of the largest producers of the diamonds in the world has an estimated production of 14 million carats, 80 per cent of which goes to the world market for sale through various channels. As against this India has the largest diamond processing capacity in the world and processes more than 100 million carats of rough diamonds out of the total estimated world annual production of 120 million carats. Having its strength in the processing, cutting and polishing of rough diamonds, India accounts for 80 per cent of the total annual trade of the polished diamonds.

Besides, Russia with an estimated production capacity of around 150 tons of gold per annum can find India a ready market because of its large consumption of gold, which is supplemented by the import to the tune of US $ 7 billion.

Conclusion

In view of the long-standing cordial, political, and economic relations between India and Russia, the prospects of strengthening Indo-Russian trade ties are bright. The frequent visits in recent years of the Russian President Putin to India is a testimony to strengthen the Indo-Russian ties. Several agreements, including a joint declaration on strengthening and enhancing cooperation in the economic, science and technology, telecom and IPR spheres were signed. The Delhi Declaration consolidated existing strategic partnership and charted out a broad agenda for cooperation in areas considered strategically important for both countries, and reiterated their commitment to tackling international terrorism. Taking a stock of the earlier agreements, leaders of both the states have recognized that there was a need to boost bilateral economic relations that have stagnated and even gone down over the last few years, and finally to take forward the long-standing defence cooperation between the two countries.

As regards trade relations, some blame can be put on to the attitude of our businessmen who have tended to take close relations with Russia for granted and did not pay much attention on the quality of their goods. This type of attitude has paved the way for other countries; especially China and Sri Lanka, to make inroads into sectors like tea and leather garments that were earlier dominated by Indian businessmen. It would be pertinent to mention that had the debt repayment mechanism not been there where Russia purchased Indian goods in return for defence purchases, the Indo-Russian trade would have been much lower. It is, therefore, high time that the Indian exporters should lay more emphasis on improving the quality of their goods and make them more competitive to make a mark in the now competitive Russian market. Concerted efforts may also be made on fostering joint ventures to enhance cooperation in education especially e-learning, banking and investment, hi-tech scientific and energy related areas.

Table 1. Trend in Indo-Russian Bilateral Trade in the Pre-Disintegration Period (1950-51 to 1990-91)

(Value: in Rs. Crore)

Year	*Exports*	*%Share*	*Imports*	*% Share*	*Total Trade turnover*
1950-51	1	0.22	0.22	0.034	1.56
1951-52	7	0.95	1	0.11	8
1952-53	1	0.17	0.24	0.036	1.24
1953-54	1	0.19	1	0.17	2
1954-55	2	0.34	2	0.30	4
1955-56	3	0.49	6	0.78	9
1956-57	16	2.58	17	1.88	33
1957-58	17	2.68	24	2.32	41
1958-59	26	4.54	17	1.88	43
1959-60	30	4.69	17	1.77	47
1960-61	29	4.52	16	1.43	45
1961-62	32	4.84	40	3.66	72
1962-63	38	5.55	60	5.31	98
1963-64	52	6.56	68	5.56	120
1964-65	78	9.56	79	5.86	157
1965-66	93	11.54	83	5.89	176
1966-67	125	10.80	112	5.39	237
1967-68	122	10.18	112	5.58	234
1968-69	148	10.90	192	10.06	340
1969-70	176	12.46	171	10.81	347
1970-71	210	13.68	105	6.43	315
1971-72	209	13.00	87	4.77	296
1972-73	305	15.47	114	6.11	419
1973-74	286	11.34	254	8.60	540
1974-75	421	12.65	409	9.05	830
1975-76	417	10.32	310	5.89	727
1976-77	454	8.83	316	6.23	770
1977-78	657	12.15	446	7.41	1103
1978-79	411	7.18	471	6.92	882
1979-80	638	9.94	824	9.01	1462
1980-81	1226	18.27	1014	8.08	2240
1981-82	1661	21.28	1137	8.36	2798
1982-83	1558	17.70	1513	10.59	3071
1983-84	1305	13.36	1659	10.48	2964
1984-85	1867	15.90	1788	10.44	3655
1985-86	1986	18.23	1677	8.53	3663
1986-87	1860	14.94	1006	5.01	2866
1987-88	1963	12.52	1608	7.23	3571
1988-89	2609	12.90	1258	4.46	3867
1989-90	4463	16.14	2038	5.77	6501
1990-91	5255	16.14	2548	6.05	7803

Source: DGCI and S Kolkata.

Table 2. Trend in Indo-Russia Bilateral Trade in the Post-Disintegration Period

Year	*Exports*	*%Share*	*Imports*	*% Share*	*Total Trade turnover*
1991-92	4041	9.18	1796	3.75	5837
1992-93	1759	3.28	737	1.16	2496
1993-94	2037	2.92	807	1.10	2844
1994-95	2472	2.99	1545	1.72	4017
1995-96	3424	3.22	2771	2.26	6195
1996-97	2717	2.29	1755	1.26	4472
1997-98	2987	2.30	2555	1.66	5542
1998-99	2786	1.99	2192	1.23	4978
1999-00	4108	2.58	2699	1.25	6807
2000-01	3968	1.97	2359	1.03	6327
2001-02	3477	1.66	3477	1.42	6954
2002-03	3479	1.38	3430	1.16	6909

Source: DGCI&S Kolkata.

Table 3. Trends in International Trade of Russia (Value: US $ million)

Year	*Exports*	*% Change*	*Imports*	*% Change*	*BOT*	*% Change*
1992	39931	-	34981	-	4950	-
1993	44047	10.3	26751	-23.5	17296	249.4
1994	63078	43.2	38600	44.3	24478	41.5
1995	77595	23.0	46399	20.2	31196	27.4
1996	83979	8.2	44504	-4.1	39475	26.5
1997	85077	1.3	52400	17.7	32676	-17.2
1998	71389	-16.1	42939	-18.1	28450	-12.9
1999	72453	1.5	30286	-29.5	42167	48.2
2000	102998	42.2	33853	11.8	69145	64.0
2001	82535	-19.9	36889	9.0	45646	-34.0
2002	107224	29.9	45507	23.4	61717	35.2

Source: Direction of Trade Statistics, IMF 2003.

References

1. Direction of Trade Statistics, IMF, 2003.
2. EIU Reports, 2003.
3. Centre for Monitoring Indian Economy, September, 2003.
4. DGCI&S, Kolkata.
5. Financial Express, December 8, 2002.

6. Narasimhual, M. "Indo-Soviet Trade in India's Planned Economic Development", Indo-Soviet Cooperation and India's Economic Development.
7. Gidadhubli, RG. "Moving Towards Consolidation—India-Russia Trade Relations" Economic and Political Weekly, January, 17, 1998.
8. Government of India, Trade Agreements between the Government of India and Government of USSR, Ministry of Foreign Trade.
9. Chisthti, S., "India's Trade with East European Countries", Indian Institute of Foreign Trade, New Delhi, 1973.
10. Chishti, S., "India's Trade with East Europe Prospects for Diversification", Indian Institute of Foreign Trade, New Delhi, 1971.
11. Kumar, Suresh, "Special Trade and Payment Arrangements" in Indo-CMEA Economic Relations, Ashish Publishing House, New Delhi.
12. www.newsfromussia.com
13. www.english.pravda.ru
14. www.indi.mid.ru
15. www.rue.ru

15

The Economic Potential and Problems of India's Trade with Russia

Professor Shri Prakash

Any worthwhile analysis of the potential of the economic and strategic potential of India's trade with Russia can only be done by mapping out the existing trends in some detail. It also requires us to analyze the factors which could enhance or reduce trade between the two countries in the future.

As things stand, both India and Russia are witnessing a period of economic growth based on factor endowments and manufacture, of products of a complementary nature which would ensure the growth of Indo-Russian trade and strategic relations.

While Russia's population has remained more or less at the same level of 149-159 millions between 1994 and 2003, that of India has increased from 883.6 million in 1994 to 1033.4 million in 2003 or by 17 per cent. A clear implication is that India's labour resources have increased and the basis for producing many of the primary products exported to Russia has grown. On the other hand due to increasing incomes from export of petroleum products from Russia and increase in oil prices as well as of other primary and manufactured goods, Russia's Gross Domestic Product measured in constant prices has grown from being 52949 million US Dollars in 1970 to 214598 million US Dollars in 1992 to 253400 million US Dollars in 2003.[1] In real terms in Russia according to Purchasing Power Parity (ppp) terms the per capita income in 2003 was 8660 US Dollars whereas in India it was only 2450 US Dollars or about 253 per cent less.

The greater income levels in Russia especially given that inequality further concentrates purchasing power in the hands of the middle class elites and those having property and/or jobs. At the present level of 7 per cent growth of the economy per annum several experts have estimated that as an economy Russia would overtake, Germany, France, Italy, and UK by 2030.[2] The size of the middle class in Russia has been estimated to range from 28 per cent of the population to 65 per cent these consisting of groups with varying levels of income, hence constituting potential customers for different categories of consumer goods, some like drugs and pharmaceuticals being needed by all.[3]

Russian Oil and Gas reserves and production coupled with increasing oil demand and a high level of oil prices will provide a central lever to sustain an increasing size of GDP. It has to be emphasized that after dropping nearly 50 per cent from the Soviet era peak, Russia's oil output has soared again to exceed 450 mil. tonnes together with gas condensates by the end of the current year making it the world's second largest producer behind only Saudi Arabia. Data concerning total oil reserves is a state secret, but the former Energy Minister estimates that Russia may have 44 billion tonnes of oil more than Saudi Arabia does. Russia currently exports over 6.5 million barrels a day. Russia is also the number one producer of natural gas in the world and has the biggest share–32 per cent of global reserves. Its companies like Gazfrom have also bought up millions of cubic metres of gas and tonnes of oil from Kazakhastan and Turkmenistan to be exploited in the future. USA will have to compete with Europe, China, Japan and Korea for Russia supplies ensuring a high level of prices and incomes. India has secured a US Dollar 1.7 billion slice off the Russia hydrocarbons of the Sakhalin Island in 2001, and can tap on more Russian oil and gas riches taking advantage of its status as Russia's most trusted strategic partner.

Table I Provides the overall direction of India's Foreign Trade which shows that USA and countries of the European Union account for the bulk of India's external trade which grew rapidly in value terms from 257737 crore Rupees in 1996-97 to 1833708 crore Rupees in 1999-2000.

Table II: Russia's Share in Indian Trade 1996-97 to 1999-2000 (In crores of Rupees)

Year	*Total Trade value in Rupees Crores*	*Russia's % share*	*Imports from Russia to India*	*Exports to Russia from India*
1996-97	257737	1.98%	2231	2880
1997-98	284277	2.13%	2521	3542
1998-99	1575865	0.33%	2295	2965
1999-2000	1833708	0.37%	2676	4123

The trend of a decline in the overall value of India's commodity trade alongwith an increase in its exports to Russia continued when in April 2002 to March 2003, India's exports to Russia totalled 4700 crore rupees but imports were 3890 crore rupees. Of course, these values do not take into account all defence related imports which would both turn Russia's deficit in commodities trade into a surplus and increase its share in the overall value of India's trade. Given the agreements on defence trade already signed, India is importing defence equipment and technology worth billions of Dollars, a trend which is likely to continue in the foreseeable future.

The most positive and noticeable aspect of the Indo-Russian trade which has potential for the future is the growth of India's commodity exports to Russia. As Table I shows from a low point of 1759 crore in 1992-93 it had recovered to 4123 crore by 1999-2000. The earlier figures for 1991-92 and 1990-91 still included India's trade with the Soviet Union so they are not strictly comparable with the latter figures.

The data relating to Russia's exports and imports trade with India is compiled for analysis in Tables III to Table VI. The first thing to notice about the commodity composition about India's exports to Russia (from Table III) is their broad base and diversity. They range from meat to fish, fruits, tea, coffee, pepper and spices, Basmati rice, tobacco, drugs, other Pharmaceutical products, leather products, a range of Textiles which after the lifting of all quotas will see an increase of volumes being exported to Russia from India. Apart from these commodities which have already proved their worth in open competition, the potential for the export of cars, automobile parts, computer software in Russian, two wheelers, hotels and tourism management agencies, cinema and audio-visual programmes dubbed in Russian - all these and more are on the future export list.

Another important dimension of Indo-Russian exports to be noticed for future consideration is the increase in volumes over a ten year period in all important commodities which may be expected to have increasing elasticity of demand in the future. A few examples with the appropriate details will illustrate the trends in relation to specific commodities which need to be concentrated on as India has a comparative advantage in them. In the period April 1993-January 1994, which may be considered to be a part of the contemporary post-Soviet phase of Indo-Russian trade India exported

31038 kgs of frozen fish valued at Rs. 8243756 which worked out to an average price of Rs. 266 Rupees per kilogram. (Table VI). However, by the period April 2002 to January 2003 not only had the volume of fish exported from India to Russia increased to 640700 kilograms which represented a massive increase of 2064 per cent over April 1993-January 1994. What is more because of better catching methods and reduction in customs duties to 20 per cent during the WTO negotiations the average price of Indian fish exported to Russia had come down from Rs. 266 per kilogram (during April 1993 January 1994) to Rs. 29 per kilogram or by 917 per cent. However, due to the enormous increase in the quantity of fish exported in the two comparable periods or by 2064 per cent the overall earnings from India's fish exports to Russia increased from Rs. 8243756 to Rs. 18410371 or by 224 per cent. (Cf Tables III and Table VI). The increase in volume made up for the decrease in prices.

The case of coffee and tea provide another example of India recapturing lost ground in the Russian markets. Between April 1993 and January 1994 India exported 55811826 kgs of Tea and Coffee to Russia at the average price of Rs. 45 per kilogram earning Rs. 2476709586. During the period April 2002 to January 2003 India exported 74106788 kgs. which was 133 per cent more than the previous period in terms of quantity. The average price of coffee and tea taken together had meanwhile fallen to Rs. 34 per kilogram compared to Rs. 45 per kilogram in the previous period (Table III and VI).

A similar scenario exists for drugs and pharmaceuticals. Between April 1993 and January 1994 India exported 2215000 kilograms of drugs and pharmaceuticals to Russia at an average price of Rs. 11785 per kilogram. Ten years later between April 2002 and January 2003, India exported drugs and pharmaceuticals products weighing 12572530 kgs. which was 568 per cent more than the previous period. The average price had declined from Rs. 11785 per kilogram to Rs. 839 per kg. or by almost 1400 per cent due to lowering of customs and excise duties and better availability of air transport, many more airlines flying between Moscow and Delhi at shorter intervals. When the prices of some goods increased because of the use of better quality yarn, or designs and materials the value of exports went down. Thus whereas in the earlier period of April 1993-January 1994 India exported 1923263 units of leather products at an average price of Rupees 327 per unit earning Rs. 627901458, between April 2002 and January 2003 India exported only 643071 units of leather products at Rs. 485 per unit earning Rs. 312081604, which was half of the previous amounts.

In other cases where the demand was higher for better quality goods a different trend prevailed. In the category of Readymade garments during April 1993 and January 1994 India exported 34575734 units at Rs. 63 per unit earning Rs. 218764465. In the subsequent period although the units of readymade garments India exported to Russia went down to 6082453 units these being of better quality their prices were higher at Rs. 109 per unit amounting to a total earning of Rs. 6643491089, this being almost 300 per cent more as it included a much larger component of silk, synthetic and handloom garments.

Overall the value of commodity imports from Russia into India have declined. The main reason is that either cheaper goods from China or better quality goods from Europe and USA have replaced the Russian goods since the Indian economy lowered its customs duties and allowed imports more freely. With the growth of joint ventures and Indian Industry raising its own quality, these also have lowered the demand for Russian goods which still is compensated for by defence imports from Russia. Still, there are examples of steel scrap, ferrite materials, newsprint in which Russia retains a large part of the Indian market. (Table V and Table IV). Still it is true that apart from defence imports the number of items being imported from Russia into India has declined and this is a cause for concern which both governments should analyse and try to remedy.

References

1. World Development Reports, 1994 and 2003, OUP, India.
2. Dominic Wilson and Roopa Purshottaman, Dreaming with BRICS, *Global Economics Paper No: 99*. 1st October 2003, p. 4.
3. Anuradha M Chenoy, *The Making of New Russia,* 2001, Har-Anand, New Delhi, p. 230.

Table 1. Direction of India's Foreign Trade (in Indian Rupees Crores)

Country	1990/91			1991/92			1992/93			1993/94			1994/95			1995/96		
	Total Trade Value	Impo-rts in Rs. Crores	Expo-rt in Rs. Crores	Total Trade Value	Impo-rts in Rs. Crores	Expo-rts in Rs. Crores	Total Trade Value	Impo-rts in Rs. Crores	Expo-rts in Rs. Crores	Total Trade Value	Impo-rts in Rs. Crores	Expo-rts in Rs. Crores	Total Trade Value	Impo-rts in Rs. Crores	Expo-rts in Rs. Crores	Total Trade Value	Impo-rts in Rs. Crore	Expo-rts in Rs. Crore
India	75751	43198	32553	91892	47815	44041	117063	63375	53688	142852	73101	6975	172645	89971	82674	229031	122678	106353
With USA	10042	5245	4797		4919	7202	16357	6219	10138	21126	9124	1254	24908	9124	15784	31382	12916	18466
UK With	5022	2894	2128	5769	2963	2806	7619	4105	3514	9144	4818	4326	10200	4895	5305	13141	6415	6726
With Japan	6284	3245	3039	8296	4136	4160	8296	4136	4160	10234	4774	5460	12768	6405	6363	15665	7411	8254
With Belgium	3977	2718	1259	5065	3422	1643	7198	5219	1979	8525	5881	2644	6893	3789	3104	9441	5693	3748
With France	2070	1304	766	2882	1516	1366	3088	1722	1366	3442	1860	1582	3761	1933	1828	5311	2812	2499
With Germany	6022	3473	2549	6977	3846	3131	8932	4799	4133	10443	5615	4828	12355	6867	5488	17134	10520	6614
With Australia	NA	1464	NA	NA	1445	NA	NA	2427	NA	NA	2068	NA	NA	2873	NA	NA	3418	NA
With Saudi Arabia	NA	2899	NA	NA	3552	NA	NA	4333	NA	NA	4836	NA	NA	4928	NA	NA	6773	NA
With Russia	7803	2548	5255	5839	1796	4043	2496	737	1759	2843	806	2037	5118	3534	1584	6360	2864	3496
With Iran	NA	1018	NA	NA	1435	NA	NA	1152	NA	NA	1191	NA	NA	1685	NA	NA	2001	NA
With Total for Asia	10698	6033	4665	11868	5365	6503	16010	6668	9342	23305	8875	1443	29702	13092	16610	40336	17723	22613
Total for with Africa			668			1441						1816			2074			3584

Source: Dg CIS, GOI, Statistics of the Foreign Trade of India.

Table 2. Direction of India's Foreign Trade (in Indian Rupees Crores)

Country	1996-97			1997-98			1998-99			1999-2000		
	Total Trade Value TTV	Imports from in Rupees Crores	Exports in Rupees Crores	Total Trade Value TTV	Imports from in Rupees Crores	Exports in Rupees Crores	Total Trade Value TTV	Imports from in Rupees Crores	Exports in Rupees Crores	Total Trade Value TTV	Imports from in Rupees Crores	Exports in Rupees Crores
India	257737	138920	118817	284277	154176	130101	1575865	178332	1397533	1833708	204583	1629125
With USA	36356	13085	23271	39096	13814	25282	45603	15314	30289	52708	15728	36980
With UK	14844	7578	7266	17038	9082	7956	18834	11028	7806	21163	11828	9335
Japan	14886	7765	7121	15028	7972	7056	17323	10373	6950	17587	10208	7379
Belgium	11873	7994	3879	14434	9916	4518	17521	12103	5418	21042	15058	5984
France	5279	2737	2542	5788	2965	2823	6518	3027	3491	7181	3194	3987
Germany	16670	10050	6620	16553	9398	7155	16798	9006	7792	15898	8089	7809
Australia	NA	4676	NA	NA	5501	NA	NA	6079	NA	NA	4677	NA
Saudi Arabia	NA	9832	NA	NA	9322	NA	NA	7705	NA	NA	9849	NA
Russia	5111	2231	2.42%	6063	2521	3542	5260	2295	2965	6799	2676	4123
			2880	2.13%								
Iran	NA	2104	NA	NA	2353	NA	NA	1993	NA	NA	4341	NA
Total for Asia	45182	18004	27178	48740	21077	27663	29754	29391	26815	69061	35881	33180
Total for Africa			3490			4082			5081			4957

Source: Dg CIS, GOI.

Table - 3
Main Commodity Composition of Indo-Russian Exports in Rupees April 2002-Jan. 2003

	Commodity	*Qty. in Kilograms*	*Value in Rs.*	*Price in Rs./Kg.*
1.	Boneless meat of Bovine animals	109906	4566758	42
2.	Fishes and Crabs	640700	18410371	29
3.	Cucumbers and Gherkins	1623574	23802136	15
4.	Mangoslices and Pulp	1001780	34120366	34
5.	Coffees of different types	3556566	238346827	67
6.	Teas of different types	70550222	2310406902	33
7.	Pepper	684670	23349008	34
8.	Rice including Basmati Rice	32040042	271120415	9
9.	Castor oil	7003545	226226792	32
10.	Tobacco of diff. types	22620595	1031709005	46
11.	Chemical Acids	744570	41886600	56
12.	Drugs/Pharma Products	12572530	10556089590	839
13.	Sacks and bags of plastics	328180	150431145	458
14.	Leather hand bags wallets etc.	643071 units	312081604	485 per unit
15.	Textiles, (Jute) Bleached, Dyed and Handlooms cloth plus	6082453 units	6643491089	109 Rs. per unit

Source: Dg CIS, GOI.

Table-4

Main Commodity Composition of Indo-Russian Trade April 2002-January 2003 Imports from Russia

	Commodity	*Quantity*	*Value in Rs.*	*Avg Price in Rs./Kg.*
1.	Natural Honey	47000	2444224	Rs. 52.
2.	Peas	29128000	383363186	Rs. 14
3.	Seeds/Coriander	44680	1154196	Rs. 26
4.	Sulphur Residues	138757000	332793213	Rs. 3
5.	Asbestos	47279191	625364390	Rs.132
6.	Zirconium Ores	242000	5359341	Rs. 22
7.	Steam coal	1000	16218330	Rs.16218 per ton
8.	Other Cokes of Coal	131060 tons	599342470	Rs.4574 per ton
9.	Carbon	4597784	9926106	Rs. 22
10.	Silicon	22000	1096695	Rs. 50
11.	Lithium	58807	14388385	Rs. 245
12.	Carbolic Acids	5013500	63093068	Rs. 13
13.	Penicillin	121149	104061425	Rs.859
14.	PVC	615906	56780485	Rs. 92
15.	Drugs eg. Isobutene	12114211	1012331589	Rs. 84
16.	Newsprint	133560385	2710495167	Rs. 521
17.	Tyre Yarn	253616	116025343	Rs 458
18.	Diamonds	1232 carats	4578474	Rs. 37163. per carat
19.	Dust and Powder of diamonds	52500 carats	1435150	Rs. 28 per carat
20.	Ferrite Materials	2856885	152888418	Rs. 54
21.	Waste and Scrap of steel	8285500	89043804	Rs. 11
22.	Flat Rolled Products and steel coils	191578008	2981483831	Rs. 16
23.	Copper and Copper Products	1038400	27881576	Rs. 27
24.	Ball bearing / Rollers	13150002 units	303985400	Rs. 23 per unit
25.	Readymade Garments	53323789 units	919606691	Rs. 172 per unit
26.	Transistors	1824000 units	850464	48 Paise per unit

Source: Dg CIS, GOI.

Table. 5
India's Imports to Russia
(April 1993 - January 1994)

	Commodity	*Qty. in Kilograms*	*Values in Indian Rupees*	*Avg Price in Rs./Kg.*
1.	Drugs and Medical Preparations	17459341 kgs	2052080609	Rs. 118 Per kg
2.	Leather and leather products	1991211 kgs	17402260	Rs. 9 per kg
3.	Ferrite Materials	428 kgs	34078	Rs. 795 per kg.
4.	Waste & Scrap of steel	3562 tons	47971597	Rs. 1468 Rs. Per ton
5.	Copper and copper products	14727554 kgs	868985885	Rs. 59 per kg.
6.	Cobalt and cobalt based alloyed	25240 kgs	207810	Rs. 807 per kg.
7.	Roller Ball Bearing	80528 units	2125991	Rs.56 per kg
8.	Photo sensitive transistors	100320 units	114870	Rs. 1.14 per unit
9.	Thermostats	4500 units	569077	Rs. 127 per unit
10.	Industrial plant project	1	37241239	
11.	Power Project	1	26434081	
	Total for Russia		6311506084	

Source: Dg CIS, GOI.

Table. 6
India's Exports to Russia (In Indian Rupees)
(April 1993 - January 1994)

	Commodity	Qty. in Kilograms	Value in Indian Rupees	Price in Rs. per kilogram
1.	Frozen fish	31038 kgs	8243756	266 Rs. per kg
2.	Cashew and Walnuts	11617 tons	246737654	21240 per ton
3.	Coffee	2844530 kgs	128421071	Rs. 45 per kg
4.	Tea	52967296 kgs	2348288515	Rs. 44 per kg
5.	Alcohols (Beer whiskey etc.)	2058809 Litres	58702742	Rs. 29 per kg
6.	Tobacco and Cigarettes	3863222 kgs	1579955867	409 Rs. per kg
7.a)	Acids as base for medicines	2215000 kgs	128110120	11785 Rs. per kg
b)	Drugs and pharma products	NA	2457373194	
			24924190	
8.	Perfumes and cosmetics	8008725 kgs	61528809	8 Rs. per kg
9.	Leather Products	1923263 units	6279014558	327 Rs. per unit
10.	Handloom/ Powerloom fabrics	2730564 sq. metres	108901769	40 Rs. per sq. metre
11.	Readymade Garments	34575734 units	218764465	63 Rs. per unit

Source: Dg CIS, GOI.

16

Impact of Developments in Russia on Indian National Movement

V.D. Chopra

It may look too sweeping a statement but there is ample evidence to the effect that when the Russian people were fighting tyrannical and despotic rule of the Czars and the Indian people were engaged in a bitter struggle against British imperialism, the people of these two countries had developed a peculiar type of emotional attachment with each other, primarily because of their cause being similar.

That explains that even in the 19th century, Indian and Russian progressive circles took keen interest in each other's affairs. The forward-looking Russians closely watched the various anti-imperialist movements in the last century and particularly India's first War of Independence in 1857 attracted their attention the most. They in fact were disappointed when the widespread risings in 1857—which the British rulers dubbed as "mutiny" - were brutally crushed. However, the Russian scholars continued to take interest in India, notable amongst them was Ivan Pavlovich Minaev, Professor of Comparative Grammar at St. Petersburg University, who paid three visits to India during 1874 and 1886. He was present as an observer at the founding of the Indian National Congress in 1885. He described this event as a significant attempt for "the development of the feeling of nationalism in India, for the unification of India".

After the Russians moved into Central Asia, the British were all the time apprehensive of Czarist invasion of India. The British used every means to stem the expansion of Russian power in areas in proximity or adjacent to India and often used it as a pretext for regular invasion or intervention as in Afghanistan. However, the people of India did not subscribe to this bogey of the Russian threat. On the other hand, a feeling started growing in India that the Russians would help India in throwing off the British colonial yoke. The Indian National Congress refused to accept Russian threat as real and consistently opposed excessive military expenditure by the British in pursuance of their "forward" policy.

In 1905, Bal Gangadhar Tilak approached the Russian Consulate and made enquires whether it would be possible for Indians to attend Russian military schools for training so that they could organise Indian patriotic forces against the British. Tilak in his speeches often admired the Russian people's rising against the Czar and advocated similar methods of defiance by the Indian masses.

Mahatma Gandhi was greatly impressed by the Russian thinkers and writers. His correspondence with Leo Tolstoy is well known. He was also an admirer of Maxim Gorky who, nevertheless, advocated methods quite different from those of Leo Tolstoy. He wrote about Gorky in 1905: "Without caring to make money, he writes with such vehemence and bitterness that authorities keep a stern eye on him. He has also been in jail in the service of the people and considers imprisonment as an honour. It is said that there is no other writer in Europe who is as great a champion of the people's rights as Maxim Gorky". Mahatma Gandhi was enthused by the First Russian Revolution in 1905. He said: "We too can resort to the Russian remedy against tyranny. The movement in Bengal for the use of Swadeshi goods is much like the Russian movement. Our shackles will break this very day, if the people of India become united and patient, love their country and think of the well being of their motherland disregarding their self interest.... We also can show the same strength that the Russian people have done".

Mahatma Gandhi prophetically declared: "If the Russian people succeed, the revolution in Russia will be regarded as the greatest victory, the greatest event of the present century".

On the other hand, Russian leaders evinced keen interest in India's struggle for independence. On the conviction of Tilak, Lenin wrote: "But the popular India is beginning to stand up in defence of her writers and political leaders. At the infamous sentence pronounced by the British jackals on the Indian democrat Tilak—he was sentenced to long term of exile—a question in the British House of

Commons the other day revealed that the Indian Jurors had declared for acquittal and that the verdict had been passed by the vote of the British Jurors—this reprisal against the democrat by the lackeys of the moneybags evoked street demonstrations and a strike in Bombay".

Similarly, Gorky wrote to Shyamji Krishna Varma on 20th October 1912, asking him to send "an article for the Russian Review that could give to the Russian democracy the knowledge of the Indian movement for liberty and justice". He said: "We must let know one people to the other that everybody who thirsts for justice, who desires to live in accordance with the intellect, should understand their unity, the unity of their aims, their spirit and would be united in one and invincible strength which will conquer finally all the evil of the world".

With his usual insight, Lenin along with other socialist revolutionaries was quick to recognise that the struggle of the Indian and other colonial peoples against their imperialist masters was a necessary part of the growth of socialism in the world.

It is significant to mention in this connection that by 1905 the situation in India had ripened for a new stage of freedom struggle and a modern method was evolved, the weapon of economic boycott, in place of the earlier technique of protests based on religious and other compulsions.

The advance of freedom movement in India during 1905-1907 was in fact, a part of the wave of the world advance of the progressive forces, following the defeat of Czarism at the hands of Japan, the first victory in modern times of an Asian nation over a European power. This led to a far reaching and lasting effect on the consciousness of the Indian people. The initial success of the First Russian Revolution further strengthened the resolve of the Indian people to do or die. Against this background the national ferment against the British rule typified by the general strike of Bombay textile workers in 1905 - the first political action of the Indian working class - needs to be understood.

The events of the First World War, the unbridled exploitation of the Indian people and the October Revolution of 1917 unleashed unprecedented mass movements for national freedom in the post war period. Just as the awakening of 1905 was generated by the world situation at large, even more so was the birth of the mass movements in India which shook the foundations of the British rule in the years succeeding 1917.

This correlation of the development of the struggle in India and the world struggle is of special importance, in view of the subjective and isolationist explanations frequently trotted out by the traditional schools of Indian political thought for interpreting mass movements simply in terms of personalities or particular groups. The bias has by no means lost its hold even today.

There is no doubt that the transformation of the political movement in India from relatively restricted sections of the population to the broad masses of the people took place in the years following 1917. And this transformation was not limited to India alone!

The World War, in the wake of the defeat of Russian Czarism by Japan a decade earlier, completed the shattering of the myth of the invincibility of Western imperialism in the eye of the Asiatic people. The spectacle of the internecine conflicts of the imperialist powers and the emergence of the Soviet Union as the first socialist state in the world aroused renewed hopes in the breast of millions of subject people that the hour of collapse of the existing empires was approaching. This made a far deeper impaçt on the minds of the Indian people and their leaders than perhaps anywhere else. The news of the February Revolution and the overthrow of the Czar, which had come to India through the British press, spurred the Indian leaders to a greater activity for they had always regarded the Russian autocracy as a phenomenon on a par with British despotism in India. A brochure published in 1917 by the Home Rule Committee and given the symbolic title "Lessons from Russia" (Home Rule Series-23) contained an appeal to the educated classes to expound to the masses of the Indian people the significance and implications of the liberation movement in Russia. The victorious revolution in Russia had truly inspired Indian nationalists to intensify their liberation struggle. Allahabad newspaper *Abhydaya* (24th March 1917) made a striking comment: "Russian revolution convinces us that there is no power in the world which an animating and life giving nationalism could not have overcome".

As the revolutionary events in Russia progressed, the British rulers and the mass media controlled by them embarked on a campaign of anti-Sovietism. However, despite all these measures of the colonial administration, the fact of the October Revolution could neither be suppressed nor denied its pull in India. "The revolution in Russia and its beginning was regarded in India as a triumph over despotism......... It has given an impetus to Indian political aspirations", confessed the Secretary of State for India, sadly though.

The demolished soldiers in India, particularly the Punjabi soldiers, returning from the battlefields of Europe and the Middle East, at the end of the War, carried the heroic story of Russian Revolution to their villages and those others who had seen action in Turkestan, Central Asia and the territories bordering on the Caspian Sea literally set the Indian hearts aflame.

It is not without significance to recall that the most influential of the national political organisations, the Indian National Congress, acclaimed the October Revolution, even though a section of leaders did not support its socio-political programme. Inaugurating the session of the Indian National Congress in 1917, Annie Besant said: "The Russian Revolution and the probable rise of a Russian Republic in Europe and Asia, have all entirely changed the conditions existing before in India".

The impact of the October Revolution on India was phenomenal. It had three distinct dimensions - stimulating the consciousness of the Indian people, widening the basis of the national movement and above all, hastening the evolutionary process of the Indian Left movement, particularly the communist movement.

This epoch making Revolution, besides shaping world events, gave a radical turn to relations between the British colonial rulers and the Indian people. The most noticeable aspect of this change was the raising of the all-important question of national self-determination and the resolve of the people to fight for it with spirit and courage. If some of the language papers editorially commenting on this Revolution hailed it as the harbinger of the dawn of a new era, national leaders of all political hues welcomed the new developments in Russia, Mahatma Gandhi, for instance, said that "Bolshevik ideals sanctified by the sacrifice of such master spirits as Lenin cannot go in vain".

Within the national movement, radicals probably had a clearer understanding about the international significance of this Revolution, a significance, which was further heightened by Lenin's breathtaking Declaration of the Rights of the People of Russia. It was, therefore, most natural that a section of the leadership of the Indian national movement should defend and stand up for the Revolution. Bal Gangadhar Tilak's newspaper Kesari spoke up for Lenin in a forthright editorial underlining the fact that the Russian people were solidly behind him and the Revolution.

This being the situation, the British rulers shrewd as they were, rightly gauged the new temper of the people and started readjusting their strategy in India. Within five months of the fall of Czarism, the British Government hastened to issue a notification, known as Montagu Declaration, and proclaimed the aims of British rule in India to be "gradual development of self governing institutions with a view to the progressive realisation of Responsible Government in India as an integral part of the British Empire" and promised suitable and speedy steps in this direction. The hasty character of this declaration was evident from the fact that real work began slowly and haltingly to concretise what was intended to be done, in producing what came to be known as Montagu-Chelmsford Report, only a year later. It is noteworthy again that the entire move was directed to creating a division among the leaders of the national movement. Nevertheless, the reaction of the national movement and the way the British rulers started changing their tactics were unmistakable proofs of the fact of the Russian Revolution and of its indelible imprint on the Indian mind.

Much of the interest of the Indian nationalists in the far-reaching developments in Russia after the October Revolution must be seen against the background of the then nationalist aspirations of the Indian people. The success of the Revolution, the withdrawal of Russia from the War and Lenin's policy proclamation had a radicalising influence on Indian thinking and actions.

The Russian Revolution had taken place precisely at a time when the Indian freedom movement had begun to acquire the status of a defined struggle is also understandable that at this stage the mass sympathy for the Russian Revolution was generally articulated by the leaders of the middle classes, they being the main instruments of the developing national movement. Hence, these were the people who were most influenced by the Russian Revolution. But as the efforts of the Soviet people for building a socialist society began to unfold themselves and as the Indian national movement started broadening its mass base, the convergence of interest of the Soviet Union and the aspirations of the colonial and semi-colonial people against imperialism came to be widely accepted by the leading forces and personalities of the national movement in our country.

In November 1927, Jawaharlal Nehru with his father Motilal Nehru attended the tenth anniversary of the Russian Revolution in Moscow. On his return, Jawaharlal Nehru wrote: "Our work in India will be easier, if Russians succeeded in the fight against poverty and illiteracy".

In 1936, while presiding over Lucknow session of the Indian National Congress, he said: "If the future is full of hope, it is largely because of Soviet Russia and what it had done. This new civilization will spread to other lands and put an end to the wars and conflicts which capitalism feeds".

Jawaharlal Nehru, in fact on the basis of this penetrating analysis of the achievements of the socialist society, was one of the first leaders of the anti-colonialist movement, who came to the conclusion that the movement towards socialism was a specific need for countries struggling for national independence. Again and again he declared that the only road of rapid development of the countries struggling for independence was through socialism. His mind was made up: "Are we to follow the English, French and the American way?" It was in this context that he firmly rejected that the developing countries could not tread on the capitalist path. "Have we time of 100 or 150 years to reach our destination?" he asked and came to the conclusion that it was impossible because "we will perish in the process".

It is axiomatic to say that in popularising socialism and lauding the achievements of the Soviet Union as a socialist state, Jawaharlal Nehru made a memorable contribution.

Scientific socialism attracted Jawaharlal Nehru not simply as a theory. The reason for its appeal was that Jawaharlal Nehru was intellectually moved and attracted by the colossal and unprecedented experiment in revolutionary changes, which were taking place before his very eyes. "While rest of the world was in the grip of depression and going backward in some ways, in the Soviet country a great new world was being built before our eyes", he said. But he did not rest at that. He opined: "We thought of the United States of America and even of some eastern countries which were forging ahead. But most of all we had the example of the Soviet Union, which in two brief decades, full of war and civil strife and in face of what appeared to be insurmountable difficulties, had made tremendous progress. Some were attracted by communism, others were not, but all were fascinated by the advance of the Soviet Union in education and culture and medical care and physical fitness and in the solution of the problem of nationalities—by the amazing and prodigious effort to create a new world out of the dregs of the old".

This attitude of Jawaharlal Nehru led to a radical shift in the Indian democratic thinking, shaped as it had been by; the influence of Russian Revolution and the achievements of socialism in the USSR.

Rabindranath Tagore was also greatly impressed by the Soviet Union in the brief span of a decade. In the words of Jawaharlal Nehru, "Even Rabindranath Tagore, highly individualistic as he was and not attracted towards some aspects of the communistic system, became an admirer of this new civilization and contrasted it with the present conditions in his own country".

"In Russia at last", wrote Tagore from Moscow on the 20th September 1930: "whichever way I look, I am filled with wonder. It is unlike any other country. It is radically different. From top to bottom they are rousing everybody up without distinction.

"Throughout the ages, civilized communities have contained groups of nameless people. They are the majority, the beasts of burden, who have no time to become men. They grow up on the leavings of society's wealth, with the least food, least clothes and least education, and serve the rest. They toil most, yet theirs is the largest measure of indignity. At the least excuse they starve and are humiliated by their superiors. They are like a lamp stand bearing the lamp of civilization on their heads: people above receive light while they are smeared with the trickling oil".

Tagore further enlarged upon the subject, in his "Letter from Russia", that "for the first time since the dawn of history the entire society, and not merely the upper portion thereof, was being illuminated by the light of civilization".

There was no doubt that the great poet was swept off his feet by "the complete disappearance of the vulgar conceit of wealth" and by provision of "equal opportunities for the entire people without any manner of discrimination" He acknowledged that without a visit to Soviet Union "my life's pilgrimage would have remained incomplete". Tagore's "Letters from Russia" were understandably proscribed by the British.

Similarly during his last years, Iqbal, another great poet turned more and more towards socialism. The stupendous progress and success of the Soviet experiment had awed him - a fact which is vividly reflected in his poetry of the last few years of his life.

Again, when Hitler invaded the Soviet Union in 1941, the Congress Working Committee in its meeting in Bardoli in December 1941, expressed sympathy and concern for Russia. The resolution passed in the presence of Mahatma Gandhi read: "The Soviet Union has stood for certain human, cultural and social values which are of great importance to the growth and progress of humanity. The Working Committee considers that it would be a tragedy if the cataclysm of war involved the destruction of this endeavour and achievement".

It is plain that the leaders of the national movement and the intellectuals continued to draw inspiration from the Soviet Union and took keener and keener interest in developments there. Jawaharlal Nehru aptly gave expression to that universal sentiment, when he said: "the presence and example of the Soviets was a bright and heartening phenomenon in a dark and dismal world".

The impact of the Russian Revolution on Indian national movement and social thought would remain incomplete without a passing reference about the rise of working class movement and the communist movement. During 1905-1909 there was a notable advance in the working class movement, parallel to the militant national movement. But after the Russian Revolution, the working class movement in India received a fresh stimulus. The strike movement, which began in 1918, engulfed the country in 1919 and 1920. These were the objective conditions in which Indian trade unionism was born, the Indian Trade Union Congress having been founded in 1920.

Despite all obstacles and initial confusion, it was after the Russian Revolution, individuals and groups in their search for building a socialist society and bringing about a synthesis between national independence and socialism, were attracted towards socialism and communism, from at least four directions.

First, there were national revolutionaries, operating from abroad in countries like Germany, the USA, Turkey and Afghanistan, who were drawn towards socialism and communism.

Secondly, national revolutionaries from the Pan-Islamic Khilafat movement came under the influence of Russian Revolution and later applied themselves to the building up of socialist and communist movements in India.

Thirdly, national revolutionaries of the Ghadar Party who were from the Punjabi emigrant labour, particularly among the Punjabi Sikhs, were inspired by the communist ideology.

Fourthly, radical minded revolutionaries in India from practically all the streams of anti-imperialist movement, the Akalis, the leaders of the Khilafat movement and elements of the younger generation of Congressmen turned to scientific socialism.

These communist groups or their representatives came together at the first Indian Communist Conference at Kanpur towards the end of December 1925 and founded the Communist Party of India (CPI).

Without going into the various phases of the history of the Indian communist movement, it must be recorded, all the same, that the Russian Revolution, its success and achievements created a tremendous enthusiasm among the national revolutionaries both in India and abroad, more specifically among those who were working in India. This laid the basis for the development of the left and the communist movement in India. Jawaharlal Nehru was keenly alive to the seminal importance of the Russian Revolution and shared this faith with other national revolutionaries, past and present. The Communist Party of India too has acknowledged this fact, though naturally in a different form: "The Communist Party of India arose in the course of our liberation struggle as a result of Indian revolutionaries who under the inspiration of the Great October Revolution were seeking paths of achieving national independence".

(*Preamble* to the *Party Constitution* adopted at its Amritsar Congress in April 1958).

Thus, the Russian Revolution laid the foundation for the building and expansion of new kind of ties between the Indian people and the people of USSR. These friendly relations naturally entered a new phase after India became an independent and sovereign state in 1947.

17

Russian Stand on Indo-Pak Conflict on Kashmir: A Historical Analysis

Dr. G.M.Shah

1. Introduction

Situated in the heart of Euro-Asian supercontinent, the erstwhile princely state of Jammu and Kashmir has an important geo-strategic location. It is surrounded by Commonwealth of Independent States in the north, Punjab and Himachal Pradesh States of Indian Union in the South, Pakistan and Afghanistan in the west and Chinese Sinkiang and Tibet in the north and east respectively. During the colonial period British India, China and Russia attached great geo-political significance to this mountainous territory lying between the Karakoram mountains in the north and the Punjab plain in the south. The highland acted as a buffer between Russia and British India. Even after the Independence of the subcontinent from the Britishers, the geo-strategic significance of Jammu and Kashmir has not diminished. The dispute over Jammu and Kashmir between India and Pakistan and the involvement of UN in this dispute has prompted both China and Russia to devise more cautious foreign policy towards the conflict.

Let us analyse the Russian response to the Indo-Pak dispute over Jammu and Kashmir. In order to study the problem in a historical context, the geo-political significance of Kashmir for Russia has been discussed right from the late Tsarist period. This paper has been divided into five sections, each section dealing with a specific aspect of the problem under discussion. The first section is an introductory dealing with geo-strategic significance of Jammu and

Kashmir for Russia, besides dealing with the frame of the study. The section deals with the Russian policy towards Jammu and Kashmir during the pre-cold war period. The third section deals with her response towards Kashmir conflict during cold war period. The fourth section deals with Russian foreign policy towards Indo-Pak dispute over Kashmir during the post cold war period. The fifth and the last section deals with the summary, conclusion and future of Russian policy towards the resolution of Kashmir conflict. A brief account of the above mentioned sections is given as under:

2. Russian Foreign Policy Towards Kashmir During Pre-Cold War Period

The princely state of Jammu and Kashmir was formed in 1846 through the treaty of Amritsar between Maharaja Gulab Singh and the Britishers. In 1870 a mission from Maharaja Ranbir Singh arrived in Taskent led by Baba Karma Prakash, who emphasized the Maharaja's desire to establish relations with Russia and said the Maharaja was ' almost a free ruler and paid only 'symbolic' tribute to the British. The Russians did not, however, take up his offer.[1]

By 1880 the British were forced to admit that their Kashmir policy had failed as Ranbir Singh did not fully cooperate with British officer on special duty at Gilgit. In 1881 the Gilgit Agency was withdrawn and the Maharaja was left to guard the northern frontier on his own.[2] Lytton's policy was that Kashmir was completely loyal to the British government in preference to both Russia and Afghanistan. The Maharaja, however was found to have dealings with both.

The Russian perspective on events in Northern India had clearly led them to take advantage of every opportunity which presented itself. Tsar Nicholas perceived that it would be to his advantage to squeeze imperial British to loosen their grip elsewhere. In 1865 the Russians had annexed Tashkent, the following year they took Khojand, two years later Samarkand and Bokhara came under Russian control. But in addition to Russia's expansion southwards into the Khanates of Central Asia, the Tsar's emissaries mere keeping a watchful eye on events in China.

In 1888 Colonel Algernon Durand went to Gilgit to work out a defensive strategy, which would utilize the recently formed Kashmir Imperial Service Troops. When Durand returned from Gilgit, he reported to his brother, Sir, Mortimer Durand, that he had heard that a Russian officer, Captain Grombchevsky had been in Hunza. This news added to British fears that the Russians could pass through the Pamirs into the sub-continent and that India, therefore, was within range of their forces. The following year, in July 1889, Durand was sent back to Gilgit to reestablish the Gilgit Agency.

No sooner had the British established themselves at Gilgit, however, than their position was once more threatened by the activities of the rulers of Hunza and Nagar, who made a temporary alliance. In 1890 another Russian delegation was received in Hunza by the ruler Safdar Ali. The following year, Uzr Khan, the heir to the ruler of Nagar, closed the Kashgar road and expelled the Kashmiri troops stationed there.

On 1st December 1890 the British forces comprising Gurkhas, Kashmir state forces, Punjab Infantry, Pathans employed on building roads and Punial irregulars with swords and shields—crossed the river Hunza at Chalt. The main gate of the fortress at Nilt was barricaded. When a well known Russian statesman heard the news of British victory, and occupation of Hunza, he said, "they have slammed the door in our faces.[3] Safdar Ali was deposed, Uzr Khan was exiled and his father continued to rule.

By the early 1930's the British had once more become alarmed at the activities of the Soviet Union in Sinkiang, which they perceived threatened Gilgit directly. Certain British Officials including Olaf Caroe, the deputy secretary in the Indian Foreign Department argued forcefully for resuming direct control over Gilgit. After over two years of discussion with the Maharaja of Jammu and Kashmir, Gilgit Agency, north of the Indus was taken on lease for a period of sixty years by the British w.e.f 26 March 1935. However, after the lapse of British Paramountcy in 1947, the Gilgit Agency came back under the control of Maharaja's administration.

3. Russian Foreign Policy Towards Kashmir During the Cold War Period

Initially the Soviet Union abstained from voting when a resolution was passed regarding Kashmir in the UN Security Council, and through the Communist Party of India was supportive of Kashmir's own nationalist stance. But as relations deteriorated between the

Soviet Union and its former allies in the Second World War, the Russians began to maintain that the British were using the Kashmir issue to keep control of both Dominions. In 1952 the Soviet representative at the Security Council said that the purpose of the United States and Britain was to convert Kashmir into a protectorate under the pretext of rendering assistance through the United Nations.[4]

In May 1954 Pakistan signed a Mutual Defence Assistance Agreement with the United States and accepted the American aid. In September 1954 Pakistan joined SEATO and the following year the Baghdad Pact (later called CENTO), whose other members were Turkey, Iran and the United Kingdom. In response to Pakistan's growing relations with the United States and Britain, the Soviet Union showed more pronounced inclination towards India. At the end of 1955 Nikolai Bulganian and Nikita Khrushchev stopped at Srinagar, where their visit marked a new phase in Indo -Soviet relations. They stated that the people of Kashmir had clearly already decided to join India. "We are so near that if ever you call us from your mountain tops we will appear at your side, said Khruschev.[5]

In 1962 Dr. Frank Graham, Dixon's successor as UN representative for India and Pakistan returned again to the sub-continent (his previous visit was in spring 1951). But the draft resolution reminding the parties of the principles contained in their earlier resolutions calling for a plebiscite was not adopted. For the first time instead of abstaining, the Soviet Union voted against the resolution. "It is now quite unrealistic to demand a plebiscite," stated the Soviet representative.

In October 1962 the unresolved dispute between India and China over their Himalayan border erupted when the Chinese overran Indian outposts and moved troops into the North-East Frontier Area (NEFA) and Ladakh. Although the immediate crisis between India and China ended when, on 21 November, the Chinese declared a unilateral ceasefire, the Indians still felt vulnerable over their long-term security. Nehru became prepared to talk in terms of a tacit air defence pact with the United States in case the Chinese resumed their offensive.[6] In return, however, the Indian government was obliged to submit to political pressure from western countries for talks with Pakistan regarding a resolution of the Kashmir issue.

At the end of November 1962 both Britain and the United States sent missions to New Delhi, in order to determine what military help India might need. The Americans and British were also anxious to reassure Pakistan regarding the extent of any military assistance to India. In a statement on 20 November, President John Kennedy said. " In providing military assistance to India, we are mindful of our alliance with Pakistan. All of our aid to India is for the purpose of defeating Chinese Communist subversion.[7] The Anglo-American team also wanted to initiate bilateral talks between India and Pakistan to help them resolve their differences, in order to present a united front against the threat from communist China. Pakistan's President Ayub Khan was, however, not convinced that such solidarity would work to Pakistan's advantage. On 2 March 1963 Sino-Pakistan Border Agreement was signed between the two governments. In July 1963, Z.A. Bhutto said in Pakistan National Assembly 'An attack by India on Pakistan involves the territorial integrity and security of the largest state in Asia.[8]

Internationally, Pakistan was beginning to emerge from its political dependence on the United States. Ayub Khan's successful visit to China in March 1965 had considerably enhanced his domestic standing. When President Johnson cancelled Ayub Khan's scheduled visit to United States, Ayub Khan at once accepted an invitation by the Russians to visit Soviet Union, making the first ever visit by a Pakistani head of government to Moscow. According to Altaf Gauhar, who accompanied the President, Ayub Khan pointed out to Prime Minister Alexei Kosygin that by using veto, the Soviet Union was 'bailing out India' in the UN Security Council, Kosygin described the meetings a turning point which will lead to further exchanges of views and to big decisions in the interests of our two countries[9]. A trade treaty was signed as well as a credit agreement on oil prospecting.

Following the 1965 Indo-Pak war the ceasefire came into force at midday on 22nd September. In January 1966 Indian and Pakistani delegations met in Tashkent where the Soviet Prime Minister Alexi Kosygin, acted as unofficial mediator. Ayub and Shastri accepted a declaration in which both countries re-affirmed their commitment to solving their disputes through peaceful means. They also agreed to revert to their positions prior to 5th August 1965.

In 1971 Soviet Union and India signed the Treaty of Cooperation and Friendship, which provided for military assistance in the event of aggression. The Soviet backing for India's effort in Bangladesh (formerly East Pakistan) in 1971 finally chilled relations between Pakistan and Soviet Union. In the late 1970s, the Soviet military intervention in Afghanistan transformed Pakistan into a frontline state in the last lap of the cold war.

Russia appeared to be improving relations with Pakistan after two decades of frozen relations. In November 1991, just before the Soviet collapse, Russia for the first time voted in the UN for a proposal sponsored by Pakistan for a nuclear-weapon free zone in South Asia, much to the consternation of India.

4. Russian Foreign Policy Towards Kashmir during Post Cold War Period

In the changed geo-political scene following the break up of the Soviet Union, Pakistan began to seem more important from Russia's pint of view. Situated close to the newly independent Central Asian republics and adjacent to Afghanistan, Pakistan seemed to be in a position to influence developments there. Some held the view that during this period 'the key Islamic actors' in the region (Iran, Pakistan and Turkey) assumed priority over India.

In December 1991, Russian Vice President Alexander Rutskoy, an Afghan war veteran visited Pakistan. As a pointer of growing warmth in Russian-Pakistani relations, an international conference was held in Moscow in April 1992 on relations between Pakistan and the CIS. Moreover, the supply of US arms to Pakistan having stopped in 1990, Pakistan was in search of new allies and sources of military hardware. It tried to move closer to Russia.

Russian policy of 'equidistancing India and Pakistan' continued until July 1994, when the day after a visit by Indian Prime Minister Narasimha Rao, the Pakistani foreign Minister came to Moscow at the invitation of Kozyrev. The two Foreign ministers finalized the draft of a bilateral treaty which was to lay the foundation of their relations in the post cold war era. It was to be signed by Prime Minister Benazir Bhutto during her Moscow visit in December 1994. However, because of Yeltsin's health problems the visit was cancelled.

The next high-level contact between Russia and Pakistan took place only in the summer of 1997 when the Pakistan Foreign Minister Gauhar Ayub Khan visited Moscow for talks with Foreign Minister Primakov. By this time Pakistan's involvement in Afghanistan through Taliban had widened the differences between it and Russia. Continued efforts to patch up bi-lateral relations precipitated a visit to Russia by Nawaz Sharif in April 1999 the first by a Pakistani head of government in 25 years.

During the early 1990's two different schools of thought existed in Russia regarding the policy towards India. One opinion favoured that the traditional "special" relationship with India should be retained. India should be given priority in the country's policy in South Asia, while at the same time developing good relations with other South Asian countries including Pakistan. The other school favoured that the epoch of "special" relations with India should be ended. President Boris Yeltsin's New Delhi visit in January 1993 removed the fog and put Indo-Russian Relations on a firm footing. There has been again a revival of the talks of Indo-Russian "strategic partnership" President Yeltsin and India's (then) Defence Minister Mulayam Singh Yadav during the latters' Moscow visit in October 1997 re-affirmed their countries' intensions to develop a strategic partnership.

After Kargil war the relations between India and Russia improved greatly as Russia was openly critical of Pakistan's aggressive designs towards India and its policy of supporting and sponsoring insurgent terrorism in Indian controlled Kashmir. Russian President Vladimir Putin in his 2000 visit referred to the 'arc of instability from the Caucasus to Southeast Asia'.

The Indian Prime Minister's visit to Moscow on 5th November 2001 came in the background of US led air strikes against Afghanistan following 09.11.2001. Vajpayee and Putin signed a new Moscow Declaration on international terrorism, which called for "completion of negotiation under UN auspices on the draft comprehensive convention on international terrorism and the convention for the suppression of acts of Nuclear Terrorism". The adoption of these conventions, they asserted would "assist in strengthening the international legal basis for effectively combating the global menace of terrorism", even while they 're-affirmed the central role of the UN in the struggle against terrorism". They supported the adoption on the basis of international law of decisive measures against all states, individuals and entities which rendered "support, harbour, finance, instigate, or train terrorists or promote terrorism." They asserted that in multi-ethnic and democratic countries like India and Russia violent actions under the slogan of self-determination in reality represented acts of terrorism which in most cases had strong international links.

Mr. Putin told newsmen that he would urge President Bush to include Pakistan-backed insurgents in Kashmir and the Chechen rebels in Russia on the list of terrorists to be targeted by the US-led coalition against international terrorism. "There are no good or bad terrorists" Mr. Putin said.

In his December 2002 visit President Putin was equally forthright when in a strong and clear message he asked Pakistan to put a stop to infiltration across line of control in Jammu and Kashmir and liquidate terror infrastructure within its boundaries. He further said "Islamabad should cut all routes of infiltration across the line of control and increase its efforts to dismantle terror infrastructure in the region" at a press conference in New Delhi.

The documents signed by India and Russia during Putin's visit in December 2002 show strategic concerns with regard to Pakistan, Afghanistan, Iraq, Central Asia and International terrorism. There are two joint working groups on terrorism and Afghanistan. Both have agreed that they will not take action detrimental to each other's security. The Delhi Declaration further significantly notes in the context of global terrorism, "we have a particular interest in putting an end to this common threat through preventive, and deterrent measures nationally and bilaterally." In his speech to the members of Indian Parliament on 4th October 2002 at New Delhi, President Putin called for urgent steps, both regional and international to counter the global sweep of 'terrorist international' that had already engulfed vast regions including Philippines, Kashmir and Kosovo. He expressed the hope that the Kashmir problem would be solved on a bi-lateral basis through compromise, with unconditional respect for the line of control and without any foreign interference. He made it clear that he was well aware of what was behind the violence in Kashmir and noted that the failure to find a solution had been feeding tension between India and Pakistan for five decades even though the peoples of the two countries had much in common.

He was categorical that there was "verified information" that the same organisation even the same individuals—were responsible for terrorist acts from the Philippines, to Kosovo, Kashmir, Afghanistan and the northern Caucasus. He put his weight behind the Indian initiative for a collective front against terrorism.

Following the Pakistani President Parvez Musharraf's Moscow visit, American war against Saddam Hussein and BJP government's pro-America inclination, Russia is taking renewed interest in improving its relations with Pakistan and the other Muslim countries. Russian desire to seek observer status in OIC is enough proof of Russia's desire of coming closer to the Muslim world. According to PTV World while attending 16-17 October 2003 OIC General Assembly meeting in Malaysia at Putra Jaya, President Putin said that during Vajpayee's meeting with him in November 2003 at Moscow, he would take up the issue of holding Indo-Pak dialogue to resolve the Kashmir conflict.

Dispelling the speculation of a pro-Pakistani shift in its position on the situation in South Asia,Russian President took, a neutral stand on Kashmir after meeting the Indian Prime Minister at Moscow. A Joint Statement issued on 13th November 2003 at the end of the three day visit of the Indian Prime Minister, Atal Bihari Vajpayee, to Moscow, urged Islamabad, "to implement in full its assurances to prevent infiltration of terrorists across the line of control" and to dismantle the terrorist infrastructure in Pakistan and Pakistan controlled territory as a pre-requisite for a purposeful dialogue between the two countries."[10]

The joint statement stated above makes it abundantly clear that Russia is trying to maintain the policy of neutrality and equidistance from both India and Pakistan. On the one hand Russia supported the Indian conditions for a dialogue with Pakistan, and on the other hand stressed the need for a purposeful dialogue with Pakistan, which means to address the core issue of Kashmir in a composite dialogue with India.

5. Conclusion

The Russian attitude towards the Indo-Pak dispute over Kashmir has been influenced more by her national ambitions and interests rather than the principles of political morality enshrined in the international law. Russian foreign policy towards South Asia in general and Jammu and Kashmir in particular has been governed by the geo-political significance of the region for Russia. Russian approach towards the Kashmir issue has always remained Anglo-America centric.

The slogans of 'Shanghai-Cooperation' and 'war against terrorism' have the twin objectives of keeping west out of Asian politics and suppressing the militant and extremist movements in the arc of instability extending from Caucasus, Afghanistan Kashmir, Nepal, North East India to South East Asia. The Russian request to seek the observer status in OIC can also be seen as an effort by Russia to strengthen the process of Eastern Alliance; as well as to contain the Chechen rebels through the cooperation of Muslim countries. In an effort to counter the growing American hegemony, Russia is discovering the possibilities of cooperation among Asian countries to develop solidarity against the process of Americanisation in Asia.

References

1. Hemen Ray; (1985), *How Moscow Sees Kashmir*, Bombay, p. 3.
2. Oglivic (193), *Memorandum on the Future of the Gilgit Agency*,18 Dec.
3. Durand, *Making of a Frontier,* p. 348.
4. Jain, (Ed), *Soviet-South Asian Relations*, Vol. p. 5.
5. Abdullah, S.M. (1993), *Flames of Chinar* translated from Urdu by Khushwant Singh), p. 134.
6. Burke, *Indian and Pakistani Foreign Policies,* pp. 166-9.
7. Altaf Gauhar, President Kennedy as Quoted in *Ayub Khan* pp. 215.fn.28.
8. Kak, *Fall of Gilgit,* p. 48-9.
9. James, *Pakistan Chronicle*, p. 126.
10. *The Hindu*, (Indian Newspaper), November 14, 2003 Column No. 2, page 11.

18

Indo-Russian Strategic Partnership Enters a New Phase

V. D. Chopra

The economic front, which has been a "weak" component of Indo-Russian strategic partnership, is expected to witness an upswing under the new Congress-led government, according to Russian experts. The fears about a slump in ongoing Indo-Russian defence cooperation are unfounded according to Felix Yurlov of the Russian Academy of Sciences' India Centre. On the contrary there would be further activity on the economic front. He said "the foundation of Indo-Russian cooperation in vital spheres including defence was laid during the rule of Indian National Congress. Prime Minister Dr. Manmohan Singh is the architect of India's liberal reforms and Russian experts are confident that the economic cooperation will further increase, which has been so far a weak component in bilateral relations. "The foundation of India's relations with Russia was laid down by Pt. Jawaharlal Nehru and Indira Gandhi and they were never a matter of debate in spite of change of governments in New Delhi," said Rostislav Rybakov, who heads the Institute of Oriental Studies - a major think-tank advising the government on Moscow's relations with the nations of Asia.

In the estimate of Russian media, no changes are expected in the traditional strategic partnership between India and Russia after the formation of Indian National Congress (INC) led coalition government in New Delhi. As far as the foreign policy of India is concerned, no cardinal changes are expected, although the coalition led by Congress President, Sonia Gandhi would carry out moderate and balanced correction in the foreign policy followed by the previous government led by the Bharatiya Janata Party (BJP), has commented *Trud* newspaper.

Kremlin has noted that during his two previous visits to India in 2000 and 2002, Russian President Vladimir Putin had met Congress President Sonia Gandhi and had established a rapport with her. On the other hand, "If regarding Russia there is any change at all in India's foreign policy, it would be only for stronger cooperation," in the estimate of Russian experts.

Not long time back before his visit to India at the end of the year 2004, Russian President, Vladimir Putin said that Russia would continue to develop strategic relations with India. "Foreign policy must be geared to the new goals and tasks and facilitate more palpable economic results," Putin noted. He said that the government must energetically uphold the interests of the Russian business abroad, especially in conditions of the European Union (EU) expansion. "An appropriate response to the challenges of international terrorism, the proliferation of weapons of mass destruction, and regional conflicts can only be given if the entire international community joins efforts, leaning on the UN and international law," Putin has underlined. "Terrorism poses a threat to people's lives and rights, destabilises countries and entire regions in the world, and hinders economic and social progress," Putin pointed out stressing that "today, international terrorism involves acts of violence and the killing of civilians."

It is relevant to mention here that despite the considerable potential of bilateral cooperation, Indo-Russian economic relations are at a low level, Director General of the Confederation of Indian Industry (CII), Shrinivasan has recently said in an interview to RIA Novosti. "Relations between India and Russia are now extremely important for us in India. But considering Russia's and India's potentials, bilateral trade is too insignificant. This is what we should worry about".

According to the Indian finance ministry, exports from India to Russia totalled 1.34 per cent of India's entire exports, not counting oil, and imports made 0.97 per cent in 2003.

"There are numerous opportunities to expand our economic cooperation, above all in science and technologies, industry and strategic areas. We are in turn ready to establish stable business ties with Russian partners," said Shrinivasan. According to him pharmaceutics, biotechnologies, and healthcare are the areas where Indian exports have huge potential. "We need a more intensive exchange in each of these domains. We should regularly exchange visits and participate in exhibitions. Now we want to arrange a large-scale exhibition of Indian produce in Russia. We also intend to help Russian companies, organise and display their procduce and services at exhibitions, we hold in India. We need to create a system of interaction between separate companies," he stressed. "Russian institute have unique technologies, and they can be forwarded to India as a basis for joint ventures and joint work," said the expert.

According to Shrinivasan, a special working group is now formed within the confederation to collect information about high technologies developed in Russian research institutes, which might arouse interest in India. He added that all the preliminary talks had already been conducted; enormous organisational efforts have been taken, including with governmental structures, so the group will be finally formed very shortly.

"There is a long-term programme of economic cooperation between India and Russia in science and technologies. This is a governmental programme. We are working in this context, attracting the private sector as well," he explained. "There is goodwill on the Russian side. Russia is quite positive about working with us. Now we are trying to win mutual trust," emphasised Shrinivasan. It is pertinent to illustrate this point.

Defence Cooperation - A New Thrust

The Russian aircraft-building corporation Irkut jointly with the Ilyushin Design Office and India's Hindustan Aeronautic Ltd. has set down to creating a new transport plane, spokesperson for Irkut Yelena Fedorova has said at the ILA'2004 international aerospace exhibition.

"The new transport, having a speed of 870 kilometres / hour, will handle a wide range of goals carrying up to 20 tonnes of freight, patrolling sea space, carrying out rescue and evacuation operations at ranges up to 2,500 kilometres. It will be distinguished by the capability to use unpaved runways", Fedorova further said.

Indian and Russian designers have completed the first stage

of work, technically shaping the plane to meet the requirements of the Indian and Russian air forces.

"The conceptual-design stage of work is now under way. Prototypes for flight tests will be made in 2006 and the first flight is set for 2008", Fedorova further said. Service of the new plane will begin in 2010.

The Irkut Corp., specialising in the manufacture of non-military and military aircraft is a vertically integrated holding.

In March 2004, it was the first enterprise of the Russian military-industrial complex to place 23 per cent of its 127 million dollar shares among Russian and foreign investors. Irkut shares have been officially put in the Moscow Interbank Currency Exchange (MICEX) and Russian Trade System (RTS) listings. The monies thus attracted have been invested in buying the Yakovlev Design Office. This shows, graphically the new trends in Indo-Russian Cooperation. There is something more to It.

India signed on an over 1.5 billion dollar deal with Russia to purchase the 45,000 ton aircraft carrier 'Admiral Gorshkov', in January 2004. The agreement was signed by the Defence Ministers of two countries on 19 January 2004. This agreement, is very significant. The deal with its complement of 28 MiG 29-K fighters and cooperation in program like BrahMos missiles, Talwar and Trishul class frigates, T-90 tanks and frontline SU-30 MKI fighters is a major landmark in Indo-Russian relationship and reaffirmation of the strategic relations between the two countries. The statement on this occasion said, "both countries discussed ways and means to develop the defence relations in new and qualitatively higher levels". This is confirmed by another fact.

India expects to significantly enhance its long-range strike abilities with the BrahMos cruise missile, jointly developed by New Delhi and Moscow. The supersonic missile, which derives its name from the Brahmaputra and Moscow rivers in both countries, has a range of almost 300 km and is designed for use with land, sea and aerial platforms. The Indian Air Force (IAF) is reportedly considering the possibility of fitting the BrahMos on its Su-30 combat jets. The production is reported to have commenced in 2003 for induction in 2004.

The BrahMos, a derivative of the Yakhont, was developed by a joint venture between India's Defence Research and Development Organisation (DRDO) and Russian NPO Mashinostroyenia. The BrahMos missile is a product of an Indo-Russian joint venture known by the same name. Registered in December 1995, the company was set up as a result of an inter-governmental agreement between Russia and India, eventually signed in February 1998, to design, develop, produce and market a supersonic cruise missile jointly.

India and Russia had planned to begin the induction of the jointly developed BrahMos supersonic cruise missile into their armed forces by the end of 2003. However, according to some reports military officials believe it is several years away from induction into the navy or the air force.

The BrahMos missile is a two-stage vehicle that has a solid propellant booster and a liquid (propellant) ram jet system.

The jointly developed Indo-Russian anti-ship cruise missile, which was successfully test-fired from Chandipur interim test range in Orissa, is a crucial step forward in India's defence efforts. This technological achievement places India among a small group of countries to acquire the capacity of producing cruise missiles. What, however, makes the jointly produced cruise missile distinguishable from others is that it travels at a supersonic speed, i.e., more than twice the speed of sound. Almost all other contemporary anti-ship missiles fly at subsonic speed.

Its unmatchable speed is its high point, making it invincible. The supersonic speed imparts it a greater strike-power as well. Possessing stealth characteristics, the 6.9-meter cruise missile weighing three tons has a range of 280 km. Its, another outstanding feature is that it is highly accurate and can be guided to its target mainly with the help of an onboard computer. This has been established by the test-flight. The computer and the guidance system have been designed by India whereas Russia has provided the propulsion system.

Test flights of the PJ-10 occurred on 12 June 2001, 28 April 2002 and in June 2002. The test firing of the cruise missile, which took place in the middle of June 2001 was described as an unqualified success. The BrahMos recorded its performance as having met technical parameters, both in terms of the flight range and hitting accuracy. Further, former Defence Minister Jaswant Singh who was present at Chandipur along with Indian and Russian scientists and technologists described the launch as a "landmark in technology partnership".

The Chandipur launch was the first in a series of test-flights of the cruise missile planned to demonstrate the capabilities of the system. A series of other test-flights will take place before the missile is simultaneously inducted into the Indian and Russian arsenals. It will also be sold to third countries in due course of time.

One of its special features is that this essentially anti-ship missile can be launched from ground, ship, submarine or air. Defence analysts underline that the eventual addition of this strategic missile is a logical follow-up of the goal set as per the country's nuclear philosophy. Stated in plain terms, it is essential for the fulfilment of India's minimum nuclear deterrent profile as outlined in the draft nuclear doctrine. The acquisition of the cruise missile, which can be tipped with a nuclear warhead, has obvious implications for nuclear weapons' delivery system.

In order to avoid controversy, both India and Russia have taken care to ensure that the production of the cruise missile did not violate obligations under the Missile Technology Control Regime (MTCR) or any of the international agreements related to proliferation. That is why the missile range is well within the 300 km limit stipulated under the MTCR.

Both India and Russia welcomed the joint development of the supersonic cruise missile with great exuberance. Elated at the successful test flight from Chandipur, the state owned Russian collaborating company, Mashinostroyenie, put the cruise missile on display at the Moscow annual air show. Mashinostroyenie designed the missile and its propulsion system, leaving the all-important software and the guidance system to its Indian counterpart - the Defence Research and Development Organisation (DRDO) of the Defence Ministry.

New Delhi described the missile as an "outstanding example of Indo-Russian joint endeavour". The former President, K.R. Narayanan and former Prime Minister A.B. Vajpayee termed it as a symbol of defence cooperation between the two countries. The development of the cruise missile takes their decades old defence cooperation and the revived post-Cold War strategic partnership to a new high. It may be recalled that during the Russian President, Vladimir Putin's visit to India in October 2000, a Joint Declaration of Strategic Partnership was issued. Two countries signed a series of agreements on the acquisition of sophisticated weapon system and for a joint production of some of them including missiles. This is how Indo-Russian defence cooperation is touching new heights.

Economic Cooperation

India and Russia historically had very strong trade ties. In fact, one important aspect of the old Indo-Soviet friendship was a special bilateral trade and economic relationship. However, after the disintegration of the Soviet Union, the economic relations between the two countries registered a steep decline. This period coincided with the transformation of Russia from a centrally planned to a market economy amid series of economic and financial crisis. The situation was further compounded by other factors, such as, collapse of the socialist system in Russia and in other East European states. Globalisation of economy and introduction of economic reforms in India, further compounded the situation. This led to a mutual decrease in the trade relations between the two countries. Besides this, the political establishment of Russia embarked on an economic path under the leadership of Boris Yeltsin, which intensified the internal economic crisis. However, the Russian patriotism asserted itself and the new Russian leadership evolved its own model of mixed economy and began to build its economic relations with its old economic partners such as India in the new historical conditions. Under the leadership of Vladimir Putin, Russia began to carve out its own position in the world economy. Russia is now once again re-emerging as a world economic power as stated in some of the chapters of this book. The crux of the problem is that both India and Russia are evolving new policies for strengthening these economic relations in the larger national interests of both the countries. It is in this setting that new trends in economic relations between the two countries need to be examined.

According to an expert, in the last decade, Indian economy had also undergone a structural transformation in the aftermath of economic reforms. In light of the transformation in both the economies, the trade basket of the two partners deserves a close re-examination in order to explore the possibilities of enhanced bilateral trade that has been languishing at US $ 1.3 billion currently as compared to US $ 5 billion in 1991.

In 2003, Russia was the 20th largest market for Indian exporters with a share of 1.3 per cent in India's total exports. Only four years back, in 2000, Russia happened to be the 9th largest market with a share of 2.6 per cent in total exports. As a source of India's imports, although Russia has lost its status compared to the heydays of the past, it has nevertheless improved its rank marginally in the past few years. In 2003, Russia was the 22nd largest market for sourcing India's imports with a share of 0.9 per cent. In 2000 it was the 22nd largest market with a share of 1.3 per cent in India's total imports.

Like Russia, India too had an insignificant position in Russia's overall trade. As a destination of Russian exports, India ranked 29th with a share of 0.7 per cent. The key markets for Russia were Germany, Italy and Ukraine with shares of 8.4 per cent, 7.0 per cent and 6.9 per cent respectively in 2001. As a source of Russian imports, India once again had an insignificant rank of 18th in 2001 with a market share of 1.3 per cent. Germany was the leading exporter in the Russian market with a share of 13.9 per cent, followed by Ukraine and USA at 9.1 per cent and 7.7 per cent respectively in 2001.

India's key exports to Russia were dominated by the traditional categories. In 2003, knitted apparel, pharmaceutical products, coffee, tea, mate and spices; non-knitted apparel, inorganic chemicals, miscellaneous chemical preparations, tobacco and manufactured tobacco substitutes, cotton, ores, slag and ash; and aircraft, spacecraft and parts were the top ten categories of exports to Russia. The top ten categories accounted for 82 per cent of the total exports. Of these, Russian markets for knitted and non-knitted apparel, coffee, tea, mate and spices; miscellaneous edible preparations, tobacco and manufactured tobacco substitutes, cotton, ores, slag and ash; and aircraft, spacecraft and parts exhibited a decline between 1997-2001. Of these India was the market leader in the Russian market for coffee, tea, mate and spices with a market share of 40 per cent in 2001. However, India's exports to Russia had declined by 13 per cent between 1997-2001. Although, a traditional stronghold, in recent times, India has been facing stiff competition from Sri Lanka, Indonesia and China.

India ranked 2nd in the Russian market for miscellaneous edible preparations with a market share of 14.2 per cent in 2001. Not only did the market exhibit a decline of 11.2 per cent between 1997-2001; even Indian exports of the category exhibited a similar decline over this period. India faced competition from German and Brazilian exporters in this market. Russian markets for non-knitted and knitted apparel were dominated by China that had shares of 37 per cent and 30 per cent in the respective markets in 2001. Indian exporters were the 8th largest suppliers in the market for knitted apparel with a share of 3.2 per cent and the 19th largest player in the market for non-knitted apparel. Both these categories had Italy and Turkey as the other key players.

India was disadvantageously placed in the Russian market for Cotton (ranked 23rd a market share of 0.1 per cent in 2001), ores, slag and ash (ranked 28th in 2001) and aircraft, spacecraft and parts (ranked 24th in 2001). However, in the Russian market for tobacco and substitutes, India ranked 6th with a market share of 5 per cent in 2001. The leaders in this category were USA, Brazil and Germany.

Of the categories where the Russian market had shown moderate to good growth, India, had a dominant position in the market for pharmaceutical products. The Russian market for this category exhibited a CAGR of 1.7 per cent between 1997-2001 and Indian exports in fact exhibited a higher growth of 4.1 per cent per annum during this period. India ranked 3rd in this market in 2001 with a market share of 8.2 per cent, following Germany and France that had market shares of 15.6 per cent and 13.4 per cent respectively.

India also had a decent 5th position in the Russian market for inorganic chemicals. This category had figured prominently in the top ten imports of Russia as well and Indian exporters exhibited a phenomenal 28 per cent average annual growth in this market and grabbed a market share of 6.5 per cent. The leaders in this market were Ukraine, Kazakhstan and USA. A closer look at the composition of Russian imports reveal that knitted apparel was a high growth category of Russian import in recent times and pharmaceutical products and inorganic chemicals were the other two leading categories of import of Russia. Since India already has an established presence in these markets; Indian exporters should work on strengthening their position in the respective markets.

The other categories of Indian exports to Russia that had exhibited good growth in the last couple of years were printed books, tanning, dyeing extracts; aircraft, spacecraft and parts; gems and jewellery, tools, implement and cutlery, manmade filaments, ceramic products and miscellaneous chemicals. Unfortunately, except for aircraft, spacecraft and parts none of the other categories figured in either the leading or high growth categories of Russian imports. In fact, despite the good growth, Indian exporters had insignificant presence in the Russian markets for all these categories. The category that had figured prominently in Russian imports basket and had shown good growth was vehicles. Russia had also been importing electrical machinery, medical and surgical instruments, articles of plastics, sugar confectionery, meat products, leather articles, clocks and watches etc. Hence, in addition to enhancing their penetration in existing established categories, Indian exporters should also think of diversifying the export basket in order to grab a larger share of the Russian wallet.

The top ten categories of India's imports from Russia accounted for almost 78 per cent of the import from that country. Russia was the leader in the Indian market for fertilisers, paper and paperboards and articles of nickel with market shares of 27 per cent, 14 per cent and 23 per cent respectively in 2003. However, the Indian import market for fertilisers declined by a whooping 21 per cent in 2003 whereas the market for paper and paperboards exhibited a meagre growth of 0.5 per cent. However, the market for articles of nickel expanded by 18.3 per cent in 2003 and Russian exports of this category also exhibited a similar growth. Hence, Russia will have to protect its share in this market where it has been facing stiff competition from Australia and Canada. Indian market for articles of rubber expanded by a decent 9.8 per cent in 2003 and Russia was the second largest exporter in this market with a share of 11 per cent in 2003. The key competitors to Russia in this market were Japan, Korea and the USA.

Russia also had a decent 6th position with a market share of 5.2 per cent in 2003 in the Indian market for salt, sulphur, stone and plastering materials. This market had grown by 15.5 per cent in 2003 and Russian exports exhibited an impressive 46 per cent growth in that year. However, the leading categories of India's imports from Russia that also figured prominently in India's overall import basket were iron and steel, gems and jewellery, nuclear reactors, boilers and machinery, inorganic chemicals and electrical machinery and equipment. It is interesting to note that except for gems and jewellery, in which Russian exports to India declined in 2003, in the other four categories Russian exports witnessed phenomenal growth in 2003. Despite the good growth, Russia remained an insignificant player in most of the markets except for iron and steel where it ranked 3rd with a market share of 9 per cent in the face of stiff competition from Japan, UK and Ukraine. In the markets for nuclear reactors, boilers and machinery, inorganic chemicals and electrical machinery and equipment, Russia ranked 23rd, 14th and 17th respectively in 2003 with market shares of 0.5 per cent, 1.7 per cent and 0.4 per cent. Hence, Russian exporters need to bolster their position in the markets that are critical from India's import perspective, an expert has pointed out.

The analysis brings out that Russia has been importing larger quantities from its neighbours. In fact, high freight cost has been a major factor in dissuading Russia from importing products from India. The recent agreement on an India-Russia transport corridor may help in reducing transport costs. Indian exporters should grab the opportunities that the growing Russian economy throws up after four long years of relative economic and political stability.

On the strength of higher commodity prices, Russian economy registered a healthy growth of 6.5 per cent in 2003 and with oil prices expected to remain firm, the growth momentum has sustained itself in 2004. Another estimate puts this rate at 8 per cent. In the domestic Russian economy, capital investments and personal consumption are up. With huge foreign trade and current account surpluses together with comfortable foreign exchange reserves, the economy looks less vulnerable to external shocks.

Similarly, the scorching pace of growth of Indian economy provides a world of opportunity to Russian exporters. India and Russia could work together in the areas of knowledge-based industries. India could use Russian expertise in the areas of infrastructure. Similarly, Russia could make use of India's knowledge in the areas of software and IT. Hence, with concerted efforts on both sides, the trade volume between these two old trade partners could grow by leaps and bounds in future.

India for instance would like to obtain access to Russia's rough diamonds and is planning to invest in the Russian diamond industry, Indian website deepikaglobal.com reported in November 2004. Kanwal Sibal, India's former Foreign Secretary and currently the Indian Ambassador to Moscow, said India would like to get the access "either through purchase or by the creation of joint ventures".

India is exporting the possibility of importing Russian technology for converting coal into gas. India has one of the largest stocks of coalmines and the Russian technology is most suitable for the Indian conditions and is also economical.

A new mechanism to boost the low bilateral trade between the two countries, which stands at US $1.8 billion, will be high on the Indo-Russian Inter-Governmental Commission (IRIGC) agenda. At the end of 2005, the countries will officially stop using the rupee and the rouble to conduct their bilateral trade and will use the dollar and other convertible currencies instead.

It is relevant here to mention another factor that the old Indo-Soviet Union trade was conducted in nonconvertible currencies. For instance, USSR contracted to sell to India a fixed volume of oil during the year under a bilateral trade protocol. The dollar value of this import was converted into rupees at the prevailing exchange rate and was credited to the Soviet account maintained by Reserve Bank of India (RBI). USSR would then allocate these rupee funds to Soviet trading organisations for the purchase of goods from India. After the collapse of the Soviet Union, India and Russia renegotiated the entire trade regime. An agreement signed in 1993 terminated the rupee trade agreement and mandated all bilateral trade transactions on hard currency. However, the rouble credit was denominated in rupees and repayment schedule was drawn up. It was agreed that India would pay about Rs. 30 billion annually to Russia for 12 years and Russia would use rupees to buy Indian goods.

Today, Indo-Russian bilateral trade is based on payment in freely convertible currencies and all Russian exports to India follow the new system. But only about 20 per cent of Indian exports follow the new route and the rest are financed through the negotiated rupee debt payment mechanism. The rupee-rouble debt payment arrangement ends in 2004 and a section of the industry feels that in future India might lose out a part of the market to competitors like China and European countries. Indian exporters would definitely not have the advantage of an assured market and would have to face stiffer competition that would necessitate gearing up on quality and cost competitiveness, an expert pointed out.

Terrorism threaten integrity of Russia and India

Both India and Russia are facing threat to their unity and integrity by terrorists and secessionists. They are handling this problem in their own specific conditions, if India is facing this new challenge in Jammu and Kashmir and Northeastern states, in Assam in particular; Russia is confronted with the same problem in Chechnya. On the other hand in Jammu and Kashmir a popular government has been installed in power through elections. In Chechnya, Alu Alkhanov, former Interior Minister has been elected Chechnya's President. His predecessor, Akhmad Kadyrov was killed by a bomb in Grozny, the capital of Chechnya in May 2004. The latest presidential election in Chechnya was shadowed by a spate of Chechen terrorist attacks, which included the downing of two Russian airliners and a bloody hostage drama at a school in Beslan, north Ossetia, in which hundreds of people died. Notwithstanding the attacks, Russian President Vladimir Putin pushed ahead with his plan to handover responsibility for ending rebel resistance to peace loving Chechens. In an interview, Alkhanov indicated readiness to negotiate with moderate rebel leaders. This shows that both Russia and India are following a realistic and practical policy to defend the integrity of their respective countries. If they are handling the terrorist menace with a firm hand, they are simultaneously negotiating with moderate leaders of secessionists.

This trend has to be seen in the context of the fact that both Russia and India are multinational, multicultural and multireligious societies. If in India for instance, about 16 per cent of the population is Muslim, in the Russian Federation this figure would be around 10-12 per cent. In this sense, defence of the unity and integrity of respective countries by integrating religious and ethnic minorities in the mainstream of the democratic structures are outstanding features of their policies. There is something more to it.

Both Russia and India are emerging as great powers and in the foreseeable future they will become significant factors in the world economy. Seen in this background, threat to their unity and integrity by foreign trained and supported terrorists and secessionists is identical to the tactics of policy of divide and rule during the colonial period. It will therefore not be incorrect to say that in the new historical conditions rise of terrorism and secessionism should be seen in isolation from the emerging new international order based on multipolarism and not unipolarism.

Let us look at the recent developments in Russia and the rising threat of terrorism and secessionism before we undertake this exercise. It is relevant to mention here that disintegration of Soviet Union was the turning point in the recent human history and the process began from Afghanistan on one side and Poland on the other side. Soon after the disintegration of Soviet Union, it was expected that this centre of the world power would disintegrate. However, after initial setbacks the Russian patriotism asserted itself and the new leadership of Russia started carving out its own position in the world politics and economy. That is why in the fight against threat to Russia's unity and integrity the Russian people are united and their President Vladimir Putin has become a symbol of this aspiration.

To understand the problem of Chechnya, a brief look at its location and historical background is essential. Chechnya is a tiny republic situated in the north Caucasus. Until the break up of the USSR it was part of the Chechen-Ingush ASSR within the Russian Federation. Other north Caucasian ASSRs were Daghestan, Kabardino-Balkaria and north Ossetia, and the autonomous region of Karacheyevo-Cherkassia. Like in other parts of the former USSR, the population of all these republics constituted mixed ethnic groups. In 1986, the population of the Chechen-Ingush ASSR was 12,22,000. According to the 1979 Soviet census there were 7,56,000 Chechens and just 1,86,000 Ingushes in the entire USSR. Traditionally, the north Caucasian people are Muslims, following in the past a tolerant Sufi variant of Islam. Grozny grew into a modern city of almost 4,00,000 with a mixed population. Under Soviet rule considerable investments were made for oil exploration and laying the pipeline from Baku in Azerbaijan to Grozny to Novorossisk in the RSFSR.

Like other nationalities in Soviet times, many Chechens received their higher education in Moscow, Leningrad (Saint Petersburg), Rostov, Kharkov and other metropolitan cities.

It was after the disintegration of the Soviet Union that terrorism and secessionism raised their ugly heads. There is something more to it than meets the eye. Chechnyan terrorists and terrorists from other countries are financed and supported from outside and their objective is to make Chechnya an independent state. This is the crux of the problem. That is why for unity and integrity of Russia, integration of Chechnyan people has become a key link. Let us not make any bones about it because we in India can comprehend how forces of disintegration are active under various labels.

This brings us to the conclusion that the war unleashed by international terrorism against Russia has left the Russian leadership with no alternative but to undertake firm measures with a view to consolidate state power to counteract effectively this global threat. This does not imply that Russia is changing its course of setting up democratic dispensations. It is relevant to mention here that in Belgium, Great Britain, Germany, Denmark, Spain, Sweden, Japan there has been successfully functioning a system of nominating a representative of the local political party, which won regional elections as a head of regional administration. A candidate appointment is then being confirmed by a local legislative body. It is this practice, which Russia has followed in the recent elections in Chechnya.

Again the United States of America after the 11th of September established unprecedented security measures, which despite significant restrictions of democratic rights and freedoms were appreciated by the American citizens. Plans of Russian government over strengthening and consolidating its power structures similar to the US administration steps also meet understanding and appreciation among Russian people.

Western business establishments too have positively responded to the various measures taken by Moscow. The reason is obvious. These measures are aimed at strengthening all political power structures of Russia, because they are conducive to sharp decrease of economic risks. The political stability in Russia including Chechnya is leading to development of foreign business and investments. Thus political stability in Russia has accelerated the economic development.

The world community, therefore, has to realise that negotiations with terrorists and secessionists on their terms is not in the larger interests of Russia as a whole and Chechnya in particular.

It is significant to mention here that the bare fact of hostage siege in Beslan where most hostages were children has completely discredited the President of Ichkerya, Maskhadov and his close associates. Presence of militants of different nationalities involved in terrorist acts points out the obvious links between Maskhadov and Chechen rebel warlord Shamil Basayev and international terrorist groups including Al Qaeda. Besides, the tragedy in the northern Ossetia has once again convincingly demonstrated that Maskhadov is unable to control bandits' activity. Therefore, it is absolutely pointless to hold peaceful dialogue with him in the estimate of Russian leaders.

Pressure is being built on Russia by certain Western politicians to negotiate with Maskhadov and his representatives. This position is not acceptable to Moscow cause it cannot afford to weaken the unity and integrity of the country by following a soft line towards terrorists and secessionists. This pressure testifies that Europe has been adhering to the policy of double standards towards international terrorism. Indian experience has also been similar.

The fact of the matter is that exponents of this policy including certain nongovernmental human rights organisations and parliament committees are supporting Chechen extremists by this course.

It is crystal clear that moral and material support by forces outside of Russia will weaken the unity and integrity of the country. The Russian people will not accept this force and the Russian political establishment has abundantly made it clear, you can have dialogues and negotiations with those who abjure the path of terrorism and secessionism and agree to become part of the national mainstream on the basis of equity and justice.

It is pertinent to say here that shocked by a series of recent terrorist attacks including the Beslan school massacre, and responding to strong statements from Russian President Vladimir Putin, all agencies of the Russian government are in the process of a major revision of security measures in the country. Russian officials have said that the recent attacks, which Basayev claimed credit for are linked to international terrorism and Moscow's response has in some cases echoed Washington's after the September 11 attacks.

Another measure under consideration in Russia is to teach civilians how to respond better to terrorism. Moscow's response to the terror attacks has ranged from Putin's call to overhaul the electoral system to give the Kremlin more control on foreigners, toughening up the criminal code and giving security organs broader power.

Recently, Russia's upper house of parliament adopted a general anti-terror measure that orders the Audit Chamber to review the effectiveness of 2002—2004 anti-terror spending and calls for increased funding for 2005.

This brings into sharp focus that both Russia and India should pool their experience of fighting against terrorism and secessionism. There are indications that during the forthcoming visit of Vladimir Putin to India, a common strategy to fight against international terrorism may come for discussions.

Indo-Russian Moscow Summit - 12 November 2003 - Joint Declaration

It is of far reaching international significance to quote here the Joint Declaration issued by the two countries after the Moscow Summit on 12 November 2003:

"The Republic of India and the Russian Federation, guided by noble purposes and principles of the United Nations Charter, relying on the provisions of the United Nations Millennium Declaration of 8 September 2000 concerning shared responsibility of States for managing threats to international peace and security and for promoting principles of human dignity, equality and justice at the global level, noting the United Nations General Assembly Resolution 57 / 145 entitled "Responding to Global Threats and Challenges" of 16 December 2002, recognising globalisation and interdependence in the world as natural processes in evolution of mankind, which offer both opportunities and challenges, taking into account the fact that uneven distribution of benefits and cost of globalisation have resulted in growing disparities among countries of the world, determined to cooperate in countering global challenges and threats, which emanate from international terrorism in all its forms and manifestations, transnational organised crime, illicit drug trafficking, money laundering and environmental and developmental challenges, proceeding from an urgent need to consolidate efforts of the international community and the role of the United Nations in eliminating these global challenges and threats, conscious of their common values and responsibilities as pluralistic democracies, desiring to continue to closely cooperate in contributing to world peace and progress, confirming their obligations in accordance with the Treaty of Friendship and Cooperation between the Republic of India and the Russian Federation of 28 January 1993, Moscow Declaration on Protection of Interests of Pluralistic States of 30 June 1994, the Declaration on Strategic Partnership between the Republic of India and the Russian Federation of 5 October 2000, the Delhi Declaration on Further Consolidation of Strategic Partnership between the Republic of India and Russian Federation of 4 December 2002, the Moscow Declaration by the Republic of India and the Russian Federation on International Terrorism of 6 November 2001 and the Memorandum of Understanding between the Government of the Republic of India and the Government of the Russian Federation on Cooperation in Combating International Terrorism of 4 December 2002.

Hereby Declare

India and the Russian Federation recognise that the aim of promoting global peace, security and stability through dialogue, consultation and cooperation among countries concerned is essential. As strategic partners, India and the Russian Federation reaffirm their commitment to cooperate bilaterally and at the multilateral level on strategic issues, and to evolve a universal effective system of countering global challenges and threats of the 21st Century. The UN should continue to play a leading role in this regard.

India and the Russian Federation as two large and influential democracies are to play a significant role in this context. Both countries are committed to promoting to the maximum extent, democratic values in international relations. India and the Russian Federation affirm that the future international order based on multipolarity, should be determined by collective and multilateral processes rather than unilateral ones. Both countries stand for building a unified, just and democratic world order and a comprehensive system of collective security based on respect for rule of law and international norms, reciprocal trust, mutual benefit, equality and cooperation.

India and the Russian Federation stress that the United Nations Organisation has a vital role in tackling major international issues.

The United Nations can and should be reformed to reflect the current realities, with a view to preserve and enhance its efficacy and efficiency. India and the Russian Federation proceed from the idea that the reform of the UN should include an early expansion of the UN Security Council. The UN should continue to play an important role in the prevention and peaceful settlement of conflicts in conformity with the UN Charter and international law.

India and the Russian Federation are convinced that greater interaction and mutual respect among diverse societies and culture will lead both to enrichment of these cultures as well as to enhanced harmony and security in the world. In this era of globalisation, it is by preserving pluralism that true multipolarity - in its political and economic as also social and cultural dimensions - will be attained. India and the Russian Federation also resolutely affirm that there is no place in today's pluralistic and diverse global village for any type of extremist ideology and intolerance. They will resist with their full might all forms of extremism, including religious extremism, which has proved to be a hot bed of terrorism in their common neighbourhood.

India and the Russian Federation are united in their fight against the evil of international terrorism. They actively cooperate with each other and with other countries in antiterrorist activities. Both countries resolutely declare that international terrorists, whatever be their stated objectives and the causes they espouse, will never succeed in bringing the world to its knees.

India and the Russian Federation believe that most urgent and essential steps in effectively and comprehensively dealing with the threat of international terrorism should be:

— creation of environment for total rejection of terrorism and absolute unacceptability of any of its forms;

— consistent and uncompromising approach to terrorism and giving up "double standards";

— preventing the flow of funds for terrorist activities;

— effective implementation of the UNSC Resolution 1373 aimed against those who support, fund, or abet terrorists or provide them shelter or asylum to engage in cross-border terrorism;

— promotion of confidence between members of the antiterrorist coalition by, *inter alia,* due consideration of interests of each one of them and ensuring that the fight against terrorism is strictly based on rules of international law and principles of the UN Charter;

— reinforcing national and international legal instruments for countering terrorism, making the existing antiterrorist Conventions genuinely universal, and earliest completion of negotiations on the draft Conventions in the UN, including the Comprehensive Convention against International Terrorism submitted by India and the International Convention on Suppression of Acts of Nuclear Terrorism submitted by the Russian Federation;

— steadfast cooperation to prevent terrorists from acquiring weapons of mass destruction, their means of delivery and materials and technology related to their manufacture;

— improvement of mechanisms of legal assistance and extradition in order to ensure the inevitability of punishment for terrorist crimes;

— efforts to promote coexistence of different religions, cultures and civilisations by stressing greater mutual understanding and respect amongst them, especially the idea that terrorism cannot be identified with any particular religion or ethnic group.

India and the Russian Federation are concerned that trafficking in illegal drugs, psychotropic substances and their precursors is assuming ever more threatening dimensions. Strong and effective measures are required by the international community to handle this threat, especially as narco-business serves as a source of financing to international terrorism. Both countries are taking specific practical steps to counter traffic in illegal drugs, psychotropic substances and their precursors, especially in their common neighbourhood.

India and the Russian Federation believe that one of the most urge challenges today is strengthening multilateral cooperation for countering the global narco-threat. India and the Russian Federation underline the urgency of the need for the development of a comprehensive strategy, under the auspices of the UN, to effectively counter this problem and reiterate their commitment for close cooperation with the United Nations and other international organisations with the framework of UN Drug Control Programme.

India and the Russian Federation support the efforts by Transitional Islamic State of Afghanistan to rebuild the nation and express full support to all international efforts aimed at promoting peace, stability, national reconciliation and economic reconstruction. It is important to adhere to the timetable, as envisaged in the Bonn Agreement, in implementation of its provisions leading to the holding of democratic elections next year. India and the Russian Federation strongly believe that Afghanistan should emerge as a peaceful strong, prosperous, united and independent nation that would be free from external interference and living in peace and harmony with its neighbours.

India and the Russian Federation are convinced that a concrete and time-bound plan of action under the UN aegis should be adopted for the earliest restoration of Iraq's sovereignty, stabilisation of political and humanitarian situation in the country, and ensuring its economic growth, through broad international efforts.

India and the Russian Federation call for the prevention of the failure of the Road Map drawn to settle the Israeli-Palestinian conflict. The failure of the Road Map may result into the situation in Israel and Palestine, as also in the entire Middle East, spiralling beyond control. This may have adverse consequences not only for the region but for the whole world.

India and the Russian Federation support the efforts of the countries concerned and the international community for a peaceful settlement of the nuclear issue on the Korean Peninsula and maintaining its non-nuclear status. They also support all efforts including the continuation of six-party talks, started at Beijing, to bring about mutually acceptable solution, as well as further development of the inter-Korean dialogue and cooperation.

India and the Russian Federation are convinced that success of the efforts aimed against contemporary global challenges and threats largely depends adequately addressing social and economic issues, such as elimination of poverty, mass unemployment, illiteracy, and racial, ethnic and religious discrimination. Both countries believe that it is essential to promote steady and sustainable development of the world economy to ensure prosperity of all countries. One of the ways to achieve this goal, as they see it, is to ensure access of the majority of people around the world to high technology - a deriving force of globalisation. Wider reach of scientific technological achievements and benefits will bring more prosperity to a larger number of people, reduce the gap between the developed and the developing world and neutralise some of the impulses which trigger conflicts.

India and the Russian Federation, which are important partners in science and high technology, possess a vast potential for joint development of alternative technologies. They are convinced that multipolarity in the world of high technology will make an immense contribution to the enhancement of political and economic multipolarity in the modern world.

India and the Russian Federation declare that through their longstanding relationship as reliable, predictable and responsible strategic partners, they are dedicated to strive for finding effective and long-term solutions and appropriate responses to the aforementioned new global challenges and threats to humanity, basing their efforts on the UN Charter and principles of international law."

Prime Minister of the Republic of India	President of the Russian Federation

The Kremlin, Moscow
12 November 2003

This Declaration shows that India and Russia are determined to "cooperate in countering global challenges and threats, which emanate from international terrorism in all its forms and manifestations". As "pluralistic democracies", they would cooperate in contributing to, "world peace and progress". Both India and Russia firmly believe that "global peace, security and stability" should be achieved "through dialogue, consultation and cooperation among countries concerned". India and Russia have reaffirmed that as strategic partners, they will "cooperate bilaterally and at multilateral level on strategic issues, and to evolve a universal effective system of countering global challenges and threats of the 21st Century". They have further emphasised that the United Nations should play an effective role in this regard.

The Declaration has further emphasised that "the future international order based on multipolarity, should be determined by collective and multilateral process rather than unilateral ones".

The Declaration has underlines that the United Nations has a "vital role" in tackling major international issues. Therefore, it should reflect the realities and that being the position, the UN Security Council should be expanded at an early date.

It has further emphasised that "in this, era of globalisation, it is by preserving pluralism and true multipolarity", in all its dimensions, this objective can be attained.

India and Russia have reiterated that in the present "global village", there is no place for "any type of extremist ideology and intolerance". Both the countries will resist with all their might "all forms of extremism including religious extremism". The Declaration did not leave at that. It brought into focus that both the countries will cooperate with each other in the fight against international terrorism. Both the countries have emphasised that the "double standards, flow of funds for terrorist activities, cross-border terrorism" should end. The Declaration brought into focus that the "draft Conventions in the UN, including the Comprehensive Convention against International Terrorism submitted by India and the International Convention on Suppression of Acts of Nuclear Terrorism submitted by the Russian Federation" should be passed by the UN.

Besides this, both the countries are deeply concerned about "trafficking in illegal drugs, psychotropic substances and their precursors, especially in their common neighbourhood". "India and the Russian Federation believe that one of the most urgent challenges today is strengthening multilateral cooperation for countering the global narco- threat".

Above all, India and Russia are deeply interested in normalisation of conditions in Afghanistan and setting up there a democratic government supported by the people. "India and Russian Federation are convinced that a concrete and time-bound plan of action under the UN aegis should be adopted for the earliest restoration of Iraq's sovereignty, stabilisation of political and humanitarian situation in the country, and ensuring its economic growth, through broad international efforts". "India and the Russian

Federation call for the prevention of the failure of the Road Map drawn to settle the Israeli-Palestinian conflict".

"India and the Russian Federation support the efforts of the countries concerned and the international community for a peaceful settlement of the nuclear issue on the Korean Peninsula and maintaining its non-nuclear status".

Most importantly, "India and the Russian Federation are convinced that success of the efforts aimed against contemporary global challenges and threats largely depends on adequately addressing social and economic issues, such as elimination of poverty, mass unemployment, illiteracy, and racial, ethnic and religious discrimination. Both countries believe that it is essential to promote steady and sustainable development of the world economy to ensure prosperity of all countries".

This shows the multidimensional character of Indo-Russian strategic partnership and its global significance. In this sense Indo-Russian strategic partnership has made a rich contribution in the thought structures and policies of creating a new global order based on peace, equality and cooperation.

Significant of Indo-Russian New Delhi Summit December 3-5, 2004

Indo-Russian strategic partnership has begun to touch a new height as is evident from Indo-Russian Summit of December 3-5, 2004. There is something more to it. Indo-Russian relations have not only assumed a multidimensional character but become a vital factor in the complex international situation and have set a new model of bilateral relations between the world's two most important countries—India and Russia. To begin with, let us sum up the contents of New Delhi joint declaration of India and Russia which was signed during the Russian President Vladimir Putin's visit to India at the end of the last year.

India and Russia took the unusual step of referring to their trilateral cooperation with China in a joint declaration signed by the Prime Minister, Manmohan Singh and the Russian President, Vladimir Putin.

While "joint declarations" are normally confined to bilateral dealings, the document said, "The sides note with satisfaction that trilateral meetings at the Foreign Ministers' level of India, China and Russia have been taking place regularly. These meetings have been useful in promoting understanding and exploring areas of possible cooperation at a trilateral and at an international level".

"The trilateral meetings have also reflected a strong concern against terrorism anywhere and in any form. The sides expressed their conviction in favour of progressive increase in trilateral cooperation, which could also result in social and economic development amongst the three countries," it added. This brings into focus that Indo-Russian, Sino-Russian and Sino-Indian relations have begun to crystallise into a new triangle in the international relations at a time when unipolarism dominates the world politics. This can be aptly described as a nucleus for multipolarism. For the first time on an official level, the importance of a triangular relationship among the world's three major powers, the two biggest Asian powers and one Eurasian power has been spelt out. This in itself is of far reaching importance.

Coming out in favour of a more democratic world order, based on a multipolar world, the declaration stressed, "Both sides recognize that their cooperation strengthens stability in Asia and the world as a whole."

Referring to energy as a key area of bilateral cooperation, the two countries said they would cooperate in the development of new oil and gas fields and the means of their transportation in Russia, India and other countries. "Both sides agree to encourage and assist investments in the energy sector by Indian companies in Russia and those by Russian companies in this sector in India," the declaration said.

India and Russia have signed an agreement during the December 3-5, 2004 visit of the Russian President, Vladimir Putin. This will transform economic relations between the two countries.

A massive $3 billion Indian investment in two oil and gas fields- $1.5 billion in Sakhalin-III and another $1.5 billion investment in the joint Russian-Kazakh Kurmangazy oil field in the Caspian - is envisaged.

The ONGC Videsh Ltd. (OVL) already has an investment of $1.7 billion in the Sakhalin-I oil field. With the new investment, India and Russia could truly speak in terms of a real partnership in the energy sector.

The Kurmangazy oil field in the Caspian Sea has the Russian State oil company, Rosneft, and the Kazakh national oil company, KazMunaiGaz, are major stakeholders. This field is estimated to have a potential of 900 million to 1 billion tonnes of oil, which according to some estimates is as high as the total oil wealth of Saudi Arabia.

During a recent visit to Moscow, the Petroleum Minister Mani Shankar Aiyar, indicated that India-Russia energy cooperation would bloom further. "In the first half century of Indian Independence Russia has guaranteed our territorial integrity, and in the second half it may be able to guarantee our energy security."

On the fight against terrorism, India and Russia emphasized the need to give substance and credibility to the global fight against terrorism and avoid selective approaches and political expediency.

"Both sides reaffirm that proliferation of weapons of mass destruction (WMD), their materials, particularly the risk of their falling into the hands of terrorists constitutes a threat to international peace and security. They highlighted the need to prevent terrorists or those who harbour them from acquiring or developing WMD, their means of delivery and related materials," the declaration said.

While calling for a central role for the United Nations in such efforts, India and Russia said they would cooperate bilaterally as well as through appropriate multilateral channels towards this objective.

The declaration said, "The (two) sides express their concern over continuing violence in Iraq and stressed the need for an intra-Iraqi dialogue aimed at building national consensus on a new constitution and on restoring stability and security in the country.

"The sides advocate strict compliance of the U.N. Security Council Resolution 1546, particularly with regard to the interim timetable of political process stipulated by it with a view to facilitating the formation of a new, democratic Iraq.

"The sides affirm their continuing interest in contributing to the reconstruction efforts in Iraq and urged a wider degree of international consultation in the ongoing peace efforts. The sides believe that it would be in the interest of the international community to restore the efficacy of multilateral approaches in addressing situations such as the war in Iraq," the declaration said.

This shows that Russia and India used the opportunity presented by Vladimir Putin's visit to raise the bilateral relationship to a higher level and remove all the irritants. This will make a significant contribution in the international arena.

It is also relevant to mention here that proposals made by Moscow for an accord to protect intellectual property rights relating to high-technology weapons, and for joint military exercise were shelved for an unconscionably long period. New Delhi has now promised to cooperate wholeheartedly in the effort to draw up a defence secrecy agreement so that it can be signed by the middle of 2005, and the special forces of the two countries will carry out joint exercises.

As for the programme for the joint development of the world class supersonic BrahMos cruise missile, India and Russia made a strategic shift from the buyer-seller equation that had characterised their relationship in the field of defence. They have now agreed to explore the scope for upgrading their economic relations in similar fashion so that the steep decline in bilateral trade can be reversed. The two countries have indicated that they would try to use the joint venture set up to develop an oil field in the Sakhalin peninsula as the template for such enterprises in the territories they control as well as in third countries. India has also promised that it would treat Russia as a market economy and support its efforts to join the World Trade Organisation. Indo-Russian trade is expected to be more than doubled during the next 2-3 years. For its part, Moscow has agreed to strengthen the mechanisms to ensure that production schedules for military equipment are met and after-sales support is provided. The two countries resolved the differences over India's practice of sourcing Russian-patented spare parts from third countries by arriving at a sensible compromise. Russia is to set up maintenance and overhauling facilities on Indian territory.

India will be gratified that President Putin expressed his support for its bid to join the United Nations Security Council as a permanent member with veto powers.

This brings us to the conclusion that the Russian-Indian relationship is an entirely new type of alliance which not only promotes the interests of the two nations, but also helps strengthen and develop democratic international relations around the world.

19

India-Russia Reiterate their Strategic Partnership

Manohar Singh Batra

The December 3-5, 2004 visit of Vladimir Putin, the President of the Russian Federation to India has been another milestone in the strategic partnership and time-tested friendship between the two countries. Apart from the multi-faceted cooperation and bilateral relations between these two major players in the world arenas, their determination to expand the area of their collaboration in the interest of their peoples and to enhance the cause of universal peace are the factors which are too important to be overlooked by the rest of the world. Mr. Putin, because of sincerity of his views and his commitment to accelerate the pace of meaningful exchanges between India and Russia, has been gaining in personal popularity in this country and his latest visit was in the nature of a home-coming. After a little hiccup, his candid and articulate support for India' s permanent membership of the Security Council in a reformed UN, with full veto power, has warmed the hearts of Indians. India being a subject country at the time of the formation of the world body in 1945, was naturally not in the reckoning for permanent membership of the UN, but since independence this country has emerged as one of the most dynamic and vibrant nations on the globe and deserves a rightful place in the world organisation. Russia's coming out with unstinted support in India's favour is a positive step in its efforts to garner affirmative votes and build a conducive world environment for this country being treated on par with other world powers. Putin emphatically said that India cannot be a permanent member of the Security Council with a second rank and it should have full rights, including the right of veto. He put an end to a controversy over the wrong interpretation of his remarks a day earlier when he had reportedly espoused India's cause for a permanent place in the Council without veto power. But on Dec 4, he corrected that misinterpretation and affirmed his country's support for India's long-cherished desire. Though the high-powered panel constituted to consider reforms of the UN system has submitted its report to the Secretary General, it has not recommended an expansion of the veto-holding membership of the Security Council and has instead proposed the creation of a new category of permanent members. But the unambiguous support of Russia should encourage the other P-5 members to ponder over India's candidature with an open mind and a spirit of realism.

In a joint declaration released after indepth talks between Dr. Manmohan Singh, India's Prime Minister and Mr. Vladimir Putin in New Delhi on December 3, 2004, it was stated that India and Russia were guided by mutual trust and respect inherent in their bilateral relations. They have drawn upon their wide-ranging tradition of cooperation since the establishment of diplomatic relations in April 1947. They have recalled the Treaty on Friendship and Cooperation signed between them on January 28, 1993. They have reaffirmed the Declaration on Strategic Partnership issued on October 3, 2000. They are convinced of the mutual desire to promote global peace and progress, and the need to counter challenges arising out of international terrorism. They confirm their adherence to the common ideals of secularism, democracy, rule of law, cultural diversity and pluralism. They also affirm their commitment to develop further and enhance the strategic partnership based on nation-wide consensus in both the countries.

The Declaration said that India and Russia, being two of the largest democracies in the world and being deeply committed to the establishment of a more democratic order based on a multi-polar world, the two sides have noted with satisfaction that the strategic partnership between them serves their long-term national interests, strengthens bilateral relations, deepens their mutually beneficial cooperation and contributes to international peace and security. They have also taken into account the major changes that have taken place in the international political landscape over the past few decades. The two countries have agreed to intensify exchanges in bilateral relations at the political and parliamentary levels, between the Security Councils and at official level. The significant degree of convergence in the overall perspective as well as interests of the two sides, have enabled Indo-Russian relations to withstand the test of time. They recognise that their cooperation strengthens strategic stability in Asia and the world as a whole.

The two countries propose to continue consultations at all levels between the Foreign countries of the two nations, including those on disarmament as well as on the United Nations issues. Priority attention will be paid to coordination of efforts through the Joint Working Group on Combating Global Challenges and the Joint Working Group on Combating International Terrorism. India regards Russia as a major and fully active member of the International community, and as a country whose voice commands respect and attention on issues of global concern. In this context, the Indian side strongly supports the earliest possible accession of Russia to the World Trade Organisation. Both sides regard this support as an important demonstration of Indo-Russian relations of strategic partnership, and express their desire to develop, after the accession of Russia to the WTO, cooperation within that Organisation, based on the principles of mutual respect, equality and mutual benefit.

The Declaration added that both sides are convinced that trade, culture and tourism promote economic cooperation, goodwill and people to people contacts between nations and they stress that the traditionally strong bilateral relations have rested on foundations of political, defence and economic exchanges of a substantial nature. In the current context, this process has to be carried forward and strengthened further. Mutual investments in industries, cooperation in IT and banking are some areas that offer a new scope.

The Declaration noted that energy constitutes an important part of the bilateral relationship. Considering the expanding energy requirements of India, both sides stress the need for employing resources that are environment-friendly and available in sufficient quantities. Nuclear power plants offer a pollution-free and substantial source of energy to provide for the sustainable development. Both India and Russia are determined to continue their cooperation in the field of nuclear energy, incorporating innovative technologies to ensure energy security, with due regard to their commitments to non-proliferation norms.

Both India and Russia recognise the considerable scope for cooperation in the hydro-electric and thermal power sectors. Russia is a major exporter of oil and gas and India is emerging as a large consumer. Both sides affirm their desire to cooperate in development of new oil and gas fields and the means of their transportation in Russia, India and other countries. Both sides agree to encourage and assist investments in the energy sector by Indian companies in Russia and those by Russian companies in this sector in India. Both sides view cooperation in energy as an area of priority attention in bilateral cooperation.

The Declaration further stated that both sides agreed that the twenty-first century presents new challenges. In a globalised world, there are inherent inter-linkages not only between countries, but also between issues. Both sides recognise the indivisibility between security and prosperity in the present-day world. They agree that the most effective way to address contemporary challenges is through multilateral approaches based on the widest possible international support. Multi-lateralism is an instrument to work towards the objective of a multi-polar world.

Since the UN system is at the centre of multi-lateralism, both sides agreed to cooprate closely at the UN and in other international organisations. In 2005 the UN would be 60 years old. Both sides emphasise the necessity of comprehensive reforms in the UN system so as to reflect both the enlarged membership in the UN and the contemporary realities. India and Russia emphasise that the expansion of the UNSC is an urgent imperative to make the Security Council more representative and effective. In this framework, the Russian Federation reiterates once again that it regards India as an influential and major member of the international community. The Russian Federation reaffirms its support to India as a deserving and strong candidate for the permanent membership in an expanded UN Security Council.

In the joint declaration, India and Russia reaffirmed their common resolve to fight terrorism. They reiterated that global terrorism in all its forms and manifestations constitutes one of the most serious threats to international peace and security, and condemn in the strongest terms all acts of terrorism irrespective of their motivation, whenever and by whomsoever committed. They underscore that there can be no justification for terrorism on any grounds, including ideological, religious, racial, ethnic or any other. They believe that the fight against terrorism has to be long-term, sustained and comprehensive. They emphasise the need for giving substance and credibility to the global fight against terrorism and avoid selective approaches and political expediency. With the recent targeting of open societies around the world, India and Russia, as two large and influential democracies, have reasons to be concerned about the vulnerability of democracies to terrorist attacks, because terrorism exploits the strengths of democracies such as the protection of human rights, freedom of expression and movement.

As per the Joint Declaration, both countries welcomed the unanimous adoption of the UN Security Council resolution 1566. Noting that it seeks to consider action against terrorists including sanctions and judicial action and aims at making the Counter-Terrorism Committee more action-oriented, both countries decided to actively cooperate with each other in counter-terrorism efforts.

India and Russia re-emphasised the need for an early adoption by the General Assembly of the Comprehensive Convention on International Terrorism and the International Convention for the Suppression of Acts of Nuclear Terrorism.

Both India and Russia reaffirmed that proliferation of weapons mass destruction, their means of delivery and related materials, particularly the risk of their falling into the hands of terrorists constitutes a threat to international peace and security. They highlighted the need to prevent terrorists or those who harbour them from acquiring or developing weapons of mass destruction, their means of delivery and related materials. As strategic partners India and Russia affirmed their commitment to cooperate bilaterally as well as through appropriate multilateral forums towards contributing to this objective. Both India and Russia reaffirmed their commitment to support efforts to prevent the deployment of weapons in outer space while preserving it for peaceful and cooperative activities aimed at developmental benefits.

In the Joint Declaration, India and Russia noted with satisfaction that trilateral meetings at the Foreign Ministers level of India, China and Russia have been taking place regularly. These meetings have been useful in promoting understanding and exploring areas of possible cooperation at a trilateral and at an international level. The trilateral meetings have also been reflecting a strong concern against terrorism anywhere and in any form. The two sides expressed their conviction that the progressive increase in their trilateral cooperation could also result in social and economic development amongst the three States.

Both India and Russia considered the situation in Central Asia and noted that security and stability in that region coincided with the priorities of our two countries for the region. Greater economic growth and democratic progress of the Central Asian states demanded the respect for their freedom to choose the models of development and implementation of reforms.

The two sides expressed concern over continuing violence in Iraq and stressed the need for an intra-Iraqi dialogue aimed at building national consensus on a new Constitution and on restoring stability and security in that country. India and the Russian Federation advocated strict compliance of the UN Security Council Resolution 1546, particularly with regard to the interim timetable of political process stipulated by it with a view to facilitating the formation of a new, democratic Iraq.

Both countries supported the objective of a lasting, just and comprehensive settlement of the Arab-Israeli conflict, based on relevant resolutions of the UN Security Council. They also welcomed the successful conclusion of the Presidential elections in Afganistan and empasised the importance of efforts at national reconciliation and unity. Both sides are also looking forward to the conduct of the parliamentary elections scheduled for April/May 2005. They would like to support a strong, united, sovereign and independent Afghanistan. They also reiterated their support for reconstruction of Afghanistan. Particularly they expressed their concern at the threat to security especially in the south and south-eastern provinces, and also over the increased cultivation, production and trafficking of narcotic drugs in Afghanistan. They underlined the need for effective steps to counteract the drug and terrorist menace.

India and Russia expressed their determination to further enhance the all-round relations of partnership and close interaction on a bilateral and multilateral basis, with other states, regional and international forums.

On December 3, 2004, President Putin delivered the Jawaharlal Nehru Memorial Lecture in New Delhi. Apart from paying tributes to Mr. Nehru as a true patriot, thinker and outstanding humanist, he praised his legacy, which belonged to all mankind. He stressed that the world was facing threats of international terrorism and organised crime. There was a great danger of proliferation of weapons of mass destruction and the weapons falling into the hands of terrorists. According to Putin no dictatorship, especially in international affairs, could solve such problems, even if this dictatorship was packaged in a pretty wrapping of pseudo-democratic phraseology. Only a balanced system of international law and the ability of the international community would ensure adherence to accepted norms. Russia and India are proactive and constructive participants in the process and we are striving for a just world order. The central coordinating role in drafting a collective response to contemporary threats should belong to the UN. It is a unique organisation embracing the entire world and has experience in acting at the global level. We expect a great deal from the UN Secretary General's High-Level Panel on Threats,. Challenges and Reforms.

According to Putin, the Russian Federation is open to sensible models of reform in the UN, particularly the expansion of the Security Council. However, any possible reforms must be conducted on the basis of broad consensus. Putin repeated Russia's principled position to support the candidacy of India as a future permanent member of the Security Council. He found this right being evidenced in this country's rapidly developing international influence and economic potential. India's independent foreign policy based on the principles of the UN charter confirmed this. Putin again felt that non-bloc interaction between Russia, India and China could make a crucial contribution to global stability and progress. Business cooperation could be an important factor in the socio-economic development of each of our countries, he said.

President Putin referred to the cooperation between Russia and India in the fight against terrorism. Our two countries, which have had serious encounters with terrorists' crimes and experienced the pain of losses, have a common understanding of the essence and principles of anti-terrorism efforts. Putin's view was that terrorism cannot and must not be used as an instrument in geo-political games or interests. He hinted at the Russian initiative in presenting Resolution 1566 in the UN Security Council, which was duly adopted, as an extremely important measure. It obliges every state to bring terrorists, their accomplices and sponsors to justice without fail. Putin pointed out that terrorism could not be identified with any particular religion or ethnic group. He warned that terrorists and their backers could gain from unleashing a conflict between civilisations and religions, and setting nations against each other.

Putin exhorted his own country and India to play a special role in solving the enormous problems facing the Islamic world today because of their huge Muslim communities, long involvement in Islamic history and culture and neighbouring leading Islamic states. He emphasized that the most important issues are of peace in Iraq, Afghanistan and the Middle East. Putin, while taking note of the situation in South Asia, referred to the long period of tension between India and Pakistan, which has hampered the solution of their problems and joint counter-terrorism efforts. He welcomed the comprehensive India-Pakistan dialogue and the new positive trends in their trade, economic, sporting and cultural exchanged and trust between the countries. His view was that taking new initiatives to solve old problems, including the Kashmir issue, would correspond to the interests of South Asia, as well as world peace and security.

Taking about Indo-Russian cooperation, Vlamimir Putin said that during the last few months our two countries have taken some serious steps and created preconditions for a breakthrough in a number of important areas of cooperation. He made a pointed reference to the Sakhalin-1 oil production project in Russia and the construction of the Kudankulam nuclear power plant in India. He believed that the future of Russo-Indian economic ties lay in the sphere of investment cooperation and the implementation of major strategic projects. He reffered to Russia's readiness to participate in major regional infrastructure projects, such as the construction of pipelines, highways and railways.

President Putin averred that Russia was interested in expanding trade in hi-tech products with India and to improve forms and methods of cooperation in the investment sphere. To bolster scientific-technical partnership such as participation in space exploration, information technologies and communications was on the top of his mind. High technologies—computers, the Internet, satellite communications and fibre option—are the driving force of globalisation. Putin strongly believed that the multi-polar world of high technologies would help to balance the evolution of human civilisation. Russia and India both have an enormous potential to develop together advanced technologies, including alternative technologies.

As a part of multilateral cooperation with India, Putin mentioned military-technical and military spheres. Russia had not been simly supplying India with armaments, military equipment and new technologies. Russia has been involved in the Joint development of new armaments. In the future, there is a strong possibility of our relations developing into full-scale scientific and technical partnership. The anted forces of both our countries have been acquiring new experience of joint exercises. Last year's joint naval exercises in the Indian Ocean are a good example of the same. Russia's assistance to India was not aimed against third countries. Strategic shipping lanes from the Persian Gulf to East Asia, China and Japan pass along the shores of India. The protection of energy supply lines in this large region and the countering of the terrorist threat and piracy at sea are all part of the common security strategy adopted by various world powers and Asian countries in particular. All the plans to ensure security on shipping lanes in the Indian Ocean would be ineffective without India's proactive participation.

India has agreed to Russian Defence Minister Sergei Ivanov's suggestion that both countries should conclude an intellectual property rights agreement on weapon systems. This would be a step forward in expanding military to military cooperation. Defence Minister Pranab Mukherjee and the three service chiefs sought assurances of lifetime support on Defence equipment from the Russians. Pranab Mukherji declared "We have decided to include the element of intellectual property rights (in defence deals). Details of the agreement will be worked out and a draft prepared for signing within a timeframe of four to five months." He announced this after co-chairing a meeting of the India-Russia inter-governmental Commission on Military-Technical Cooperation with his Russian counterpart Sergei Ivanov. The two sides signed a new protocal on military-technical cooperation. Over 70 per cent of equipment available to the Indian military is of Russian origin. Russia has been insisting on this agreement for the last two years.

Russia's head of the Federal Space Agency, Anatoly Perminov said in Moscow on December 1, 2004 that India and Russia would join hands in building a space navigation system and using it for civilian and possibly military purposes. An Agreement on long-term cooperation in the field of joint development and use of Russian global navigational satellite system GLONASS for peaceful purposes has signed in New Delhi.

An agreement on visa free travel between India and the Russian Federation for mutual travel by holders of diplomatic and official passports was also signed.

An agreement on cooperation between the city of Mumbai, Republic of India and the City of St. Petersburg, Russian Federation, which would facilitate cooperation between Mumbai and St. Petersburg city in the field of trade, economy, industry, tourism, culture and education was inked.

An MoU was initialled between ECGC and Exim Bank and Vnesheconom Bank to establish a framework for cooperation between the business, trading companies in supporting and encouraging trade and investments between India and Russia. Another MoU was signed on cooperation between SBI and Sber Bank to facilitate direct banking relationship between the Indian and Russian companies. Similarly an MOU on Cooperation between Ganara Bank and Sber Bank to facilitate commercial and bank to bank payments was initialled. Still another MoU was signed between GAIL and STROITRANSGAZ which envisaged underground storage project in India, Russia and third countries. The next on the agenda was an MoU between GAIL and Skochinsky Mining Institute in Russia, which covers development of pilot project on lignite gasification in Tamil Nadu and Rajasthan, transfer of technology and training. All these accords were signed after wide-ranging talks between Prime Minister Manmohan Singh and President Putin.

Putin said that all problems in military-technical cooperation between the two countries had been resolved. "Very detailed two-day negotiations have resulted in settling virtually all problems in our military-technical of cooperation. There are no problems that could obstruct our movement forward in this sphere now", Mr. Putin told Defence Minister Pranab Mukherji.

India and Russia approved the development of the air-lauched version of BrahMos, the supersonic cruise missile jointly developed by both countries. This version of BrahMos will be integrated with Sukhoi-30 MKI (Mark India) multi-role fighter airoraft. The time-frame for providing this version is two years. In due course the Indian Air Force will be equipped with BrahMos. Vladimir Putin visited the BrahMos Aerospace Headquarters complex in New Delhi on December 4, 2004. He visited various centres like the BrahMos design group, training and documentation, project management, international cooperation and an exhibition. The following day, President A.P.J.Abdul Kalam visiting the complex stressed on the staff that thrust should be given to the marketing of BrahMos. He described BrahMos the most competitive missile system which should be marketed early for friendly countries of the Third World.

The IAF version of BrahMos will be lighter than the Naval version, which weighs three tonnes. The range of course would be the same. The IAF version will have an improved booster and a modified nose cap. An army version of BrahMos is under process and it would be fired from a mobile launch complex on ground towards a land target. Mr. Putin has called BrahMos "a real joint venture between Russia and India, which showcases the strength of both the countries." Mr. Putin was happy that all its eight flights were a success.

During his two-day visit to Bangalore, before his departure for home, Mr. Putin witnessed India's aeronautics capability, at Hindustan Aeronautics Limited. Paying an official visit to India's public sector aeronautics giant, Putin saw the flying prowess of the Light Combat Air-craft (Tejas), Intermediate Jet Trainer and Advanced Light Helicopter (Dhruv). The Russians have expressed interest in tying up with India for developing a fifth generation fighter aircraft.

Putin had signed the Declaration on Indo-Russian Strategic Partnership during his first visit to India in the second half of the year 2000, which had laid strong foundations for further development of multifaceted relations between the two nations. Highlighting that India stood at the top of his foreign policy agenda, Putin had said "comprehensive strengthening of our cooperation with India has always been and remains a priority one of the top priorities of Rassian foreign policy. We have always maintained contacts at the high level." Emphasising India's role in the international field, Putin said, " we take a long-term view that as one of the largest countries in Asia and in the world, India is a crucial factor in stability in the region and in the world as a whole. Russia would like to see India play a genuinely important role in international affairs." Virtually all of Indian navy's submarines have been built in St. Petersburg. The killo class, state of the art submarines, frigates owned by Indian navy have been built in St. Petersburg's Baltisky Zavod. Putin once said "I am the greatest friend of India". Under Putin's Russia the relations between India and Russia have been going from strength to strength and higher and higher goals are being set.

In economic relations, the customer-seller mode of interaction is seeing a positive shift towards joint license production, transfer of technologies, research and development with further movement towards joint promotion of product range of Russian and Indian defence industries on foreign markets.

As regards Indo-Russian collaboration in military aviation, the Su-30 MKI epitomises a "universal air warrior", capable of accomplishing a wide variety of combat missions at significant distances from the home base, in any weather conditions and severe jamming environment, both by day and night. The multirole aircraft is adequately fitted for the entire spectrum of tactical and operational combat employment scenarios. As per the Gorshkov contract, the Indian Navy has acquired some MiG-29KUB, ship borne combat trainer. The two-seater MiG-29KUB can perform a wide spectrum of tasks.

In sum, the Indo-Russian cooperation in all fields has crystalised into a strong strategic partnership between these two countries with an enormous further scope of its widening in strength and dimension.

Appendix

Russia-India: Joint Declaration by the Russian Federation and the Republic of India

The Russian Federation and the Republic of India, hereinafter referred to as the Sides,

Guided by mutual trust and respect inherent in bilateral relations,

Drawing upon their wide ranging tradition of cooperation since the establishment of diplomatic relations in April 1947,

Recalling the Treaty on Friendship and Cooperation between the Republic of India and the Russian Federation of 28 January 1993,

Reaffirming the Declaration on Strategic Partnership between the Republic of India and the Russian Federation of 3 October 2000,

Convinced of the mutual desire to promote global peace and progress, and the need to counter challenges arising out of international terrorism,

Confirm their adherence to the common ideals of secularism, democracy, rule of law, cultural diversity and pluralism,

Affirm their commitment to develop further and adherence the strategic partnership based on nation-wide consensus in both the States,

Declare as follows;

I

India and Russia, as two of the largest democracies in the world, are deeply committed to the establishment of a more democratic world order, based on a multi-polar world, which takes into account the major changes that have taken place in the international political landscape over the past few decades. The two Sides note with satisfaction that the strategic partnership between them serves their long-term national interests, strengthens bilateral relations, deepens mutually beneficial cooperation and contributes to international peace and security.

The Sides agree to intensify exchanges in bilateral relations at the political and parliamentary levels, between the Security Councils and at official level. The significant degree of convergence in the overall perspective as well as interests of the two sides, have enabled Indo-Russian relations to withstand the test of time. Both sides recognise that their cooperation strengthens strategic stability in Asia and the world as a whole.

The Sides propose to continue consultations at all levels between the foreign ministers of the two countries, including those on disarmament as well as on the United Nations issues. Priority attention will be paid to coordination of efforts through the Joint Working Group on Combating Global Challenges and the Joint Working Group on Combating International Terrorism.

The Indian Side regards Russia as a major and fully active member of the international community, and as a country whose voice commands respect and attention on issues of global concern. In this context, the Indian Side strongly supports the earliest possible accession of Russia to the World Trade Organisation. The Sides regard this support as an important demonstration of Indo-Russian relations of strategic partnership, and express their desire to develop, after the accession of Russia to the WTO, cooperation within that Organisation, based on the principles of mutual respect, equality and mutual benefit.

The Sides are convinced that trade, culture and tourism promote economic cooperation, goodwill and people-to-people contacts between nations. The Sides stress that the traditionally strong bilateral relations have rested on foundations of political, defence and economic exchanges of a substantial nature. In the current context, this process has to be carried forward and strengthened further. Mutual investments in industries, cooperation in IT and banking are some areas that offer a new scope.

Energy constitutes an important part of the bilateral relationship. Considering the expanding energy requirements of India, both Sides stress the need for employing resources that are environment-friendly and available in sufficient quantities. Nuclear power plants offer a pollution-free and substantial source of energy to provide for the sustainable development. Both Sides are determined to continue their cooperation in the field of nuclear energy, incorporating innovative technologies to ensure energy security, with due regard to their commitments to non-proliferation norms. The Sides also recognise the considerable scope for cooperation in the hydro-electric and thermal power sectors. Russia is a major exporter of oil and gas and India is emerging as a large consumer. The Sides affirm their desire to cooperate in development of new oil and gas fields and the means of their transportation in Russia, India and other countries. Both Sides agree to encourage and assist investments in energy sector by Indian companies in Russia and those by Russian companies in this sector in India. The Sides view cooperation in energy as an area of priority attention in bilateral cooperation.

II

The Sides agree that the 21st century presents new challenges. In a globalised world, there are inherent inter-linkages not only between countries, but also between issues. Both Sides recognise the indivisibility between security and prosperity in the present day world. They agree that the most effective way to address contemporary challenge through multilateral approaches based on the widest possible international support. Multilateralism is an instrument to work towards the objective of a multi-polar world.

The UN system is at the centre of multilateralism. Both Sides agree to cooperate closely at the UN and in other international organisations. In 2005 the UN will be 60 years old. Both Sides emphasise the necessity of comprehensive reforms in the UN system as to reflect both the enlarged membership of the UN and the contemporary realities. India and Russia emphasise that the expansion of the UN Security Council is an urgent imperative to make the Security Council more representative and effective. In this framework, the Russian Federation reiterate once again that it regards India as a influential and major member of the international community. The Russian Federation reaffirms its support to India as deserving and strong candidate for the permanent membership in an expanded UN Security Council.

III

India and the Russian Federation reiterate their common resolve to fight terrorism. They reaffirm that global terrorism in all its forms and manifestations constitutes one of the most serious threats to international peace and security, and condemned in the strongest terms all acts of terrorism irrespective of their motivation, whenever and by whomsoever committed. They underscore that there can be no justification for terrorism on any grounds, including ideological, religious, racial, ethnic or any other. They believe that the fight against terrorism has to be long-term, sustained and comprehensive. In this regard they emphasise the need for giving substance and credibility to the global fight against terrorism and avoid selective approaches and political expediency. With the recent targeting of open societies around the world, India and the Russian Federation a two large and influential democracies, have reasons to be concerned about the vulnerability of democracies to terrorist attacks, because terrorism exploits the strengths of democracies such as, the protection of human rights, freedom of expression and movement.

Both countries welcome the unanimous adoption of the UN Security Council resolution 1566 [piloted by the Russian Federation]. Noting that it seeks to consider action against terrorists including sanctions and judicial action and aims at making the Counter Terrorism Committee more action-oriented, both countries decided to actively cooperate with each other in counter-terrorism efforts.

India and the Russian Federation re-emphasise the need for an early adoption by the General Assembly of the comprehensive Convention on International Terrorism and the International Convention for the Suppression of Acts of Nuclear Terrorism.

IV

Both Sides reaffirm that proliferation of weapons of mass destruction (WMD), their means of delivery and related materials, particularly the risk of their falling into the hands of terrorists constitutes a threat to international peace and security. They highlighted the need to prevent terrorists or those who harbour them from acquiring or developing WMD, their means of delivery and related materials. Both sides emphasised the necessity to further address this threat on national basis as well as through forward looking multilateral long term efforts by all partners against proliferation with the central role of the United Nations. As strategic partners India and Russia affirmed their commitment to cooperate bilaterally as well as through appropriate multilateral forum towards contributing to this objective.

Both Sides also reaffirm their commitment to support efforts to prevent the deployment of weapons in outer space while preserving it for peaceful and cooperative activities aimed at developmental benefits.

V

The Sides note with satisfaction that the Trilateral Meetings at the Foreign Ministers level of India, China and Russia have been taking place regularly. These meetings have been useful in promoting understanding and exploring areas of possible cooperation at a trilateral and at an international level. The Trilateral Meetings have also reflected a strong concern against terrorism anywhere and in any form. The Sides express their conviction in favour of progressive increase in the trilateral cooperation, which could also result in social and economic development amongst the three countries.

VI

The Sides considered the situation in Central Asia and note that security and stability in that region coincides with the priorities of India and Russia for the region. Greater economic growth and democratic progress of the Central Asian States demand the respect for their freedom to choose the models of development and implementation of reforms.

VII

The Sides express concern over continuing violence in Iraq and stressed the need for an intra-Iraqi dialogue aimed at building national consensus on a new constitution and on restoring stability and security in the country. The Sides advocate strict compliance of the UN Security Council resolution 1546, particularly with regard to the interim timetable of political process stipulated by it with a view to facilitating the formation of a new, democratic Iraq.

The Sides affirm their continuing interest in contributing to the reconstruction efforts in Iraq and urged a wider degree of international consultation in the ongoing peace efforts. The Sides believe that it would be in the interest of the international community to restore the efficiency of multilateral approaches in addressing situations such as the war in Iraq.

VIII

The Sides support the objective of a lasting, just and comprehensive settlement of the Arab Israeli conflict, based on relevant resolutions of the UN Security Council. The sides encourage the resumption of peaceful negotiations as soon as possible in accordance with the Road Map worked out by the Quartet of international intermediaries and approved by the UN Security Council in its resolution 1515.

IX

The Sides welcome the successful conclusion of the Presidential elections in Afghanistan and underline the important efforts at national reconciliation and unity. Sides also look forward to conduct of a parliamentary elections as scheduled in April-2005. They express support for a united, sovereign and independent Afghanistan and underline the importance empowering the Central authority in indigenous security institutions.

The Sides reiterate their support for reconstruction process in Afghanistan. Sides express their concern at the continue threat to security, especially in the South and Southeastern provinces and also over the continued increase in the cultivation, production and trafficking of narcotics drugs in Afghanistan and underlined the need of effective steps to counteract the drug terrorist threats.

X

The Russian Federation and the Republic of India are convinced that their bilateral cooperation in all forms, and their strategic partnership, contributes to the strengthening of the regional and global goodwill and cooperation. They are determined to further enhance in every possible way the relation of partnership and closely interact on bilateral and multilateral basis, with the states, regional and international forums.

Prime Minister of the Republic of India	President of the Russian Federation

Index

H

I

J

K

S